Marlborough's
Irish Dragoons

Marlborough's Irish Dragoons

The 5th Dragoons in Ireland, the Low Countries and the War of Spanish Succession 1688-1711

Walter Temple Willcox

LEONAUR

Marlborough's Irish Dragoons
The 5th Dragoons in Ireland, the Low Countries and the War of Spanish Succession
1688-1711
by Walter Temple Willcox

FIRST EDITION

First published under the title
The Historical Records of the Fifth (Royal Irish) Lancers

Leonaur is an imprint of Oakpast Ltd

Copyright in this form © 2014 Oakpast Ltd

ISBN: 978-1-78282-323-0 (hardcover)
ISBN: 978-1-78282-324-7 (softcover)

http://www.leonaur.com

Publisher's Notes

Contents

MARLBOROUGH'S IRISH DRAGOONS

DEDICATED

TO THE PAST & PRESENT

OFFICERS

NON-COMMISSIONED OFFICERS AND MEN

OF THE

FIFTH LANCERS

TITLES OF THE REGIMENT

Wynne's (Enniskillen) Dragoons
1689.
Ross' Dragoons
1695.
The Royal Dragoons of Ireland
1704.
The 5th (or Royal Irish) Dragoons
about 1752.

Introduction

Shortly after my appointment as Honorary Colonel of the 5th Royal Irish Lancers, it was a source of satisfaction and pleasure to me to learn that the historical records of the regiment were being compiled, for I consider it essential that every officer, non-commissioned officer, and man should be conversant with the history of his regiment, in order that he may gain that "*esprit de corps*" with which it is so important that all ranks should be imbued—an element which forms, I am glad to say, one of the strongest features of the British Army.

The study of such historical records, recounting the deeds of those who have helped to make their country's history, fosters and maintains this spirit, and is an incentive to all ranks to endeavour to sustain the good name and high state of efficiency for which their corps were celebrated in the past.

Surely, therefore, the present record of the exploits of past members of the 5th Royal Irish Lancers must prove most interesting and instructive to those now serving in the regiment.

The author tells me that his aim has been to recount facts of interest to other cavalry regiments, as well as to his own, for he thinks that, while "*esprit de corps*" should be nurtured in each individual regiment it should also be cherished throughout the British Army as a whole.

I cannot speak too highly of the care and trouble which Captain Willcox (recently promoted to a majority in the 3rd Hussars) has taken in the production of this record.

His self-imposed task has occupied him for three years, and it has been most admirably performed. Everyone who has served or is still serving in the regiment must owe him a deep debt of gratitude.

T. A. Cooke, Major-General.
Hon. Col. 5th (Royal Irish) Lancers.

September, 1906.

5TH ROYAL IRISH

Preface

It may be a popular belief that a soldier as a rule has but little inclination towards a literary effort. The belief, if such there be, is possibly justifiable, for a soldier should undoubtedly live by his sword rather than by his pen. On the other hand, nowadays the profession of arms entails a large amount of study and some literary effort on the part of her sons.

Such study, outside purely professional subjects, should, we are told, take the form of history in its connection with war. I would, however, venture to add that the first historical study to which a young officer should devote himself on first obtaining the honour of His Majesty's Commission is the history of his own regiment; and not only the officer but the recruit should surely know of the actions of his predecessors.

To recall, however, a possibly forgotten past is quite a waste of time if no useful lessons or fruitful results are forthcoming from the labours which the effort entails. As regards the lessons to be learnt much depends upon the ability of the would be historian, but fruitful results in the furtherance of that *esprit de corps* for which British regiments are so justly famed, will always follow in the course of any effort in the publishing of a regimental history.

To this end some three years ago, as at time of first publication, the following story of the regiment was considered, thought out and commenced.

One may be allowed to say that the difficulties of the undertaking were great. Our regiment is now the 5th Lancers.

We were raised in 1858. When we were so raised we took the place, the titles and the traditions of that historical and unfortunate old regiment, the 5th Dragoons, which was disbanded in 1799.

The records and references relating to the 5th Lancers were all plain sailing, but this can scarcely be said of those of the 5th Dragoons.

Our gallant predecessors, as the following pages will show, were disbanded for an act of "presumed delinquency,"—the words are not mine,—and His Majesty George III ordered that their place in the army should remain a blank for all time as a standing reproach. In 1858 this order was cancelled by Her late Majesty Queen Victoria, and the regiment was again brought into existence.

Meanwhile, however, Cannon had written by Royal Command the history of nearly every regiment in the British Army, but for the foregoing reason he left untouched that of the 5th Dragoons. For the same reason, no doubt, many records of the later years of the 5th Dragoons are not forthcoming, and it is consequently difficult to trace back much of interest until the times of Blenheim and Malplaquet. From there we go fairly easily to the more early days of the regiment under the command of Ross, and back still further to its birth as dragoons of Enniskillen raised and commanded by the gallant James Wynne. It is just previous to this period, when the irregular levies fighting in the defence of Enniskillen were not yet formed into regiments of the Standing Army of Britain, that we commence our story.

There are two points in the history of the Regiment which require some clearing up.

The first point is the Battle of the Boyne. In a modern historical work on the army a copy of the plan of the line of battle of William of Orange's Army at the Boyne is given, nowhere in which is Wynne's regiment of Enniskillen Dragoons shown. The author gives the 6th Dragoons as being in the right and left wings of both the first and second line. In his copy of the plan, the author has given the modern numbers of such regiments engaged as are still in existence, and in that I venture to think is the possibility of an error. The plan of the line of battle is said to have been executed about the year 1694 or 1695, before the system of numbering regiments came into being. I have personally seen the plan of the line of battle at the Boyne in the Print Department at the British Museum, and I find that "Enniskillen Dragoons" are placed in the right and left wings of both the first and second line.

There were three mounted regiments of Enniskillen fighting for William of Orange at the Boyne, *viz.* The Enniskillen Horse, (disbanded some few years later), and two regiments of Enniskillen Dragoons, one being Wynne's (later the 5th Royal Irish Dragoons and now the 5th Lancers), and the other Cunningham's, which became the 6th

Dragoons and has throughout its distinguished career retained the name of Inniskilling.

Tending to confirm my argument that a possible error has been made in not mentioning the presence of Wynne's Dragoons at the Boyne, I note that more than one writer of the War in Ireland states that Wynne's Dragoons were at the Dundalk camp a few days before the Battle of the Boyne with the remainder of William's army, and that the regiment took part in the review at Finglas a few days after the battle, where its strength is given.

In this matter of the Boyne I have to thank Major E. S. Jackson, late of the 6th Inniskilling Dragoons, for his opinion, which bears out the foregoing argument.

The second point to be mentioned is the operations in Flanders from 1743 to 1748, and more especially the battle of Fontenoy. Certain writers state that the Royal Irish Dragoons served at Fontenoy, but in no detailed account of the battle can it be discovered that such was the case, and in the lists of killed and wounded the regiment is not mentioned, while an entry in Lord Stair's Order Book (Add. M.S. 20,005) is a paragraph giving the regiment as being in Ireland.

In the following pages there will be found but little reading from Ormonde's abortive campaign to the Irish Rebellion of 1799. For the reasons already mentioned, and because a continuous list of changes of stations and mere matters of detail are dull reading, and also for want of space, that period has been but lightly touched upon.

The account of the great rebellion of 1799 in Ireland tells its own tale, and in its relation my object is "neither to vindicate, nor to set down aught in malice."

I regret exceedingly that a sudden departure for India prevents my obtaining the biographies of certain officers who have been at the head of the regiment, more especially that of Lord Rossmore and of his Lieutenant-Colonel, Stewart, who later, in the Peninsula wars, rose to great distinction. For the same reason I am unable correctly to check the list of officers who have served in the old and present regiment, and I must tender my apologies for any mistakes in the Roll.

I have met with the greatest kindness and help on all sides; I would especially thank Brigadier-General Allenby C.B., Commanding the 4th Cavalry Brigade, for his encouragement and help at the commencement of my labours, and also my thanks are due to Lieutenant-Colonel H. Graham D.S.Q. and the officers of the 5th Lancers for coming forward and taking over the final work of publication, which, owing to the exigencies of the Service, I am prevented from doing. With them, too, I have to thank my stepfather, Mr James Dodds, for his promise of co-operation. I have made much use of the departments at the British Museum and the Public Record Office, and have experienced the greatest kindness from the officials at both those institutions. The advice of the Librarian at the War Office was most valuable, while the Royal United Service Institution and the Prince Consort's Library at Aldershot were of the greatest help. My thanks are also due to Mr W. Morris Colles, of the Authors' Syndicate, for his sound advice and practical help.

To Major-General Cooke C.V.O., Colonel of the Regiment, my thanks are due, for his sympathy in my undertaking.

That this story might have better told I well know, but should it prove of interest to my comrades the officers, non-commissioned officers and men of the 5th Lancers, I should feel that the labours of the past three years have not been in vain.

I have only to add that my effort is but a small thank offering for the extremely happy thirteen years which I have passed in the regiment, and which end today.

W. T. W.

West Cavalry Barracks
Aldershot.
17th December, 1906.

CHAPTER 1

The Irish Revolution 1688-1691

At the close of 1688 the Earl of Tyrconnel foresaw the possibility of a struggle in Ireland between William of Orange and King James and set himself to organise a Jacobite army in Ireland. His efforts were so successful that he was able to attach to the Jacobite cause no less than 19 regiments of infantry, 4 or 5 of cavalry, 20,000 stands of arms and several guns.

Tyrconnel's successful efforts in organising this Jacobite army had the result of arousing the suspicions of the North of Ireland, and the people of the North immediately began to organise on their part on behalf of King William the Third.

There were a number of minor engagements in the North in which the people of the North were mostly defeated, although they were more or less successful in some. King William's adherents however, seeing it was useless to carry on these detached actions in the open, proceeded to concentrate their forces, chiefly at Derry and Enniskillen.

Andrew Hamilton, in his pamphlet entitled *The actions of the Enniskillen Men*, writes that the inhabitants of Inniskilling and of the country round that town received orders early in December 1688 from Lord Tyrconnel to provide quarters for two Foot Companies of Irish which he proposed to send to the town, and on Friday the 14th December, news arrived that the two companies of foot whose presence they so much feared, were within 18 miles of Enniskillen. On the 15th December, the men of Enniskillen wrote the following letter to the officers commanding in Londonderry:—

Gentlemen,
The frequent intelligence we have from all parts of this King-

dom, of a general massacre of the Protestants, and two companies of foot of Sir Thomas Newcomen's regiment. . . . being on their march to garrison here, and now within 10 miles, hath put upon us the resolution of refusing them entrance our design being only to preserve our own lives, and the lives of our neighbours, this being the most considerable pass between Connaught and Ulster; and hearing of your resolutions, we thought it convenient to impart this to you, as likewise to beg your assistance both in your advice and relief especially in hewing us with some powder, and in carrying on a correspondence with us hereafter, as we shall with God's assistance, do with you, which is all at present, Gentlemen, from your faithful friends and fellow Christians.

The Inhabitants of Enniskillen.

On Sunday the 16th at 10 a.m., word reached the town that the two companies they so much feared had arrived at Lisbellaw. Most of the inhabitants were in church at the time, but soon got under arms, resolved to advance and meet the enemy. On being drawn out they were found to amount to some 200 infantry and 150 horse, and the sight of the Enniskillen men was sufficient to drive the two companies, headed by their officers, to Cavan, where they remained until they received orders from Tyrconnel to march to other quarters.

On the 18th December Gustavus Hamilton was appointed governor of the town, and under him was formed a garrison drawn from the town itself and the surrounding districts.

This garrison soon consisted of 12 Companies of Horse and Foot:

Upon which they thought fit to regiment themselves under Gustavus Hamilton and Thomas Lloyd, and to send to England for arms and ammunition, meanwhile causing a great number of pikes to be made, and beating out old scythes, they fixing them on poles.

In the news of the accession of William and Mary in March 1689, Andrew Hamilton states "we rejoiced unspeakably."

When James II landed at Kinsale in March 1689 with some 1800 followers from France, the situation stood briefly thus:—

The Earl of Tyrconnel, James' Lord Lieutenant, had been stirring to prevent the Protestants from "concentralisng" so as to become formidable, and he had occupied in King James' name as many stations as he could. The Protestants, on the other hand, were endeavouring to hold their own until support should arrive from England. Both parties were very determined and rancorous, because their quarrel was religious as well as political and national. The Irish had it all their own way in the South, and were also predominant in Connaught and Leinster, but in the North the Protestants were more numerous, and were banding themselves together for resistance.

James arrived in the North of Ireland in April, and appearing before Derry, demanded the surrender of the town. The answer he received was: "No surrender" accompanied by the discharge of every description of firearm, whereupon the forces of King James laid siege unsuccessfully to the place for 105 days, until it was relieved by a force from England.

Meanwhile the people of Inniskilling, in spite of the manifestations of Lord Gilmoy, the threats of King James and of the non-arrival of arms from England, remained firm in their defence of the city.

On the 6th May 1689, Lieut.-Colonel Lloyd with 12 Foot Companies and some horse went towards Ballyshannon, and meeting the enemy's horse near Beleek, soon put them to rout; killing about 120 of them and taking prisoners and 2 small pieces of cannon, several horses and some good arms, without the loss of a single man.

This was the first time our men encountered the enemy in the field and having had so great success in the beginning it encouraged our men very much.—Andrew Hamilton.

Redhills and Ballinacarg in the county of Cavan, were taken by Lloyd with 1500 Horse and Foot. The taking of these places spread consternation amongst the Irish, and Lloyd returned to Enniskillen with 3000 cows and oxen, 2000 sheep and some horses, again without losing a man.

On June 4th, the Governor of Enniskillen, hearing that the Irish Army besieging Derry had sent a great many of their horses to graze near Omagh, despatched two troops of dragoons under Captains Gore and Crosby to the parish of Kilskerry, where they stayed two days, and picked up a troop of Horse and two companies of foot that were quartered there. In the evening, at about sunset, they proceeded together towards Omagh, and before eight o'clock the next morning they returned with 80 good horses, and nearly as many more smaller and inferior horses fit for labour, and 300 cows. By this enterprise they dismounted about three troops of the enemy's horse, and would have

IRISH DRAGOONS

surprised their foot at Omagh, if notice of their coming had not been sent to the enemy, which gave the latter time to secure their position, but not to save their cattle.

On the 10th of June, the Governor of Enniskillen, hearing of the dreadful state of the Protestants in Londonderry, who, it was generally thought, would be obliged to surrender in a few days if not relieved, marched with 2000 of his men towards that city. At Omagh he possessed himself of the whole of the town except the fort, which he invested. In a few hours, however, urgent messages were received from Enniskillen that Colonel Sarsfield with 5000 or 6000 men had advanced and laid siege to Ballyshannon, and that Colonel Sutherland had appeared with another army before Belturbet. Each of these places being within 20 miles of Enniskillen, the danger of an attack from these armies appeared imminent. A consultation was at once held, when it was agreed that it was their imperative duty to return to the protection of their own town, and not to proceed, according to their previous purpose, to the relief of another. The next day, therefore, the whole party returned to Enniskillen.

On the 15th of June, the Enniskilleners received intelligence that Colonel Sutherland's force at Belturbet was daily increasing, as the Irish were flocking to him from all parts of the country. Colonel Lloyd was ordered to march against Sutherland with the greatest strength of Horse and Foot he could collect, and on the 17th he arrived at Maguire's bridge, half way between Enniskillen and Belturbet, with his little army, which Irish rumours had swelled to the imaginary number of 15,000. From McGuire's bridge a spy fled on Lloyd's approach, and informed Sutherland that all the forces of Enniskillen were in full march to attack him. Sutherland had with him at Belturbet only two regiments of foot, a regiment of dragoons, and a few troops of Horse. He gave credit to the exaggerated numbers of his opponents, and no longer considered it safe to remain in Belturbet.

There was no place of any strength there but the church and the graveyard about it, the latter being but weakly fortified, and not nearly large enough to contain the men he had with him. He therefore retreated towards Monaghan, leaving a detachment of 80 dragoons and 200 foot under the command of Lieut. Col. Edward Scott to defend Belturbet. The next day happening to be remarkably wet, Lloyd's army could not march from their quarters, and so the retreat of Sutherland was effected without a pursuit; but on the succeeding day the Enniskilleners appeared before Belturbet. Colonel Lloyd, advancing at the

CAVALRY CHARGE

head of his men against the town, ordered Captain Robert Vaughan and Capt. Hugh Galbraith, with their two troops of Dragoons, on the forlorn hope. When within two miles of the town, they were fired on by a troop of dragoons, upon which they alighted from their horses and lined the ditches upon both sides of the road, "which unusual manoeuvre," together with the appearance of the main body of their army coming up at the moment, caused the enemy to retreat to Belturbet. Here, with the rest of their party, they took post in and about the church, and in the Archbishop of Dublin's house adjoining it; but after two hours skirmishing, they held out a white flag and surrendered upon the condition that their lives should be spared, but that the common soldiers should be stripped of their red coats. The officers were not included in this stipulation, and had all their money, under ten pounds each, returned to them.

The prisoners taken numbered 300, including Colonel Scott and 13 other officers. Two hundred of the meanest prisoners were next morning discharged, the victors being unwilling to have the trouble of maintaining them, and the rest, with their officers, were brought to Enniskillen, together with about 700 muskets, some gunpowder, 80 dragoon horses, with all the accoutrements belonging to them, 20 horse loads of biscuit, 50 barrels of flour, 120 barrels of wheat, and as many red coats as served two companies of men, who were in much need of such clothing.

Early in July, General Kirk, who had arrived from England with a fleet for the relief of Londonderry, sent a ship round from Lough Swilly to Ballyshannon, for the purpose of ascertaining the wants of the Enniskillen garrison and offering a supply of ammunition and other necessaries. Whereupon on the 4th July an expedition was sent to inform him of their wants, and to bring back arms and ammunition. With the expedition was sent a statement of their strength, as follows:—

17 troops, 30 Foot Companies and some few troops of Dragoons; our Foot are indifferently well armed, but our Horse and Dragoons not so well.—Andrew Hamilton.

Kirk had but few arms fit for horsemen, but, on July the 12th he gave the Enniskilleners 20 barrels of gunpowder, 600 firelocks, and a thousand muskets, together with bullets and match, 8 small pieces of cannon and a few hand grenades.

Major General Kirke, gave us commissions for a regiment of

21

horse consisting of 16 troops, and 50 private men in each troop besides officers, for a regiment of dragoons consisting of 12 troops and the like number of private men in each troop, and for 3 regiments of foot each consisting of 18 companies of 60 private men in each. He told us he could spare none of his private men, but gave us some very good officers, *viz.*—Col. Will Wolseley to be our commander-in-chief and Colonel of Horse, Colonel Will Berry to be Lieutenant-Colonel to our Horse: Captain James Wynne, a gentleman of Ireland, but then a Captain in Col. Stuart's Regiment, to be Colonel of our Dragoons: and for our 3 Regiments of Foot, Governor Gustavus Hamilton, Lieut. Col. Lloyd and Major Tiffan were made Colonels.[1] These regiments were brought on to the establishment of the Regular Army on 1st January 1689 by the following Royal Warrant[2]:—

W. R.

Whereas we have thought fitt to forme a regiment of horse together with two regiments of dragoons and three regiments of foot out of our Inniskilling Forces, and to take them into our pay and entertainment. We do hereby make and pass this our establishment for the said forces to commence the first day of January 1689, in the first year of our reign.

Then follow the establishment charges, those for a Regiment of Dragoons being:

FIELD AND STAFF OFFICERS

		£.	s.	d.	
Colonel as Colonel.		£.	15.	0	per diem.
Lieut.-Colonel as Lt.-Col.			9.	0	„
Major, who has no troop for himself and horses		1.	0.	0	„
Chaplain			6.	8	„
Adjutant			5.	0	„
Chirugion			6.	0	„
Gun Smith 4s — and 1s for his servent.			5.	0	„

ONE TROOP

			s.	d.	
Captain 8s and 3 horses 3s			11.	0	„
Lieutenant 4s 2 „ 2s			6.	0	„
Cornet 3s and 2 „ 2s			5.	0	„
Quartermaster for self & horse.			4.	0	„

1. Andrew Hamilton.
2. Harl. MSS. no. 4847.

3 Sergeants, each 18d & 3s horses . .	7.	6	„
3 Corporals, each 12d & 3s „ . .	6.	o	„
2 Drummers, each 12d & 2s „ . .	4.	o	„
60 Dragoons, 18d a day for man and horse. 4.	10.	o	„

A regiment of Dragoons to consist of 8 troops.

The above mentioned Royal Warrant called into existence Wolseley's Inniskilling Horse—disbanded in 1697.

Wynne's Inniskilling Dragoons—afterwards the 5th Royal Irish Dragoons, disbanded in 1799, and re-embodied as the 5th Royal Irish Lancers in 1858.

Cunningham's Inniskilling Dragoons—now the 6th Inniskilling Dragoons.

Hamilton's Inniskilling Foot

Lloyd's   „   „

Tiffan's   „   „   now the 27th Inniskilling Fusiliers.

The following officers were appointed to the regiment on formation, commissions bearing date 20th June 1689.

               Captains

Jas. Wynne   —Colonel

. . . . . .   —Lt. Colonel

. . . . . .   —Major

Hugh Galbraith

Percy Gethin

Chas. Newcomen

Hugh Caldwell

Chas. Ross

               Lieutenants

Robt. Drury

               Cornets

Mat. Watts

Mat. Wells

Although it has no immediate connection with the dragoons of Enniskillen, it may not be out of place here to turn for a moment to the famous siege of Derry. The following market prices, taken from *Walker's Diary*, testify to the extent of the sufferings from famine of the garrison, and the degree of heroism which animated them in their refusals to surrender.—Horse flesh, each pound, one shilling and eight pence. A quarter of a dog, fattened by eating dead bodies, five shillings and six pence. A dog's head, two shillings and six pence. A cat, four shillings and six pence. A rat, fattened by eating human flesh, one shilling. A mouse, six pence.

Walker, Bishop of Derry, governor of that city and garrison. Colonel of volunteers and the last warrior Bishop of English history, says that by the 27th July, the defenders of Londonderry had no prospect of subsistence otherwise than by eating the bodies of the dead; and he mentions a fat gentleman of his acquaintance who hid himself for several days, because he imagined that some of the soldiers who were perishing by hunger, looked at him with a greedy eye.

The regiments of horse in the place had been reduced to foot; having in their extremity been forced to kill and eat their horses.

At this time the Irish General McCarthy was besieging the Castle of Crom on Lough Erne; and another Irish force under Colonel Sarsfield was at the same time close to Ballyshannon, the design being to effect a junction before Enniskillen and to crush that stronghold. In order to prevent this junction, and to force a separate action with one or other of these leaders. Colonel Wolseley at Enniskillen detached Lt.-Col. Berry on the 30th July with some four troops of horse, two of dragoons, and three companies of foot, to turn McCarthy.

On the 31st of July Berry came up with the enemy about four miles beyond Lisnaskea. Finding they far outnumbered his own detachment, he despatched an orderly to Wolseley at Enniskillen asking for assistance; he meantime retreated past Lisnaskea so as to take up a position a mile from the town, where he would have a bog to cover his front. The causeway over the bog was scarcely wide enough to allow of two horsemen riding abreast. He placed his dragoons and infantry in a thicket of underwood at the end of the causeway, drawing a body of horse a little further off as a reserve, with which he proposed to support the other, and he gave the word "Oxford."

The pursuing Irish soon came into view. McCarthy had ordered Colonel Anthony Hamilton with a force to attack Berry at once.

On arriving at the bog, Hamilton dismounted his dragoons and gallantly led them along the causeway on foot. Both parties opened fire. The Enniskilleners were concealed in the thicket, while Hamilton's men were in full view on the narrow causeway. Hamilton was very soon wounded, and his successor in the command was immediately after shot dead. Deprived of their leaders, and with their comrades dropping around them, the Irish began to retreat, while the Enniskilleners "raising a shout, and crying out that the rogues were running," took the bog on each side of the narrow road over which their reserve of horse galloped, and quickly turned the retreat into a flight, and chased the fugitives through the streets of Lisnaskea, killing some 200 and taking 30 prisoners, and capturing a large number of arms.

It was still but nine o'clock, and Berry returned to his ground and rested his men until a message arrived at about noon from Wolseley, ordering him to effect a junction with him at Lisnaskea. On the junction of the two bodies, Wolseley called the officers together, and also consulted the men, and explained the risk they ran of being caught between McCarthy and Sarsfield, and of their shortness of provisions, and that their only alternative to fighting McCarthy at once was to return home. They were unanimous in giving the preference to "fighting their way to the enemy's provision carts, rather than return to Enniskillen for their dinner," (*Siege of Derry*).

McCarthy's force consisted of some 6000 men, horse, foot and dragoons, while with Wolseley were 16 troops of horse, 3 of dragoons, and 21 companies of foot, in all barely 2000 men.

Accordingly, having given the word "No Popery," this gallant little band marched towards the enemy.

McCarthy had raised the siege of Crom and was advancing towards the Enniskilleners, but on coming in sight of them between Donagh and Newtown-Butler, he retreated on Newtown-Butler, and took up a position about half a mile from that place, on a steep hill with a bog in front of it.

The forlorn hope of the Enniskilleners led their advance by half a mile, and on reaching the enemy's position. Colonel Tiffan with his battalion of foot entered the bog on the right of the causeway, while Colonel Lloyd's battalion moved on the left, and Colonel Wynne's dragoons, divided into two parts, supported Tiffan and Lloyd on foot. Berry, with the horse, advanced along the causeway, and Wolseley came on in the rear with the main body.

McCarthy allowed the van of the Enniskilleners to cross the bog before opening fire, but before they could climb the hill he retired through Newtown-Butler (which was set fire to) to a similar position about a mile beyond the town. McCarthy posted his guns so as to cover the causeway across the bog, and checked the advance of the Enniskillen horse along the causeway. Wolseley recalled the horse, and ordered his infantry across the bog in extended order, Tiffan on the right, and Lloyd on the left, with Wynne's dragoons (dismounted) again supporting either wing. The Enniskilleners crossed the bog with some loss, captured the cannon and "killed the cannoneers," who had courageously maintained their fire to the last moment. The horse then came along the causeway in support.

The brunt of the Enniskillen attack was borne by the Irish right. McCarthy, seeing this, sent orders to a regiment on the left to move to the right. There was some mistake in the delivery of the order, and the regiment, instead of facing to the right, went to the right about. The troops in rear of this regiment imagined they were about to retreat. The Irish cavalry promptly turned and galloped off, leaving the infantry to their fate. The regiment that had faced about, seeing the cavalry go off, ran too, whereupon the right threw down their arms and fled also. By this time the Enniskillen Horse had reached the spot, and there ensued a most bloody rout. The majority of the fugitives made towards Crom, and crossing a bog took refuge in a wood near Lough Erne, where they were followed by the Enniskillen Foot, who gave no quarter to any but the officers. Rendered desperate, 500 of the fugitives took to the waters of the Lough, and only one escaped drowning.

Of McCarthy's 6000 men, 400 were captured, 2000 killed and 500 drowned. McCarthy, who had striven in vain to rally his troops, was captured, and all the Irish guns, ammunition and colours were taken. The loss amongst the Enniskilleners did not amount to a hundred.

> There was a very remarkable stroke given by Captain William Smith in the battle: with one blow of his sword, he cut off the upper part of a man's skull, just under the hat. As much of the skull as was within the hat, with all the brains it contained, was struck away from the under part of it, and not so much as a fibre of skin remained to keep them together, (*Siege of Derry*).

> After this victory, the name of the Enniskillen men became a terror to the Irish, (Andrew Hamilton).

> The Enniskilleners having made their name a terror to the Irish, had only to rest and refresh themselves, and regiment themselves according to the commissions which General Kirk had sent them, (*History of Ireland*).

Londonderry was relieved by Kirk on the 4th of August, and on the 7th, that general sent orders to Wolseley at Enniskillen to send him 500 horse and 200 dragoons to escort his infantry to meet the Duke Schomberg, who was on his way from England to Belfast Lough with an army which King William had raised in England.

According to these orders our horse and dragoons came to Derry, and "marched before the major-general till his party joined Duke Schomberg at Carrickfergus," in other words, the horse and dragoons acted as Kirk's advanced guard.

Schomberg landed near Bangor on the 13th of August with 10,000 men, and on the following day started for Carrickfergus, arriving at that place on the 15th August; and, besieging it for eleven days, captured it on the 26th.

The arrival of the Inniskilling Horse, Dragoons, and Foot, and 3000 more men from England, made up Duke Schomberg's army to 15,000 men.

There arc two incidents recorded in the Siege of Carrickfergus which are of interest.

The first is that its defenders discovered the Duke Schomberg's tent, and waiting until he was at dinner, they fired two or three 6 lb. shot at the tent. A writer points out that this was a gross breach of manners and of military etiquette. The other incident is curious. A breach was made in the wall of Carrickfergus, and was about to be rushed, when the inhabitants of the town drove a large herd of bullocks towards the breach. The guns were turned on the bullocks, killing them, and earth being thrown over the beasts they formed a rampart which was defended for some considerable time.

By the terms of the surrender of Carrickfergus, the garrison was permitted to march out to Newry, to the great chagrin of the Enniskilleners.

On the surrender of Carrickfergus, the English Army marched to Belfast, and on the 2nd of September continued the march to Newry *via* Dromore and Lough Wickland.

The Enniskillen Horse and 5th and 6th Dragoons formed the advanced guard.

These regiments, whose exploits had often been talked over by the English soldiers, were the subject of great curiosity when they first joined Schomberg's force. Everyone expected to see a perfectly equipped and admirably drilled body of men. Instead of this, there rode into camp three regiments of irregulars without uniforms, mounted on all sorts of horses. Some men had holsters, while others carried their pistols stuck into their belts; and the majority of the privates had their servants riding behind them on small country ponies called "garrons."

Another eyewitness writes:—

The Inniskilling Dragoons came there to us. They are but middle sized men, but they are, nevertheless, brave fellows. I have seen them like masty (mastiff) dogs run against bullets.

Story, an army chaplain, in his *Impartial History of the War*, gives us the following anecdote in connection with that advanced guard of Enniskilleners. He met the dragoons, who had received orders to find the enemy's outposts and to establish contact with them and to report to Schomberg. To use his own words:

They showed me the enemy's scouts upon a hill before us; I wisht them to go and beat them off, and they answered 'with all their hearts; but they had orders to go no further than where they saw the enemy's scouts;' though they seemed to be dissatisfied with it, and added, they should never thrive so long as they were under orders.

Schomberg had formed a high opinion of the Enniskillen's, and reposed more confidence in them than in the freshly raised English regulars. He had sent to England for uniforms for them.

On the approach of the English Army, the Duke of Berwick abandoned Newry after setting fire to the town, and retreated to Drogheda, where he joined King James. Schomberg sent "a trumpet" to Berwick, to say if any more towns were thus wantonly burnt, his army would give no quarter for the future; a timely hint of which Berwick availed himself. The word trumpet, as used here, meant a message sent by a cavalry trumpeter; a message sent by a drummer was termed a "drum."

After two days rest at Newry, Schomberg's army proceeded to Dundalk, where they arrived on the 7th September, and pitched their camp about a mile North West of the town, on extremely damp, low-lying and marshy ground.

The Enniskillen horse, foot and dragoons, together with the Guards and some artillery, were posted on the Northern side of the town to protect it from attack.

Meanwhile, King James had collected an army at Drogheda, and on the 21st September he appeared before the camp at Dundalk, but Schomberg refused to entertain any idea of fighting. Fever had broken out in his camp, and he was doubtful of the loyalty of the French troops with him. He found out afterwards that there was a conspiracy amongst them.

Diversions were made by King James all along Schomberg's right towards Sligo, and it was during one of these, on the 27th September, that a force of Enniskillen horse and dragoons about 1000 strong under Colonel Lloyd, succeeded in utterly routing an Irish force of some 5000 men near Boyle and Sligo.

Duke Schomberg was so delighted to hear of the gallantry and success of the men from Enniskillen, that:

> Having ordered all the Enniskillen horse, foot and dragoons in his camp to be drawn out, he rode along the line with his hat off, and caused the Dutch guards and the Enniskillen foot to make three running fires, which were answered by the Enniskillen horse and by the cannon upon the works, as also from the ships that lay at the mouth of the river, as an honourable mark of his approbation, (*Impartial History of the War*).

The camp at Dundalk was now getting into a most insanitary condition; a raging sickness of fever, occasioned by the unwholesome situation of the camp, a wet season, bad provisions and want of medicines, clothes and comfortable bedding, swept away and disabled a great number of Schomberg's officers and soldiers. King William wrote several letters to Schomberg, pressing him to move on Dublin, but Schomberg alleged many good reasons for not doing so.

In addition to the sickness, his English troops were in a bad state of disorganisation and training. The confidential Report on the state of the army throws some light on the deplorable condition of some of the regiments. The report on one reads:

> The colonel ill, and as incapable as all the other officers, who are usually absent; as bad a regiment as possible, except . . . . . . which is worse.

Another:

> The major very assiduous, but the colonel neglects the regiment.

One regiment is accused of much debauchery and drinking; while another "has hardly any good officers, an entire absence of good order, and badly clothed." Another regiment has;

> A very assiduous colonel, but he is too easy to the officers, who are the most negligent that can be imagined. Often he is the only officer present with the regiment, which he never quits;

yet the regiment is in a bad condition; arms almost useless.

One regiment has a colonel who "has a good opinion of himself, but is not really efficient."

The question of the payment of the army was another of Schomberg's difficulties. Not only did the military officers rob their men, but the commander-in-chief could get but little money. For this, the Treasurer of the Army, a most shameless individual, was responsible. The only corps in the force which was regularly paid, was an independent troop of cavalry, which this official, by name William Harbord, had, by some jobbery, contrived to "raise" and command. The troop in reality only consisted of himself, two clerks, whom he put down as officers, and a standard which he kept in his bedroom; and yet he managed to draw pay regularly for it as a complete troop of cavalry.

It is not to be wondered at that Schomberg considered his army unfit to advance, and that it showed itself equally unfit for the monotony of a standing camp.

In the beginning of November, the Irish Army went into winter quarters, and Schomberg lost no time in following their example, and on 5th November the camp was broken up.

On the 4th December, Belturbet was taken by Wolseley with a force of Enniskilleners, and the dragoons of Enniskillen went into winter quarters there on the 12th of that month.

The loss of life in the camp at Dundalk stood thus:—

Total of Army in Camp		14.000
Losses—Died in Camp	1.700	
Died in course of removal to Belfast	800	
Died in Hospital at Belfast	3.800	6.300
Survivors		7.700

Story writes:

> Death has become so familiar in the camp at Dundalk that men were only sorry when their comrades were carried away for burial, because their dead bodies had been used to stop the chinks in the huts, (*Impartial History of the War*).

The same author writes that during the march of a foot regiment to winter quarters, some men were lodged one night in a stable, and the morning two of them were dead. The chaplain visited the stable, and found the survivors had arranged the bodies of their two dead comrades to serve as seats round a fire.

On the 12th February, 1690, the Duke of Berwick reinforced the Irish garrison at Cavan with some three to four thousand men, with the object of next day dislodging Wolseley's force from Belturbet. Wolseley, however, had received notice of this design, and marched from Belturbet in the same evening that Berwick entered Cavan, with 3 troops of horse, 2 of dragoons, and 700 foot, in all about 1000 men.

Wolseley's only chance of success lay in surprising his enemy; he accordingly made a detour so as to cross the River Annalee a couple of miles above Ballyhaise. This entailed a march of 14 miles over bad roads and a deep ford, "over which the horse were obliged to carry the foot," and it was daylight before he came within a mile of Cavan. The approach of the Enniskilleners was perceived, and the garrison beat to arms. The advanced guard of cavalry was checked in a narrow lane, and retreated on the infantry, some of whom. Story relates, were so furious at the idea of running from Irishmen, that they fired at the cavalry and killed several of them.

Wolseley now brought forward his foot, and the enemy retired on the main body, which held a fortified position on a hill near the town. The Enniskilleners deployed to the attack. After a while the enemy, giving a yell of victory, fired a volley and charged, but the balls flew harmlessly overhead, and before they could reload, the Enniskilleners poured in such a brisk fire that the Irish fled. The victors, instead of pursuing the enemy into the fort, began to loot the town, which gave the Irish an opportunity to sally out of the fort and attack them.

Wolseley 's reserve of some 300 men kept the enemy at bay, while he and his officers endeavoured to rally their men in the town. They found this more difficult than they imagined, and they had to set fire to the town to compel the men to leave the burning houses.

The Irish infantry were again driven into the fort, while the horse fled and disappeared altogether. The magazines were blown up, and stores destroyed, and Wolseley returned to Belturbet; his men being too fatigued to attempt the capture of the fort, having been marching and fighting since 4 p.m. the previous day.

Wolseley captured 200 prisoners, and killed 10 officers and 300 men, the Enniskilleners only losing about 30 men.

The following order, issued by the Duke of Schomberg to the English Army in Ireland, is interesting:

A PROCLAMATION

By Frederick, Duke of Schomberg
Lord General of Their Majesties forces &c.

Whereas the horrid and detestable crimes of profane cursing, swearing, and taking God's Holy Name in vain, being sins of much guilt and little temptation, have, by all nations and people, and that in all ages, been punished with sharp and severe penalties, as great and grievous sins: And we, to our great grief and trouble, taking notice of the too frequent practice of these sins by several under our command; and that some have arrived to that height of impiety that they are heard more frequently to invoke God to Damn them than to Save them; and this notwithstanding the heavy and dreadful judgments of God upon us at this very time for these and our other sins, and notwithstanding the penalties enjoined by Their Majesties' Articles of War on these offenders; and we, justly fearing that their Majesties' Army may be more prejudiced by these sins than advantaged by the conduct and courage of those guilty of them, do think fit strictly to charge and command all officers and soldiers under our command that they and every one of them from henceforward do forbear all vain cursing, swearing, and taking God's Holy Name in vain, under the penalties enjoined by the aforesaid Articles, and our further displeasure; and that all officers take particular care to put the said Articles of War in execution on all under their respective commands guilty of the said offences, as they will answer the contrary at their utmost peril.

Given at our Headquarters. . . . the 18th January 1690.

Schomberg.

From March to June 1690, the military operations consisted of the nature of raids and counter-raids, attended with considerable loss of life on both sides, and captures of cattle by Schomberg's forces.

In April, Schomberg besieged the fortress of Charlemont, but the Enniskilleners were not employed in the investment. The place fell to Schomberg, but some days before its capture, a "trumpet" was sent to summon it to surrender. "Tell your gineral," shouted O'Regan the governor, "that he is an owld knave, an' by Sin Patrick, he shall not have the town at all, at all."

This Teague O'Regan; an old gentleman, must have been somewhat of a character. Story writes that on the surrender of the town, O'Regan,

32

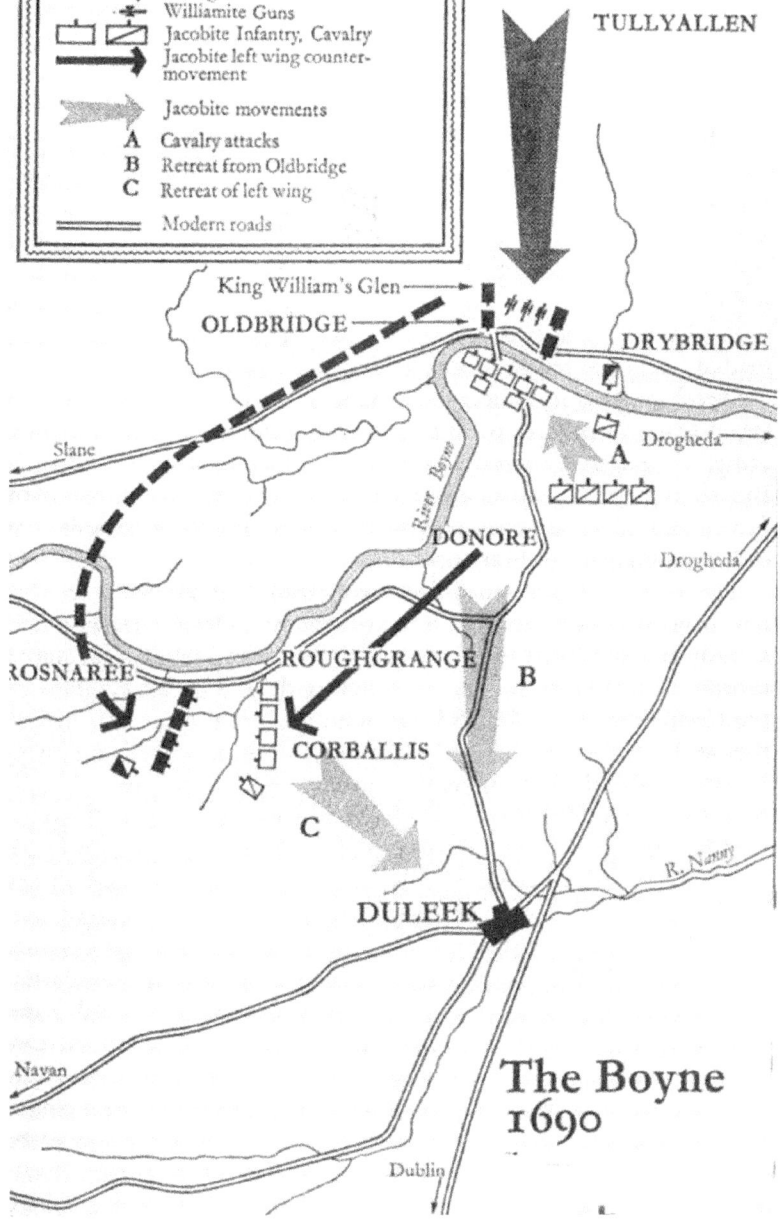

The Boyne 1690

Legend:
- Williamite Infantry, Cavalry
- Williamite attack at Oldbridge
- Williamite turning movement through Rosnaree
- Williamite Guns
- Jacobite Infantry, Cavalry
- Jacobite left wing counter-movement
- Jacobite movements
- A Cavalry attacks
- B Retreat from Oldbridge
- C Retreat of left wing
- Modern roads

TULLYALLEN

King William's Glen
OLDBRIDGE
DRYBRIDGE
Slane
Drogheda
A
River Boyne
DONORE
Drogheda
ROSNAREE
ROUGHGRANGE
B
CORBALLIS
C
R. Nanny
DULEEK
Navan
Dublin

riding out to meet the duke, wore an old red coat, a worn out, long, ill dressed wig, on which was perched a narrow brimmed white beaver hat, much too small for him and cocked on one side; a yellow cravat round his scraggy throat, and a muff hanging round his neck, and he had evidently "drink taken." He was mounted on a very old and starved stallion, which was very lame, and had an unpleasant trick of kicking and squealing when anyone approached him. The two generals, the Duke Schomberg and Teague O'Regan, met and began to exchange the usual compliments, which, however, were cut short by Teague's vicious stallion, which drowned every syllable with his squeals, clearing a ring round him by lashing out on all sides. As soon as the ridiculous scene was over, and he could control his laughter and speak, the duke observed that if Teague's horse was very mad, Teague himself was very drunk. O'Regan was afterwards knighted by King James.

All this time, regiments, recruits, and reinforcements, and also an artillery train had been arriving at Belfast from England and the Continent for the English Army.

King William himself landed at Carrickfergus on the 14th June, having left London on 4th June, and before a week was over, the army was assembled between Armagh and Newry. The king occupied himself in making minute inspections of the different regiments, which he formed into brigades, and in gaining a knowledge of his generals and staff. By the 27th, his army was concentrated on Dundalk. The following list from Story gives the strength of the army, and shows the English regiments that took part in the Battle of the Boyne River. In giving this list. Story makes the following note:

> Because several people may be curious to know what number of men we had at the Boyne, and also how many the enemy were, I have inserted the exact number of our horse and foot, as it was taken at Finglas.

HORSE.

	Men.
Life Guards 1st & 3rd Troops & Horse Grenadiers.	368
Oxford's Blues (Royal Horse Guards)	368
Lanier's (1st Dragoon Guards).	360
Villiers' (2nd „ „).	245
Coy's (5th „ „).	236
Byerley's (6th „ „).	244
Schomberg's (7th „ „).	242
Russell's	242
Langston's (Princess Anne's,	225

Wolseley's (Enniskillen)	423
Harbord's Troop	38
Total Horse.	2,991

DRAGOONS.

Hayford's Mathews' (1st Royal Dragoons) . . .	406
Leveson's (3rd Dragoons, now 3rd Hussars) . . .	246
Wynne's Enniskillen (5th Dragoons now 5th Royal Irish Lancers)	260
Cunningham's Enniskillen (6 Inniskilling Dragoons) .	358
Total Dragoons.	1,270

FOOT REGIMENTS.

Douglas'	648
Kirke's (2nd Queen's).	666
Trelawney's or Queen's Regt. (4th King's Own) . .	553
Lloyd's (5th Northumberland Fus.) . . .	652
Babington's (6th R. Warwickshire) . . .	416
Beaumont's (8th King's Liverpool) . . .	526
Stuart's (9th Norfolk)	660
Hammer's (11th Devonshire)	593
Brewer's Wharton's (12th Suffolk) . . .	571
Hastings' (13th Somersetsh. L. I.). . . .	606
Meath's (18th Royal Irish)	678
Gus. Hamilton's (20th Lancs. Fus.) . . .	560
Bellasis' (22nd Cheshire)	628
Herbert's (23rd R. Welsh Fus.)	600
Deering's (24th S. Wales Borderers) . . .	600
Tiffan's, Enniskillen (27th R. Inniskilling Fus.) . .	625
Fowke's	439
Lisburne's.	611
Earle's	693
Mitchelburne's	664
S. John's	589
Drogheda's	660
Geo. Hamilton's	583
White's	600
Hamilton's	600
Total.	15,021

French Forces, Horse	395
Foot	2,231
Total.	2,626

Dutch Forces, Horse .	.	.	.	.	.	.	1,683
Dragoons	.	.	.	.	.	.	621
Foot .	.	.	.	.	.	.	3,704
					Total.		6,008

Danish &c. Forces, Horse .	.	.	.	.	.	.	812
Foot	.	.	.	.	.	.	4,581
					Total.		5,393

SUMMARY.

English Forces including 1700 for Officers & Sergeants and 300 killed at the Boyne	21,282
Foreign Forces including 1200 for Officers & Sergeants and 700 killed at the Boyne	15,927
Grand Total of K. William's Army	37,209

The list from Story was taken on 5th July after the Battle of the Boyne, and, consequently, addition has been made for killed and wounded.

The strength of the Irish Army north of the Boyne at this time is doubtful; Walton puts it down as 45,260, (Foot 32,950, Horse 12,310), but other writers bring it nearer 30,000.

James retreated before the advance of William, who arrived at the Boyne on the 30th of June, and found James in position on its southern bank.

During the march of William's Army to the Boyne, the Enniskillen Horse and Dragoons (5th and 6th) were always in the advanced guard. The two regiments of Enniskillen dragoons were at this time clothed in grey.

On the march, an Irish *gossoon* was hanged for kidnapping English soldiers, for whom he received half a crown a head. His practice was to promise to show the soldiers where cattle and loot were to be found, and so induce them to follow him. He wore an English dragoon's hat and waistcoat, the owner of which he had stabbed in the back, while his worthy father held the man in conversation.

Just before being hanged, the boy, bent on a little business combined with amusement, offered to hang one of his own countrymen, a prisoner, for six pence.

At daybreak on the last day of June, William started his army in three columns, and himself rode forward to reconnoitre the Boyne. In

BATTLE OF THE BOYNE

their position on the southern bank of the river, the Irish army possessed a good front and a safe line of retreat.

On James' right lay Drogheda, held by his soldiers, and on his left was a very difficult bog. In his front was the river Boyne, with its rugged steep banks and difficult fords. The Irish position was on a series of terraces, on the summit of which was the village of Donore commanding the view to the North.

Three miles south of Donore is the village and pass of Duleek, through which lay the high road from Drogheda to Dublin. Some three miles higher up the river, and on the left of the Irish camp, is the bridge of Slane, and an extensive bog lay between the Camp and the bridge, and one narrow road crossed the bog. In the centre of the position, and close to the river, was the hamlet of Oldbridge, to which was a good ford.

During King William's reconnaissance, the enemy opened fire on him with two six-pounders from near Oldbridge. The incident is thus related in *The Field of Mars:*—

> King William. . . . as he reconnoitred their situation, was exposed to the fire of some fieldpieces, which the enemy had purposely planted against his person. They killed a man and two horses close by him, and the second bullet rebounding from the earth, grazed upon his right shoulder, so as to carry off part of his clothes and skin, and produce a considerable contusion. This accident, which he bore without the least emotion, created some confusion amongst his attendants, which the enemy perceiving, concluded he was killed, and shouted aloud in token of their joy. Their whole camp resounded with acclamations. . . . . William rode along the line, to show himself to his army after his narrow escape.

William, meanwhile, ordered his escort to dismount and rest beside their horses in full view of the enemy. Some of Coy's and Byerley's horse and Life Guards were there, and for some hours did the king make them remain on the spot exposed to the enemy's artillery fire. Eventually he ordered them to a more sheltered position, saying: "Now I see that my men will stand."

At 9 p.m., William held a Council of War, and declared to his generals his intention of forcing the river. Schomberg opposed the idea as being too hazardous, but was over-ruled. Schomberg then suggested that a strong force should be at once sent to occupy Slane Bridge, so that in the morning it might move along the Dublin road and cut off the enemy's line of retreat at the pass of Duleek. This was opposed, and William decided against it, whereupon the duke retired in high dudgeon to his tent, and when, later, the order of battle was brought to him, he growled that it was the first he had ever had to receive since he commanded armies.

The road from Slane Bridge to the pass of Duleek was undoubtedly the key of the position, and, curiously enough, James was also advised by one of his generals to send immediately a large force to secure the bridge, which advice was also over-ruled, and a weak force of a regiment of dragoons only was sent on this duty.

In the order of battle for the English Army, King William was to lead the left attack towards Drogheda in person, the Duke Schomberg the main or centre attack on Oldbridge, while his son. Count Schomberg, was to lead the right attack against Slane Bridge.

The two armies were dressed so much alike that William ordered his men to wear a green sprig in their hats, while James' troops wore a white cockade in theirs.

Before retiring to bed at midnight. King William rode through the camp by torchlight, and gave the word "Westminster" for the night.

The 1st of July, a lovely summer morning, "as if the sun itself had a mind to see what would happen," was to witness the first pitched battle fought by the Standing Army of England. In the battle of the Boyne we shall chiefly confine ourselves to the doings of the dragoons of Enniskillen.

William's left attack was composed of all the Enniskillen Dragoons, (Wynne's and Cunningham's), and Villiers', Mathews' and Leveson's regiments of horse.

It was to move towards Drogheda, and crossing at the fords, was to hold the Irish right, and, as the centre or main attack developed, to harass the enemy.

Early in the morning the right attack under Count Schomberg forced the river at Slane Bridge and by the ford of Rosnaree just below it, and at ten o'clock, William, learning of this success, ordered the advance of the old Duke Schomberg's main attack on Oldbridge, and the king himself rode off to lead the left wing.

A short account of Schomberg's main attack will not be out of place, as during it that fine old soldier met his death.

The band of the Blue Dutch Guards struck up a march as the Dutch and French regiments marched into the river, supported by the Enniskillen Foot and Hanmer's and Nassau's brigades. The Dutchmen climbed the opposite bank and engaged the Irish Foot Guards at Oldbridge. Schomberg's regiments pressed on out of the river and the Irish regiments retreated before them. The Irish Horse then made some gallant charges, cutting their way through various regiments, finally being repulsed by Hanmer's men. These several charges had told on the whole front; the Frenchmen were nearly broken; the Dutch had received a check; the Danish horse was routed; the English brigade held its own, but made no progress.

Considerable confusion arose, and Duke Schomberg, noticing the crisis and that Caillemotte had fallen, without waiting to put on his armour, rode into the river and placed himself at the head of the leaderless French Protestants, and urged them on. It was soon after this that Schomberg was killed. There were numerous reports as to how he was shot. In Graham's *History of Ireland*, we find that the French refugees, having allowed some of the Irish Horse through their lines, thinking them friends, but, perceiving their mistake, commenced firing rashly, by which means they shot the duke in the neck. A report current in the army to this day was, that the duke was shot by a trooper in King James' Guards who was a deserter from Schomberg's regiment a year before.

Walton, in his *History of the British Standing Army*, gives the following tradition he heard from an inhabitant of Oldbridge:—

On the appearance of the English Army on the north bank of the Boyne, the inhabitants of Oldbridge abandoned their homes, many of the men joining James' army,—all except one poor deformed lame man or "*bokkha.*" This *bokkha* refused to leave, and damning the heretics who were coming to lay waste his home, he swore he would have a shot with his old duck gun at the bloody-minded Prince of Orange. On the morning of the battle he concealed himself in a double ditch by the Oldbridge ford. Lying low in his hiding place, he made out the principal personages in the enemy's army, and bided his time until he could get a shot at some important person. He watched the charges of the Irish horse, the wavering of the French regiments, and the fall of Caillemotte. He then perceived with joy a horseman ride down to the river, who was wearing a richly laced coat, an embroidered sword belt and plumes in his hat. This, he thought, must be William of Orange, and he was about to ride close by his hiding place. He examined the priming of his duck gun, and seeing the officer point the soldiers towards his empty home, decided, even if he were not the Prince of Orange, he was quite worth killing. Chance favoured the *bokkha*, for the officer turned in the saddle to speak to the soldiers, and his horse pulling at the reins stooped for a long drink. Taking a deliberate aim, he fired, and Schomberg fell, never to rise again.

History does not relate what happened to the *bokkha*.

Duke Schomberg, the gallant old soldier, and one of the greatest captains of his time, was buried in St. Patrick's Cathedral, Dublin, and two hundred and fourteen years later, the successors of Wynne's Enniskillen Dragoons, who fought under Schomberg, and under him shared the horrors of the pestilential camp at Dundalk, erected a monument close by his grave to their comrades in the 5th Royal Irish Lancers who fell in the South African War of 1899-1902.

To return to the Battle of the Boyne, at about 11 o'clock King William, with his left wing of cavalry, was putting into effect his movement against the right flank of the enemy. Placing himself at the head of the dragoons from Enniskillen, William told them that they should be his guards that day. "Gentlemen," he said, "I have heard much of your exploits, and now I shall myself witness them;" and he led his division down to the river side. Here a number of them, including the king, got bogged. William was obliged to dismount while Private David M'Kinley, of the Enniskillen Dragoons, extricated his horse. A regiment of Irish Dragoons on the other side of the river, howled in derision at the endeavours of the horsemen to reach the stream. "Pass if you can!" they shouted. Local tradition gives this as the reason for the passage being still called the "Pas-if-you-can."

At length they got into the water, and the Irish regiment retired upon its supports, when the Enniskilleners, deploying into line, charged with such fury, that they not only broke the enemy, but became so scattered in pursuit that they in turn were driven back on to the Danish Horse, by a fresh body of Irish Cavalry. William was now at the head of the Danes, who, overwhelmed by fleeing friends and pursuing foes, gave way, carrying the king with them, on to a British regiment whose immovable rock of seventeen-foot pikes turned the tide of battle: William was able to rally the flying troopers, and the Irish squadrons were cut to pieces.

CAVALRY DUEL

The Irish Foot now got the order to charge and drive the main body of William's infantry back into the river. They advanced, but only the Irish foot guards actually charged, for a murmur was passed along the ranks that the army was taken in flank by cavalry. The Irish foot-soldiers saw the grey uniforms of the relentless Enniskilleners on their right, and turning about, pressed back up the hill as fast as they could go.

In vain their officers endeavoured by example shown in sacrificing their own lives, to rally them. "The Horse, the Enniskilleners!" was all that the panic-stricken infantry would reply.

The gallantry of the Irish horse at this point saved a rout. With such effect did they charge that they gained time for their foot to re-form at Donore. But it was only for a short time; a rapid and disorderly retreat on Duleek was commenced. Two regiments of Irish dragoons were ordered to the front to check the pursuit, but both turned and followed the foot. The Irish horse regiments, however, behaved with the greatest gallantry. Time after time they charged down the grassy slopes endeavouring to check the pursuit.

At Platin House, halfway between Donore and Duleek, General Hamilton had drawn up a body of Irish cavalry in a field, into which a gap from a by-road was the only entrance. Eight troops of Enniskilleners under Wolseley came riding along this byroad in advance of the army, and two troops promptly entered the field. Wolseley ordered the men, by mistake, to form to the right, thus bringing the men with their backs to the enemy. Orders to wheel to the right were given, but the result was confusion. The Irish charged, and cutting down some fifty troopers, drove the others pell-mell on to the crowded troops in the lane, who were quite incapable of resistance and were chased out of the lane. King William, coming up with some Dutch cavalry, rode up to the Enniskilleners and asked them "What they would do for him." The soldiers turned their faces to the enemy again, and, re-forming with the Dutch, charged their pursuers, who were now joined by more of the Irish cavalry.

The hardest fighting of the day took place now. Ten times did the gallant Irish Horse charge to gain time for the retreat of their panic-stricken infantry, and ten times did the equally gallant Enniskilleners and Dutchmen beat them back. Numbers of the Irish officers were killed, and the Irish Life guards and other troops were literally cut to pieces. Eventually they had to retire, but no troops could have done more than they did.

While this action was taking place. General de Ginckell, with Cunningham's Enniskillen Dragoons, Leveson's Dragoons and some Dutch cavalry, had encountered the enemy still more to the left towards the Drogheda road. Here again the Irish Horse displayed their accustomed valour, and de Ginckell and his Dutch regiment were driven pell-mell down a lane. The Enniskillens and Leveson's Dragoons promptly dismounted and lined the hedge, besides manning a house that overlooked the lane, and by their unexpected and heavy fire drove back the Irishmen.

The whole of the Irish Cavalry at length retreated, after having thus fought for half an hour against superior numbers. This half hour saved King James' army from annihilation.

Count Schomberg's attack on the right joined the rest of the army in Duleek. The cavalry followed up the enemy for some three miles, but the retreat was so excellently covered by the French troops on the Irish side, that the enemy suffered little loss.

Almost all the baggage and stores were seized by the conquerors. The Enniskilleners had taken not less than three hundred cars, and found among the booty ten thousand pounds in money, and much plate, many valuable trinkets, and all the rich camp equipage of Tyrconnel and Lanzon.

King James II fled through Dublin to Waterford, where he took ship to France, his army retreating southwards through Dublin. Of the Irish army, the Irish Horse and the French regiments of Lanzon were the only troops who marched through Dublin with any sort of order, with their kettledrums and trumpets sounding a march.

On the 5th of July King William's army encamped at Finglass, a suburb of Dublin, and on the 7th and 8th he held a very particular muster, or review of his troops. On the 9th the army marched southwards, the main army with the king to Limerick, while a detached force under Lieutenant-General Douglas was sent to invest Athlone. Douglas' detached force consisted of Langston's, Russell's and Wolseley's (Enniskillen) Horse, Wynne's and Cunningham's (Enniskillen) Dragoons and ten regiments of Foot, in all some 7,500 men.

While the king was at Dublin, he published a proclamation offering protection to those of the Irish peasantry who should remain neutral. But the men of Douglas' division plundered indiscriminately on the march, and this violation of the king's protection papers had a most baneful effect on the people. It is told that on one occasion four soldiers were caught looting, and Douglas ordered their execution. He was asked to reduce the sentence, which he did by making the malefactors throw dice, and the holder of the lowest throw alone suffered the death penalty.

On the 17th of July Douglas arrived before Athlone and summoned the place to surrender. "These are my terms," replied Governor Grace, firing a pistol at the messenger: "these only will I give or receive; and after my provisions shall be consumed, I will defend Athlone until I eat my boots."

Douglas proceeded to invest the place, but was not long in discovering that its strength had been underestimated. He had only a dozen guns, the heaviest of which were 12 pounders, and he was without sufficient powder for these. He also heard that Sarsfield, with 15,000 men, was on the march to cut off his communication with Dublin and the main army.

Douglas was considered one of William's best officers, but that he was very illiterate, his letter to the Earl of Portland will show, (*History of Ireland*):—

> My Lord,
> I have done my best endeavours at Athlon. The necessaries which belong to our train wer so smal, that even pouder was scarce. At the beginning wee had hot eighteen barrill of pouder for tenn piece of cannon and two houitzers.
> They mak head at Rachray, which is fourteen myles distant from my camp. All their passes on the Shannon and many more, the enemie had possessed before I came here, or at least the nixt day after, so that it is generally believed that they will endeavour to keep the Province of Connaught for their winter quarter, and hereby prolong the war, or obteen terms for themselves— this reasons is lykways my not having pouder to mak a breach on their retrenchments makes me judge it absolutely necessary at present to reteir to Molengair. . . .
> James Douglas.

The besieging army had by this time grown dispirited from a continuance of fruitless efforts to take the town, and sickly from scanty provisions. At midnight of the 24th and the 25th of July Douglas raised the siege and marched towards Limerick to rejoin the king. Captain Rapin, Douglas' quartermaster-general, says that the valour displayed on both sides was admirable.

Douglas' retreat was not accomplished without difficulty. Walton writes:

> Ignorant of the strength of the enemy in the vicinity, obliged to take precautions against possible pursuit by the garrison of Athlone or a surprise by Sarsfield's reported force, Douglas had to accept for his route those roads where he would be least likely to fall in with the enemy, and where he would have the advantage of passes capable of defence by so small a force. This restriction to by-roads, on which there were few farms and no towns, caused such a failure in the supply of provisions that for four days together, the army was without bread.

Douglas rejoined King William on the 27th of July, at Cahirconlish, a place about six miles from Limerick.

On the 8th of August William's advanced guard, 200 horse and dragoons in the van, marched towards Limerick, and very early next morning came into contact with the Irish outposts. The army pressing forward gradually drove in the outposts, and the king called on Limerick to surrender. Major General Boisleau, who commanded the garrison, replied that he was surprised at the summons, and that he thought the way to gain the Prince of Orange's good opinion was by a vigorous defence of the city with which His Majesty King James II had entrusted him.

On the same day General de Ginckell, with a force of dragoons and foot, reconnoitred the ford of Annaghbeg, two miles above the town, and discovered it strongly held by the Irish. However, it was abandoned during the night, and in the morning de Ginckell secured the passage.

King William had brought with him nothing but field guns, but there was on the road from Dublin a train of ammunition wagons and siege guns, and a set of tin pontoon boats. The escort for this valuable convoy, moving through an enemy's country, consisted of only two troops of Villiers' Horse under Captain Poulteney. Naturally the Irish had information of the approach of the convoy.

On the morning of the 11th, Mr. Manus O'Brien, an Irish Country gentleman, arrived in camp with the news that Sarsfield from Limerick had passed the Shannon in the night by the bridge at Killaloe, with a body of five or six hundred horse and dragoons, "designing something extraordinary." The English officers laughed at the news, and suggested Sarsfield was hunting mares' nests in the mountains; while one great officer commenced asking about a possible cattle raid in the country, to which O'Brien replied he was sorry to see King William's honour regarded less by general officers than cattle were. He was, however, taken to the king, "who grasped the situation in a moment, understanding at once that the Irish must have had news of the convoy, and that Sarsfield had been sent to waylay it; he instantly ordered Sir John Lanier to take a body of five hundred horse to meet the convoy and escort it to camp." Sir John Lanier failed in his orders, for he did not start until about two o'clock in the morning, and then in a most leisurely fashion.

Sarsfield, meanwhile, left Limerick on the night of the 10th with eight hundred cavalry, and crossing the river at Killaloe, marched quietly towards Cashel until he received certain news that the train was at that town.

> All the 11th he lurked in the mountains along the course to be taken by his prey. In the afternoon the train halted at Ballynedy Castle, seven miles from Limerick: the men of the escort turned their horses loose to graze, detailed the usual corporal's guard, ate their suppers, smoked their pipes and went to sleep; they had never marched alone in an enemy's country before, they had no practical military education, and therefore they merely complied with routine orders and trusted to luck. Not a sentry, not a vedette was posted beyond the precincts of the camp, not a word of notice of approach had been sent on to headquarters.

Sarsfield, arriving quietly at the spot, effected a complete surprise, the escort and wagoners being either cut to pieces or running away. The Irish drew the carriages and guns together, and filling the latter with gunpowder, fixed their mouths in the ground and set fire to the whole heap, which blew up with a "most astonishing explosion."

Sir John Lanier viewed the flash of the explosion from a distance of three miles. He wheeled half his force to the left, and the other half under Villiers towards O'Brien's bridge, in order to intercept the Irish retreat over the Shannon, "but Sarsfield marched another way and got into Limerick."

This well executed success greatly inspirited the Irish, and the want of guns greatly delayed the English works. Other guns were ordered up from Waterford, while a force of three hundred foot, mounted on ponies, kept the road.

On the night of the 17th of August the trenches were opened, and the Irish beaten out of an advanced redoubt, and the next night the besieged made a sally. The two English regiments, having relieved the right of the trenches, were ordered to lie down, and the majority of the officers and men falling asleep, the enemy were able to surprise them. The English soldiers, suddenly aroused, began firing at everything and everybody.

> Some Danish troops, who manned the trenches to the left, finding themselves fired upon, took the English for the enemy and returned the fire, while the Irish fired on both. This confusion lasted for over an hour before the English and Danes discovered the true state of affairs, when they united in the charge and repulsed the sallying party.

During the following days the siege gradually progressed, the semi-circle of guns and trenches surely closing in until they were within a range of eighty yards. For three days and nights before the 27th, a storm of shot, shell and red hot balls rained upon the town, and on this date a breach appeared in the walls near St. John's Gate. During this period of the siege, a heavy and continuous rain poured down. So heavy was it that:

> To mount fresh batteries was an impossibility: the trenches were knee deep in mud: the soldiers were never dry: sickness increased to a plague: the camp became a swamp, and those who could afford it burnt bowls of spirits in their tents to keep down the damp.

These facts and the near exhaustion of ammunition, rendered it imperative to carry the place at once or raise the siege.

An assault under General Douglas was determined upon, and at 3.30 p.m. on the 27th of August the signal was given by three guns. Five hundred grenadiers, drawn from every regiment, rushed to the counterscarp and "showered grenades and bullets on to the Irish, who replied with cannon and musket." Captain Carlisle, of Drogheda's regiment, who had been twice wounded before reaching the top of the glacis, was first into the ditch, and was instantly shot, and his subaltern took his place; the covered way was quite in the hands of the besiegers, and the supporting regiments followed up the success. The grenadiers then impetuously rushed on to the breach, while, unfortunately, the supporting regiments followed those of the Irish, who were retiring along the covered way to St. John's Gate, which they reached only to have the gate shut in their faces. By this time the grenadiers were well within the town, but the Irish, seeing how few they were, and unsupported, rallied and returned to the fight.

The Brandenbergers were the first to support the grenadiers, and had actually taken the Black Battery, when, with a horrible explosion, the enemy's powder there blew up, killing and wounding many. The grenadiers had now to fall back and regain the covered way, and for three hours did a sharp fight continue, in which the Irish women boldly joined; and when they failed to obtain more deadly missiles, threw stones and broken bottles. At length when the ammunition was spent, while the Irish fire increased, the troops were recalled from the covered way. In this assault of a little over three hours' fighting, one thousand five hundred men had fallen on the side of the besiegers alone, of whom five hundred were left dead on the spot.

On the 29th the rain came down again in torrents, with every appearance of continuing. A Council of War was held, and on the 31st of August the king raised the siege, and with a rear guard of five thousand men, marched to Cahircoulish, first blowing up all the shell etc. that could not be taken away.

The following description of the siege by Corporal Trim is related by Sterne, and is evidently taken from some old soldier who was present:—

We were scarcely able to crawl out of our tents at the time the siege of Limerick was raised, and had it not been for the quantity of brandy we set fire to every night, and the claret and cinnamon and Geneva with which we plied ourselves off, we had both left our lives in the trenches. . . . . The City of Limerick, the siege of which was begun under His Majesty King William himself, lies in the middle of a devilish wet swampy country; it is surrounded with the Shannon, and is by its situation one of the strongest fortified places in Ireland; it is all cut through with drains and bogs; and besides, there was such a quantity of rain fell during the siege, the whole country was like a puddle; 'twas that and nothing else brought on the flux. Now there was no such thing after the first ten days, as for a soldier to lie dry in his tent without cutting a ditch round it, to draw off the water: nor was that enough for those who could afford it, without setting fire every night to a pewter dish full of brandy, which took off the damp of the air, and made the inside of the tent as warm as a stove.

A curse to William's army during this campaign of 1690, were the Rapparees, who were bodies of armed peasantry independent of the armies, and who hung around the flanks of the English forces, stripping the dead, murdering and looting the wounded, and pillaging when opportunity offered.

They were extremely cunning, and when they feared detection, the Rapparees would sink down into the long grass or other cover, and how they would dismount the locks of their pieces and stow them away in their clothes or some dry spot, how they would then stop the muzzles with corks and the touch holes with small quills and chuck away the piece confidently into a pond or other equally secure hiding place; and then you may see an hundred of them without arms who look like the poorest humblest slaves in the world, and you may search without finding a gun; and to do mischief, they can all be ready in an hour's warning. (Story).

The English Army now retired into winter quarters.

King William having returned to England, and Marlborough having arrived in Ireland and captured Cork and Kinsale and returned to England, the Spring of 1691 found General de Ginckell in command of, and busily reorganising the English Army in Ireland, in preparation for the third and final year of the Irish War. It is with de Ginckell that we continue to follow the doings of Wynne's dragoons. Both armies were eagerly making preparations for the approaching campaign.

Tyrconnell, in January, offered every trooper or dragoon who would desert from the service of the "Prince of Orange and repair to Limerick, or any other Irish town, two *pistoles* of gold or silver, and every foot soldier a *pistole* in like coin."

An attempt was made by the Irish to erect defences on the roads leading to Athlone; but de Ginckell, hearing of this, ordered out a body of troops to force them, which was successfully done. It is to be noted that with this force was a corps of wounded infantry called Monk's dragoons, composed of a few picked men taken from each company of Kirk's regiment of foot, who were mounted, and ordered to do dragoon duty under Lieutenant Monk of the same regiment.

In May the campaign opened, and on the 6th of June de Ginckell marched from Mullingar to Rathcondra, sending forward a strong body of cavalry to Ballymore, to prevent any attempted relief of that fort.

Just before arriving at Rathcondra, Douglas with Wolseley's horse, and Wynne's and Cunningham's dragoons, and eight regiments of foot, joined the main army.

The next day the united forces marched to Ballymore and invested the place.

When de Ginckell appeared at Ballymore, the wretched starving aged men and women and children, who had been expelled over the frontier by the Irish, came flocking round the troops and were to be seen eagerly picking up the offal and refuse of the camp, and devouring dead horses.

Story relates a little incident which occurred about this time. He narrates that his brother was killed in an attack upon a certain fort, and the Irish irregulars captured the body. The soldiers of the company sent and asked for their officer's body, that they might bury it. The request was refused, but the soldiers were told that "their officer was a brave man and they, (the Irish Irregulars), would bury him themselves." They added that "his own company drummers were to beat the dead march before him, but that they would fire three volleys over his grave themselves to show their appreciation of his bravery."

De Ginckell's army arrived before Athlone on 19th of June, having besieged and captured the fort at Ballymore on the way.

Athlone stands on either side of the Shannon, and the two portions of the town are called English town and Irish town, the two being connected by a stone bridge. The Irish had considerably strengthened the defences of Irish town, but curiously enough, no great endeavour had been made in the defences of English town.

The enemy's outposts were met and driven in, and batteries were erected against English town on the rising ground to the North west, and, by noon next day, a wide breach appeared in the North west bastion. A Council of War resolved that English town should be stormed, and a force of foot, with a body of cavalry in readiness to support, advanced to the assault at 5 p.m. the same day. The advance party was led by a French subaltern, and after a short and severe fight, English town was in the hands of the attackers, and batteries were erected against Irish town.

A desperate struggle now took place day by day for the possession of the bridge connecting the two towns, the Irish contesting it to the utmost, and the English gaining ground only inch by inch.

The English general having information of a ford higher up the river by which he might cross and take the enemy in rear, despatched a small party under a lieutenant of horse to reconnoitre, with orders to return directly he had tested the ford by crossing it. The young officer crossed the ford and went on after a herd of cattle he espied in the distance. The enemy consequently discovered the party's proceedings, and within a few hours the newly found ford was strongly defended by Irish earthworks. The lieutenant was tried and cashiered.

In the daily desperate fight for the Bridge of Athlone, the English were continuously gaining ground and repairing the captured arches as they were taken, and by the night of the 26th, with the exception of the broken arch on the Irish side, the bridge was in their possession. On the 27th, the breastwork erected by the Irish on their end of the bridge was burned by the English grenades, and on that they succeeded in laying planks over the gap of the ruined arch. Next morning the enemy observing this, a sergeant and ten Scottish soldiers of Maxwell's regiment volunteered to wreck the English work over the gap. Putting on armour, they boldly set about their daring task in the face of an appalling fire, but every man of them was killed. Another party of ten equally gallant fellows took their place, and under the close and heavy fire of the English actually succeeded in throwing all the planks into the river, but only two of them returned.

On the 30th, at a Council of War, it was decided to carry the place by assault.

To ascertain the depth of a ford, three Danish soldiers under sentence of death were promised their pardon if they would try whether it was fordable or not. They readily consented, and putting on armour, entered the river at distances from each other, the English firing at them all the time as if they were deserters. The Irish, thinking such was the case, left them alone until the Danes facing about, the design became apparent, when a hot fire was opened on them from the other side of the river.

It is satisfactory to know that all three got back safely with a well earned pardon, two being slightly wounded. They had discovered that the ford did not reach their breasts. The river had not been known so low in the memory of living man.

A little before 6 o'clock on the evening of the 30th, "instead of the usual relief of the guards," there marched down to the English trenches some two thousand men, every man carrying fifteen rounds of ball and having a green bough, the "sign of battle," to place in his hat. [3] De Ginckell went to the trenches to encourage the soldiers, and "distributed a bag of guineas as some sort of acknowledgement among those who were thus foremost in danger."

At length the signal rang out,—the toll of the bell from the church steeple—and instantly 60 men in body armour left the trenches and entered the river, and close upon them followed the remainder of the storming party. So unexpected was the attack, that the Irish were driven through the town, and their own gates shut in their faces, and by half past six o'clock the whole place was in the hands of the English.

> St. Ruth, in command of the Irish forces, was astounded no less at the audacity, than at the success of de Ginckell's stroke; and early next morning he left, leaving the castle, which had not yet surrendered, to fall into the hands of the English.

During the attack, the English found the streets encumbered by rubbish and masonry knocked down by their own cannon, and the bumps they received as they fell over the ruins "occasioned the soldiers to utter volleys of oaths," which drew a memorable rebuke on them from Major-General Mackay, "a veteran officer, noted for religion and virtue, as well as for valour and conduct."

> Soldiers, ye have more reason to fall upon your knees and thank God for your victory, than to blaspheme His Name; you are brave men, and would be the best of men if you would swear less.

St. Ruth crossed the Shannon from Athlone and went to Aughrim, while de Ginckell, having put the place in a state of defence, left there on the 10th of July for Limerick, which city he intended to capture. He arrived at Ballinasloe on the 11th, and found St. Ruth in position at Aughrim, distant 3½ miles.

De Ginckell reconnoitred the Irish position and found St. Ruth strongly posted on the top of Aughrim or Kilcommodon Hill, occupying a front of two miles. His left rested on the castle of Aughrim which was strongly held, while his right rested on Urachree. An extensive bog lay across the foot of the slope of the hill. The only passes suitable for cavalry were the Ballinasloe Road, which passed over the front of the Urachree ridge and dipped between the extensive bog and

---

3. It is interesting to note that the ancient practice of donning a badge as a "sign of battle" had not quite expired in King William's reign; for throughout the wars in Ireland, and in the subsequent campaign in Flanders, it was the custom of the English soldiers on going into action to fasten a green bough in their hats, an emblem which originated at the Battle of the Boyne.

another bog between Aughrim and Urachree, and passed close under the castle; and a road which diverged from the Ballinasloe Road along the Urachree ridge, and skirting the bog between the two ridges, ran along the rear of the Aughrim hill. There were several foot tracks by which infantry could avoid the worst places of the bog.

On the evening of the 11th de Ginckell issued orders for an advance against the enemy in the morning; the baggage was to be left behind under a guard of two regiments. The force was to be early under arms without beat of drum, "the arms to be clean and bayonets fixed," and a good quantity of ammunition was to be taken; the grenadiers were to be on the right and left of each regiment, with two grenades per man, and five pioneers were to march at the head of each regiment, to be ready to act when called for. The word that night was "Dublin."

At 6 a. m. on the 12th of July the troops marched out of Ballinasloe, and as they crossed the River Suck, they were formed in a double line of battle.

The English Cavalry formed the right wing, and the left wing cavalry consisted of French and Danish Horse.

These, with twenty-eight foot regiments in the centre, gave the English strength as some 19,000 men.

The Irish Army of some 20,000 men was drawn up in two lines, with the infantry in the centre and cavalry on both flanks. A reserve of cavalry was posted to the left rear, under the command of Sarsfield.

AUGHRIM

THE LINE OF BATTLE 12TH JULY 1691.

1st Line.

SCRAVEMORE. / MAJOR-GENERALS. TITTAM. MACKAY. / BRIGADIERS. LA MELONIÈRE. BELLASYSE. VILLIERS.

VILLIERS.
- Leveson (3rd D. G.)
- WYNNE (5th Lan. 2 squad.)
- Oxford (Blues)
- Langston
- Rovigny
- Villiers (2nd D. G.)

BELLASYSE.
- Kirk (2nd Foot)
- Gus. Hamilton (20th Foot)
- Herbert (23rd Foot)
- Lord G. Hamilton
- Ffoulks
- Bellasyse (22nd Foot)
- Breiver (12th Foot)

LA MELONIÈRE.
- La Melonière
- Du Cambon
- Belcastell
- Greben
- Danish Foot
- Do
- Do

2nd Line.

RUVIGNY. / MAJOR-GENERALS. NASSAU. TALMACE. / BRIGADIERS. PRINCE OF HESSE. STUART. / LEVEROE.

LEVEROE.
- Cunningham (6th Drag.)
- WYNNE (5th Lan. 1 squad.)
- Lanier (1 D. G.)
- Wolseley
- Byerley (6th D. G.)

STUART.
- Stuart (9th Foot)
- Earle (19th Foot)
- Tiffan (27th Foot)
- Crighton
- St. Johns
- Lisburn
- Meath (18th Foot)

PRINCE OF HESSE.
- Nassau Regiment
- Lloyd (6th Foot)
- Cutts
- Danish Foot
- Do
- Do

LA FORREST.	EPPINGER.		HOSTAPLE.	SCHACK.	
		La Forrest's Dragoons			Schack's Dragoons
		Schested			Nieuhense Do
		Donep			Zohistern Do
		Boncour			Reidesell Do
		Montpouillon			Ginckell Do
		Eppinger			Eppinger Do

St. Ruth, seeing that the English were determined to give battle, ordered masses to be said in every part of his army, while the priests obliged the soldiers to promise they would give no quarter.

A heavy fog hung over the swamp until about noon, when it lifted and discovered the two armies in battle array.

In the early afternoon de Ginckell detached a small force of Danish horse to force the pass of Urachree, who, however, were beaten back, and a party of two hundred Enniskillen dragoons, (chiefly Cunningham's), were ordered down to prevent the Irish from crossing while the infantry of the centre advanced.

It was evident to de Ginckell that to render the centre attack of any avail, either the Ballinasloe or Urachree road must be forced, and the Enniskilleners were therefore ordered to force the ford and fall upon the right flank of the enemy. They forced the ford, and driving the enemy from the cover of a house, were in turn overwhelmed by his supports, and driven back on to Eppinger's dragoons, who had been sent to reinforce them.

The Irish were reinforced, and Enniskilleners and Eppingers were now in so tight a corner that the Blues had to be sent to their assistance. Portland with the latter regiment charged the Irish, and the combined efforts of the three regiments drove the enemy back over the stream, which they did not cross again.

The English generals now met in a Council of War, and considered whether the attack should be delayed until next day, and orders were sent for the tents at Ballinasloe. Eventually, however, it was decided not to delay, but to bring the Irish to a decisive action.

The plan of action was that Aughrim, being the key of the position, was to be captured at all costs. The Irish right at Urachree was to be threatened, while an infantry holding attack was to be directed on the centre, and the main and decisive attack was to be delivered against the Irish left upon Aughrim.

At 4.30 p.m. the English line advanced, and at 5 p.m. the firing recommenced at Urachree, and the cannon of both sides was playing on the main body of either army. The fighting was desperate, both sides displaying great courage, and it was not until 6.30 p. m. that the Irish

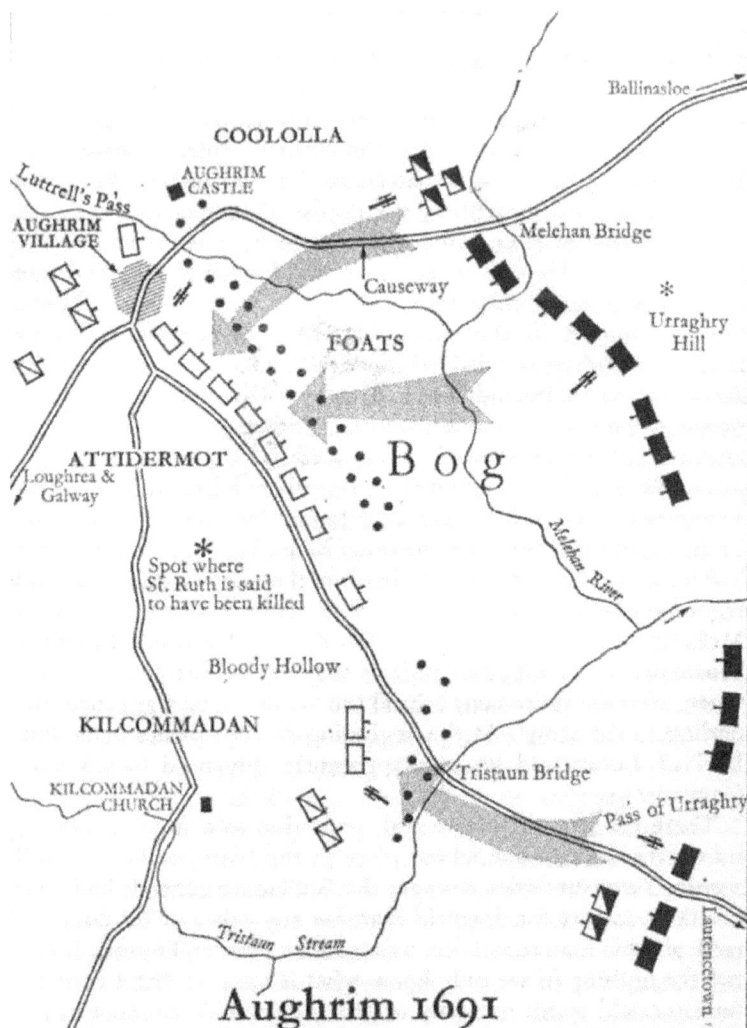

COOLOLLA

Ballinasloe

Luttrell's Pass

AUGHRIM
CASTLE

AUGHRIM
VILLAGE

Melehan Bridge

Causeway

Urraghry
Hill

FOATS

B o g

Melehan River

ATTIDERMOT

Loughrea &
Galway

Spot where
St. Ruth is said
to have been killed

Bloody Hollow

KILCOMMADAN

KILCOMMADAN
CHURCH

Tristaun Bridge

Pass of Urraghry

Laurencetown

Tristaun Stream

Aughrim 1691

Limerick

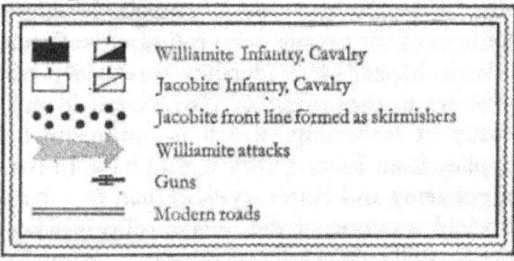

		Williamite Infantry, Cavalry
		Jacobite Infantry, Cavalry
		Jacobite front line formed as skirmishers
		Williamite attacks
		Guns
		Modern roads

right had sufficiently given way to admit of the centre or holding attack being developed.

The centre attack consisted of Wharton's, Herbert's, Creighton's, and Earle's Foot regiments, supported by Stuart's and Ffoulks' Foot. The men got so elated at their success at first that they could not be restrained, and the attack developed into a severe frontal one and was carried into the Irish position, when they found themselves confronted by a mass of Irish cvalry, who came pouring down on them through the gaps in the fences, as had previously been arranged by St. Ruth. The English regiments, in spite of the greatest gallantry, were overwhelmed, and beaten back into the bog, leaving so many of their men mingled with the Irish dead, that the spot on the hillside was known afterwards as "The Bloody Hollow."

Meanwhile, the attack had been extended along the right by the Enniskillens, St. John's, Hamilton's, Meath's and the French Foot. The Irish remained concealed and held their fire until the English were within twenty yards, when from the hedges came a terrible fire. In spite of frightful losses, the English and French steadily drove the Irish, who fought gallantly, from hedge to hedge, until at length the regiments became so intermingled and confused, that when the Irish foot cleared away for their cavalry to swoop down, the victorious but disordered regiments had to retire.

De Ginckell next sent Lanier's and also de Ruvigny's Horse from his right to assist his hard-pressed infantry on the left, in their feint against the Irish right at Urachree. St. Ruth, seeing this, and thinking the English main attack was about to develop against Urachree, reinforced his right from his left at Aughrim.

De Ginckell, discovering this, ordered the centre attack forward again, and commenced his main or right attack on Aughrim. This consisted of Wynne's Enniskillen Dragoons, the Blues, Cunningham's Enniskillen Dragoons, Leveson's Dragoons, Villiers' and Byerley's Horse, supported by Kirk's and Gus Hamilton's Foot regiments.

The English cavalry rode steadily forward under an incessant fire from the hedges on the Irish position, and following a byroad which branched off from the Ballinasloe road to Aughrim, reached a very narrow passage across the bog. This pass, with slippery and boggy sides, would only permit of two horses crossing at a time, and with showers of bullets in front and a heavy press of men and horses behind, it required steady and brave troops to attempt it.

When St. Ruth saw the cavalry making for the crossing, he could not believe they were going to attempt it, and when he saw them actually reach the place, he cried, "By Heaven, they were gallant fellows, and it was a pity they should thus court death." The horse and dragoons successfully leapt or scrambled their horses over the stream, and led by the Blues, they charged along the firm ground that bordered the bog, under a close fire from Aughrim Castle; and Kirk's and Hamilton's Foot regiments managed to reach a large dry ditch close under, and more or less covered from, the fire of the castle.

Meanwhile, the desperate fight between the infantry continued on the bog, the Irish and English alternately gaining or giving ground.

St. Ruth, seeing the successful crossing of the English cavalry, rode off to his left and brought away some Irish horse to oppose the English at Aughrim, and on the hill side just above the Bloody Hollow, he was killed by a chain-shot or round-shot.

Walton, in his *History of the British Standing Army* says the "chain-shot asserted to be the fatal shot is preserved in St. Patrick's Cathedral."

The English infantry on the right was meanwhile reinforced, and under General Talmach pressed forward, and an advance of the whole line of infantry taking place, a heavy enfilading fire was poured in on the Irish left.

St. Ruth had not communicated his plans to a successor, and the Irish Army without a leader, broke, and, pursued by the English, fled in utter confusion, until kindly night ended the horrid slaughter.

Walton relates that just before the Irish gave way, their ammunition ran short, and on a fresh supply being brought up, it was found that the bullets had been cast too small for the calibre of the fire arms; whereupon the Irish soldiers tore the buttons from their coats and tried to make them serve as bullets.

Historians do not agree in the losses incurred during this battle, but the Irish losses during the fight and pursuit are said to have amounted to 7000 killed, and the English to some 2000.

In the official lists furnished to the general two days after the battle, it is noticed that Wynne's Dragoons are shown as not having lost a single officer, man, or horse, but as at this time "there were several pecuniary inducements to officers to conceal the vacancies in their regiments," it is quite possible that these lists were not to be trusted.

The cavalry regiments especially mentioned for gallantry at the battle of Aughrim were: the Blues, Wynne's and Cunningham's Enniskillen Dragoons, and de Ruvigny's French Horse, which rather leads one to believe the foregoing statement as to the correctness of the official lists.

Mr. Story, the historian, writing of the bravery of English soldiers at this battle, says:

> That they marched boldly up to their old ground again from which they had lately been beat; which is only natural to Englishmen: for it is observable that they are commonly fiercer and bolder after being repulsed than before; and what blunts the courage of other nations commonly whets theirs, I mean the killing of their fellow soldiers before their faces.

Though using the word "Englishmen," he writes of the whole of the British troops.

The Irish too, horse and foot, fought gallantly at Aughrim. "Captain Parker, an eyewitness of the battle, says:

> Never did the Irish fight so well in their own country as they did on this day.

Story relates a great many of the dead were left unburied on the ground, and large numbers of dogs fed on the carcases of horses and men, which made them so savage that people found it unsafe to pass that way alone. He tells a pretty story of a greyhound, the property of a fallen Irish officer. This dog would not suffer his master's body to be touched, and when the other dogs left the place, this one remained guarding his master's bones, obtaining food at night from the houses about. For six months did he keep watch, until one day a soldier happened to pass close to the Irishman's remains, whereupon the dog flew at him, and the soldier, alarmed at the attack, shot the poor beast with his firelock.

The remains of the Irish Army, after their defeat at Aughrim, retreated as best they could to Limerick.

De Ginckell, four days after the battle, marched by way of Loughrea and Athenry on Galway, which surrendered with the honours of war, being permitted to march out of the town to Limerick "with their arms, six pieces of cannon, drums beating, colours flying, match lighted, and bullet in mouth." Wynne's Dragoons were employed in the reduction of Galway, and on the 20th July, as soon as it was dark, formed part of a force which were floated over the river on pontoons, about two miles north of the town, but met with no resistance except from a small force of dragoons "who fired on the first and then retreated." Upon the attack by de Ginckell, next morning, the city surrendered.

De Ginckell them moved slowly to Limerick with his cavalry, reconnoitring down the line of the Shannon.

The following account of the siege of Limerick is taken from *The Field of Mars* published in 1801:—

The general (de Ginckell) next marched to this town (Limerick), and while Captain Cole sailed up the Shannon with a squadron and some frigates, he drove the enemy from their advanced posts. The batteries were opened, and a line of contravallation was formed on the 25th August, 1691, while the Irish Army lay encamped on the other side of the River Killala, and the fords were guarded with four regiments of their dragoons. After the town had been almost reduced to a heap of ruins, and large breaches made in the walls, the guns were dismounted, the outposts evacuated, and all such other motions were made as if the English were inclined to abandon the siege; for on the 17th September, it was warmly debated in a Council of War, whether they should prosecute the siege, or turn it into a blockade, and in the meantime pass over the Shannon and destroy the enemy's forage in the county of Clare. It was so far carried for the latter, that an engineer was ordered to go with a guard to Kilmallock, and fortify that place, but was countermanded and a great number of palisades brought to Mackay's fort . . . . . as if the army intended to winter there. On the 19th a party was ordered to pass the river, either to prosecute the siege with vigour, or if not found feasible, to burn their forage and prevent all supplies.

A battery was raised between Mackay's fort and the Old Church, to flank the Irish, in case of a sally from St. John's Gate, and four mortars were brought from the great battery to this fort, it being judged the best for bombarding, as the whole town lay in a line from it. When the ships that came up the river with Captain Cole had appeared, and fired into the Irish horse camp, the enemy could scarcely credit it, having been persuaded that either the English had no ships there, or else that the *dauphin*, with a strong fleet from France, would soon destroy them; which was industriously propagated and hourly expected, so infatuated were the credulous Irish in the favourite opinion of succours from the French king.

On the 20th most of the heavy cannon were sent on shipboard, which caused it to be generally believed that Limerick would not be taken this year. But Ginckell, far from desponding, exerted all his military capacity on this arduous occasion; for in two days after, he pressed with most of the horse and dragoons, over a bridge of boats they had laid, into the county of Clare, on the other side of the river, leaving Mackay and Talmash to the command on this side, while the enemy fired on them all the morning from several batteries without any effect. In the afternoon a party of English troops was attacked by a superior force of the enemy, till, being sustained by four regiments of foot, they drove and obliged them to retire under their cannon. Then the English were commanded to advance and attack the works that covered St. Thomond's Gate, and other smaller fortifications, from which the Irish played their cannon, and made such discharges with their small shot, that the English were ordered not to approach so near: the grenadiers, notwithstanding, pressed so hotly on the reinforced detachments, that they drove them to the draw-bridge, which the officers, fearing the English would enter instantly, drew up, and thus sacrificed the Irish who were on the outside, to the fury of the English, who killed or drowned most of them.

The English then lodged themselves within ten yards of the bridge; and the Irish, finding all communication cut off between them and their horse, and despairing of the French succours, began to open their eyes and think seriously of capitulation. In the meantime the siege was carried on with great fury, and the fire was excessive hot on both sides the next day, though it rained and blew incessantly; but towards night, on the 22nd, the rain began to cease, and both storms ended together, for about six o'clock the Irish beat a parley. The next day Sarsfield and Wachope desired a cessation of arms for three days, till they could send to Lieutenant-Colonel Shelden, who lay with 1,600 horse at Six mile Bridge, in order that he and his men should be included in the articles of capitulation, which was granted, and the English prisoners in the town were released. On the 26th Sarsfield and Wachope dined with General de Ginckell and it was agreed to exchange hostages.

The next day the Irish sent out their proposals, which were so high, that de Ginckell sent word, that though he was a stranger to the laws of England (being a Dutchman), yet from the face of the demands, he was sure they could not be listened to; and so ordered a new battery to be raised: but upon the request of the Irish, he sent twelve articles, which in the end proved to be the sum of the capitulation; which put an end to the French intrigues for holding out the siege, and thereby the war. This step was also mortifying to some English, who hoped this war, if continued, would end in the total destruction of the Irish interest, whereby they might enjoy the forfeited lands.

On the 1st October, the Lords Justices came into the camp, and after some conferences with the commissioners, on the part of the garrison, and their troops in the County of Clare, the articles for the surrender of the City of Limerick, with the castles of Ross, Clare, and other places, were finally concluded on the 3rd. By these the Irish, who chose to stay in that kingdom, and take the oaths of allegiance to William, were restored to all their estates which they enjoyed under King Charles. They were freed from the oath of supremacy, as they always look upon the Pope as the head of the church. Not only the French, but as many of the Irish as pleased, had liberty to go over to France, with safe transportation, and free passage. So that about 12,000 choice troops, of the Irish alone, were shipped off, being the original of those Irish forces which have so much strengthened the French Army. . . . . thus ended the second siege of Limerick, having in the two sieges (which may be reckoned as one), held out fifty six days against many furious attacks.

On the 24th of August Graham relates that two men of Lanier's regiment of horse were condemned to death for having robbed Captain Watts, an officer of the same regiment, and a country sutler was likewise condemned to death for having bought the captain's watch from the troopers.

After the siege of Limerick, Wynne's dragoons, and other regiments marched north to winter quarters.

The treaty of Limerick [4] was signed on the 3rd of October 1691, by Sir Charles Porter, Thomas Coningsby Esq., Lords Justices of Ire-

---

4. By this the Irish were indemnified, with certain qualifications, for their losses, and had restored to them all they enjoyed in king Charles's reign, on condition of taking the oath of allegiance to William and Mary. A free passage to France, with the French troops, was also promised to such as desired to go.

land, and the Baron de Ginckell, Commander-in-Chief of the English Army in Ireland, on the one part; and the Earl of Lucan, Viscount Galmoy, Colonel Purcel, Colonel Cusack, Sir Toby Butler, Colonel Dillon and Colonel John Brown, on the other part: and with it ended the War in Ireland.

CHAPTER 2

Campaigns in Flanders, 1694-1697

During 1692 and 1693 Wynne's Dragoons remained in Ireland, but there is no trace of any particularly interesting events during those two years. On the 15th and 22nd of May, 1694, Wynne's dragoons sailed from the Thames for Flanders.[1] Early in June the regiment joined the Allied armies which were camped near Meldert under the command of King William III. The following is a list of the British Regiments serving in this campaign:—

HORSE

		Regiment	Squadrons.
General.		THE EARL OF PORTLAND.	
Major-Generals.		THE DUKE OF ORMOND.	
		THE EARL OF COLCHESTER.	
		THE EARL OF SCARBOROUGH.	
Brigadier		**Regiment**	**Squadrons.**
L'Etang	Life Guards.		4
	Horse Grenadiers.		1
	Dutch Life Guards.		2
Leveson	Leveson's (2.D.G.)		2
	Wood's (3.D.G.)		2
	Wyndham's (6.D.G.)		2
	Galway's		2
Lumley	Lumley's (1.D.G.)		2
	Langston's (4.D.G.)		2
	Coy's (5.D.G.)		2
	Duke of Leinster's (7.D.G.)		2

1. The following letters relate to the embarkation of the regiment:—To Commissioner of Transport "It is His Majesty's will and pleasure that you provide shipping for Colonel Wynne's regiment from the river Thames to Willenstadt; which troops are to embark 22nd day of this instant May."

To Colonel James Wynne:—"His Majesty having thought fit that the recruit horses for Flanders should embark on Friday 15th, I desire you should give me notice as soon as may be what number of horses will be ready by that time."

DRAGOONS

Brigadier	Regiment	Squadrons.
Mathews	Mathews (1.D.)	4
	Scots (2.D.)	4
	Fairfax (3.D. & Hussars)	4
WYNNE	Essex (4.D. & Hussars)	4
	WYNNE's (5.D. & Lancers)	3
	Cunningham's (7.D. & Hussars)	4
	Eppinger's	5

INFANTRY

Major-Generals.   LORD CHURCHILL.
                SIR H. BELLASYSE.
                RAMSEY.

Brigadier	Regiment	Battalions.
C. Churchill	1st Foot Guards	2
	2 ,, ,, (Coldstreams)	1
	3 ,, ,, (Scots)	2
	Dutch Guards.	2
Earle	Hamilton's (1st Foot) 1st Battalion.	1
	Selwyn's (Queen's)	1
	Churchill's (Buffs)	1
	Trelawny's (R. Lancs)	1
	Fitzpatrick's (R. Fus.)	1
	Brewer's (12th Suffolk)	1
	Earle's (19th Yorks).	1
Stuart	Granville's (10th Lincoln)	1
	Tidcombe's (14th W. Yorks)	1
	Lesley's (15th E. Yorks)	1
	St. George's (17th Leicester)	1
	Castleton's	1
	Lauder's.	1
	Lloyd's (Northumberland Fus.)	1
	Stanley's (16th Bedford)	1
	Hamilton's (18th R. Irish)	1
	Ingoldsby's (23rd R. W. Fus.)	1
	Tiffan's (27th R. Inniskilling Fus.)	1
	Collingwood's.	1
O'Ffarrel	O'Ffarrel's	1
	Maitland's (25 K.O.S.B.)	1
	Fergusson's (26 Cameronians)	1
	Buchan's	1
	Mackay's	1
	Graham's.	1
On Command	1st Foot. 2nd Battalion	1
	Argyle's	1
	Strathnavor's	1
	G. Hamilton's.	1

The artillery train consisted of 60 guns and 6 mortars and some 2400 men, which brought the British Contingent of the Allied Army up to some 30,000 men.

A squadron of horse or dragoons had a strength of 150 men, and a battalion of foot 600.

Altogether the Allies had in the field a force of 32,000 cavalry and 57,000 infantry, besides strong garrisons at Ghent, Liége, etc.

An innovation of this year of the wars in Flanders was that the artillery, some 130 pieces of cannon, was divided amongst the various brigades, instead of marching in one body as they had hitherto done.

During June the king selected Colonel Wynne to be a brigadier of dragoons.

The French Army, consisting of 22,500 horse, 6,700 dragoons, 55,300 foot, in all some 84,500 men, under the *dauphin* and de Luxemburg, was at this time camped at Gemblours.

The French were sorely handicapped in their preparations for the coming campaign owing to the scarcity of forage and supplies, and to the fact that their treasury had been exhausted by a long series of wars. Also their altered frontier compelled them to find large garrisons for Mons, Charleroi, Namur and Huy. The Allies on the other hand had fewer garrisons to keep up, and had received large reinforcements from England; hence the strength of the two opposing armies in the field was brought more on an equality than in the campaigns of the preceding years.

The main hope of the French for the coming campaign was the capture of Liége, and accordingly on the 8th of June they marched to Joudrain with the object of getting between the Allies and Liége.

On the 10th of June the king reviewed the dragoons of Lord Essex and Brigadier Wynne;

"The latter wanted two troops that had been left in England, and his horses were very much fatigued in twice crossing the sea the last winter, and their continued motion through Ireland and England, to come to this country."

At the Liége entrenched camps were 24,000 allies, and William had every confidence in their strength. From Meldort he could scarcely prevent the interception of the French, but for better observation he moved to Tirlemont.

On the 10th de Luxemburg marched to St.Tron, which was almost directly between Tirlemont and Liége. At the same time de Boufflers advanced across the Meuse with a corps from Dinant, and encamped near Warem, within a short march of the main army. Another corps under the Marquis d'Harcourt in the Duchy of Luxembourg was ordered to approach the Meuse with instructions to be ready to co-operate.

Both armies remained quiet for the rest of June. Neither side would risk an engagement, the intervening country being so intersected by rivers and streams that the attacker would be placed at a great disadvantage.

During the winter the French had collected a large quantity of siege material at Huy, in readiness for use down the Meuse, but de Luxemburg was of opinion that the siege of Liége was too formidable a task to be undertaken in the face of the Allied Army. Without a second army to cover his operations he could have little chance of success. De Luxemburg apparently had no particular plan of campaign at this time, unless it were that he hoped to prevent the Allies from moving towards the coast.

William on his side was perfectly content to see the French helping him to consume the forage of the district, thereby raising a serious difficulty in their future movements.

In his list of the Allied troops in the Confederate Camp during July, D'Auvergne puts Wynne's and Mathews' brigades of Dragoons in the Reserve of the line of battle. This reserve consisted of the Dutch and English Dragoons under Major-General Eppinger. The historian writes of them:

> You must observe that at first coming to the camp of Mount St. Andrée, all the dragoons encamped on the left, where the left is the post of honour; 'tis for this reason that the English dragoons in this list fall after the Dutch."
> "Of the dragoons especially I may say that such a body, either for number or the good order they were in, has hardly ever been in the field.

The French on the 1st of July marched to the Jaar, halting between Warem and Tongres, and on the 13th the Allies moved towards Huy, halting at Ramillies. On this, de Luxemburg moved to Vignamont, so covering Huy without losing his hold over Liége. Both sides threw up entrenchments along their positions, and the Allies placed their guns on the Ramillies heights, which enabled them to command the Huy road for a long distance.

D'Auvergne writes that on the 28th of July:

We surrounded a party of enemies in a wood. This was a voluntary party of dismounted troopers that had a great mind to ride some of our horses, and to mount themselves at our own cost; they got a partisan with them, who when they came near to our camp inquired whereabouts our horses grazed; a Boor (countrymen and farmers in Flanders were called Boors) told them they were every day by the wood, and that if they would lie there in ambuscade that night they would not fail of horses next morning. They took his advice and the Boor came immediately to advertise my Lord of Athlone of it, who thereupon commanded a detachment of dragoons and some foot to surround the wood and give no quarter.

Twenty of the enemy were killed, but at last they gave quarter to seventeen.

Forage was scarce, and de Luxemburg had had to send part of his cavalry beyond the Meuse to find food. The Allies were between the French and their frontier lines on the Scheldt, and as soon as all the forage should be exhausted William could march direct to the Scheldt without further anxiety for Liége.

William not only had a start in the straight race for the Scheldt, but his position prohibited the French from following the same route as himself without affording him an opportunity of fighting; and as soon as Luxemburg should march westwards, the garrison of Liége could join William, and give him an overwhelming preponderance of force. To reach the Scheldt without coining into contact with the Allies, de Luxemburg would have to cross the Sambre, which would increase the start already gained by his opponents.

In anticipation of the race for the Scheldt, both armies had sent their heavy baggage to the rear. Wynne's dragoons accompanied that of the Allies, their horses being in such bad condition with the voyage from Ireland and subsequent bad feeding, that they were not fit to take the field. In relation to this D'Auvergne writes:—

> On the 5th August our heavy baggage was commanded away towards Louvain under the escort of Brigadier Wynne's regiment of dragoons, which was sent to garrison in Ghent, because their horses were out of order for reasons we have before alleged.

On the 8th of August the Allies marched to Sombref, where they halted for a day. The march had been a severe one, and the rest was absolutely necessary.

On the same day de Luxemburg crossed the Mehaigne, and advanced to near Namur. On the tenth he crossed the Sambre near its junction with the Orneau, having bridged it the previous day. After the crossing the army was broken up into nine or ten different corps, and to each was assigned a separate route; all, however, were to halt each day within a certain circumference, so as to facilitate a speedy junction if necessary. Three thousand dragoons had been sent to Charleroi, and these, on hearing of the departure of the Allies from Ramillies, hurried to reinforce the Marquis de la Valette at the lines.

William marched to Nivelle on the 10th, to Soignies on the 11th, and to near Ath on the 12th.

At Soignies a man who had been detected in attempting to fire the ammunition wagons, suffered the penalty of incendiarism.

Having first been put to the torture, with a view to discover his employers, his right hand was cut off and burnt before his eyes, and he himself was then cast into the flames alive.

De Luxemburg marched on the 12th, his columns being greatly impeded by difficult and woody country, full of streams swollen by rain, and heavy roads. The next day his infantry was so knocked up that it could not go on; but the cavalry under the Dauphin pushed on with great energy, and reached Tournai on the evening of the thirteenth.

On this day William crossed the Dender at Ligne, halted at Frasnes, and sent on General Tettau with 5000 men, to prepare bridges at Hauterive.

De Luxemburg on the thirteenth was marching to Saint Ghislain beyond Mons. His men were so tired that they were ordered to throw away their knapsacks, and, to revive them, a ration of brandy and beer was every now and again served out. At Saint Ghislain de Luxemburg received a message from the *dauphin*, to the effect that not only was the Allied Army close to the lines, but Tettau was actually on the Scheldt, and the Elector of Bavaria had crossed the river above Oudenarde. The French general appealed to his men, with the result that the grenadiers and the major part of the battalion companies at once came forward and expressed their readiness to proceed that night, and the exhausted army struggled on, being plied with brandy at every halt. The next morning the main body of the French Army was in Tournai.

Tettau, on reaching the banks of the Scheldt, was surprised to find de la Valette's force strengthened by the 3000 dragoons from Charleroi; but still more astonished was he to see the brigade of Guards, which had been forced on to Condé, and thence forwarded in boats. Tettau sent for guns and opened fire, but he was effectually hindered from laying his bridges.

On the morning of the 14th William marched to force the river at Hauterive. About midday the Allies reached the river, and to their dismay and disappointment found Villeroi well entrenched on the other side, and the half of the French Army winding through the Lines to join him. Before nightfall the whole of de Luxemburg's army was united on the banks of the Scheldt.

The French had left Huy at midday on the 8th, and on the morning of the 14th were ready on the other side of the Scheldt to oppose the passage of the Allies. They had covered, in the five days and a half, a distance of about 120 miles through a difficult country, had crossed the Mehaigne, the Scarpe and the Scheldt, and had twice crossed the Sambre. The distance marched by the Allies in the same time was scarcely 80 miles.

This famous march was a great triumph for de Luxemburg, but the cost was dear. The French cavalry was ruined for any further service, and it is said the French lost some 3000 men: the course of the march could be tracked by the dead bodies of men and horses.

D'Auvergne writes:—

> The French Army might have been followed by the scent which they left behind of dead men and horses, which were to be found all along the road it went.

William, foiled in his designs on the Lines, marched to Escanesse and Melden, detaching four brigades to strengthen de Würtemberg's force on the heights of Peteghem, between Oudenarde and the enemy on the other side of the river.

The next day William crossed at Oudenarde, and halted half way between that place and the Lys.

De Luxemburg moved to the Lys, halting at Courtrai; and on the 17th he crossed that river, and encamped with his right on Courtrai and along the Lys to the Heulle River, while his left stretched at right angles with the Lys as far as Moorseele.

De la Valette occupied the lines from the Scheldt to the Lys with some 5000 men; and de Villeroi those from the Lys to the town of Ypres with some 12,000 more; while 15,000 men were placed in garrison at Furnes, the place being made ready for defence.

William crossed the Lys and encamped at Rousselaer, his object being to detain the French Army North of the Scheldt by threatening Furnes and Fort Knoque.

The historian writes:

> Our heavy baggage came up to the camp on the 19th August; it had been sent away on the 5th under the convoy of Brigadier Wynne's Dragoons, They marched by Louvain, Vilvarde and Ghent, and so joined us in this place.

On the 24th the heavy baggage was sent back to Ghent.

On the 7th of September all the English horse and dragoons came up to Rousselaer from their camp at Wonterghem.

> Wynne's Dragoons, that had been sent from the camp by Mont St Andrée to Ghent, to get their horses in better case, being now refreshed from the fatigues they had endured, came up to the camp along with them, and on the 8th they were all sent to canton upon the villages between our right and Dixmude.

The English horse and dragoons were reviewed by the king on the 10th of September near Dixmude, and the troops "appeared in very good order" after their trying marches.

Huy, in the meantime, was besieged by a detached portion of the Allied Army under the Duke of Holstein, to whom the garrison capitulated after a short and feeble resistance.

During the summer of this year an expedition was fitted out from England for the purpose of harrying the French Coast, but without any good result. On the 6th of June an attempt on Brest resulted in complete failure, the troops being re-embarked with great difficulty.

From the middle of September the Allied Army began to move into their winter quarters. Wynne's Dragoons, together with the regiments of Eppinger, Mathews, Livingstone, Essex and Cunningham, were quartered in the villages between Ghent and the Sas Van Ghent.

The main feature of the campaign of 1694 was the famous march by de Luxemburg from the Meuse to the Scheldt, which William had regarded as a physical impossibility.

This great general was an extremely ugly man with a deformed figure. Upon its being reported to him that William had once exclaimed "What! am I never to beat this hump-backed fellow?" de Luxemburg observed, "How should he know the shape of my back;

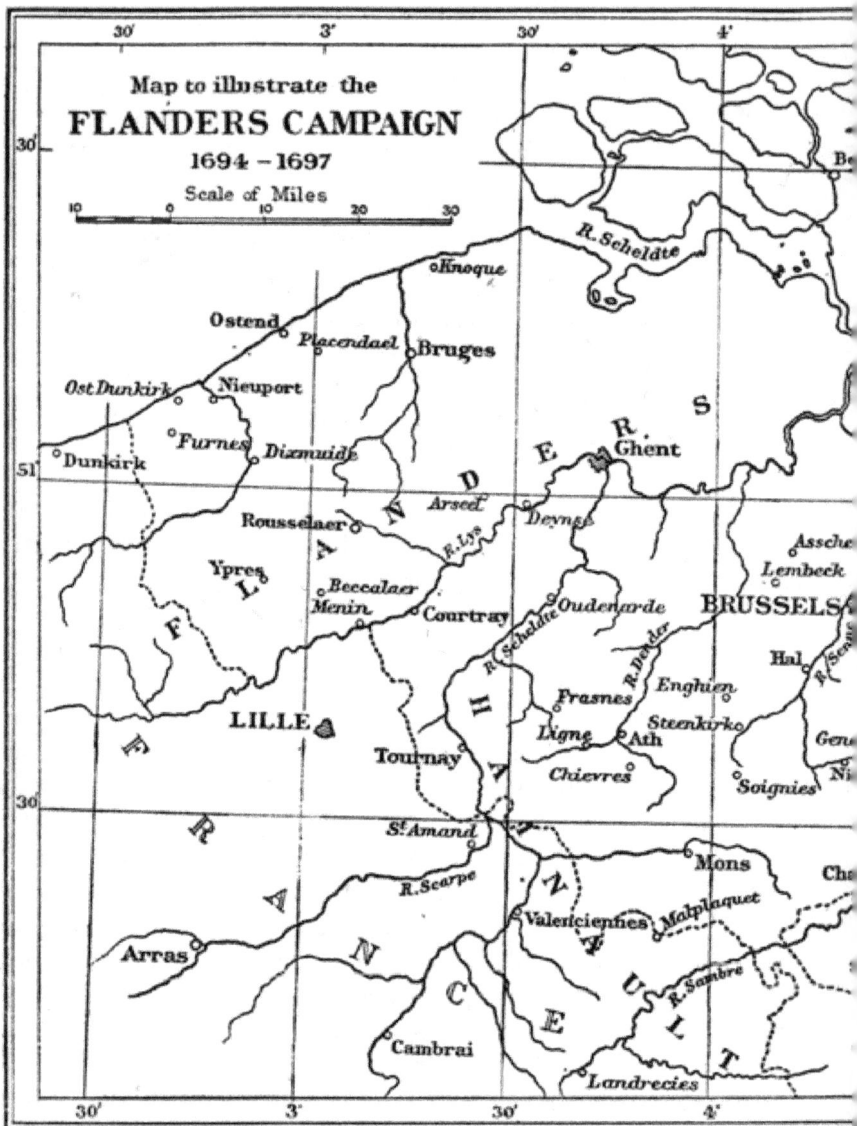

Map to illustrate the

FLANDERS CAMPAIGN
1694 – 1697

Scale of Miles

10   0   10   20   30

R. Scheldte

Knoque

Ostend

Placendael   Bruges

Ost.Dunkirk   Nieuport

Furnes   *Dixmuide*   Ghent

Dunkirk

F   L   A   N   D   E   R   S

Arseel

Rousselaer   *Deynse*

R.Lys

Ypres   Assche

Beccalaer   Lembeck

Menin   Courtray   Oudenarde   **BRUSSELS**

R.Scheldte

R.Dender   Hal   *R.Seine*

LILLE   *Frasnes*   Enghien

Ligne   Steenkirk   Gene

Tournay   Ath   Ni

Chievres   Soignies

F   R   A   N   C

St. Amand

Mons   Ch

R.Scarpe

Valenciennes   Malplaquet

H   A   I   N   A   U   L   T

Arras   *R.Sambre*

Cambrai

Landrecies

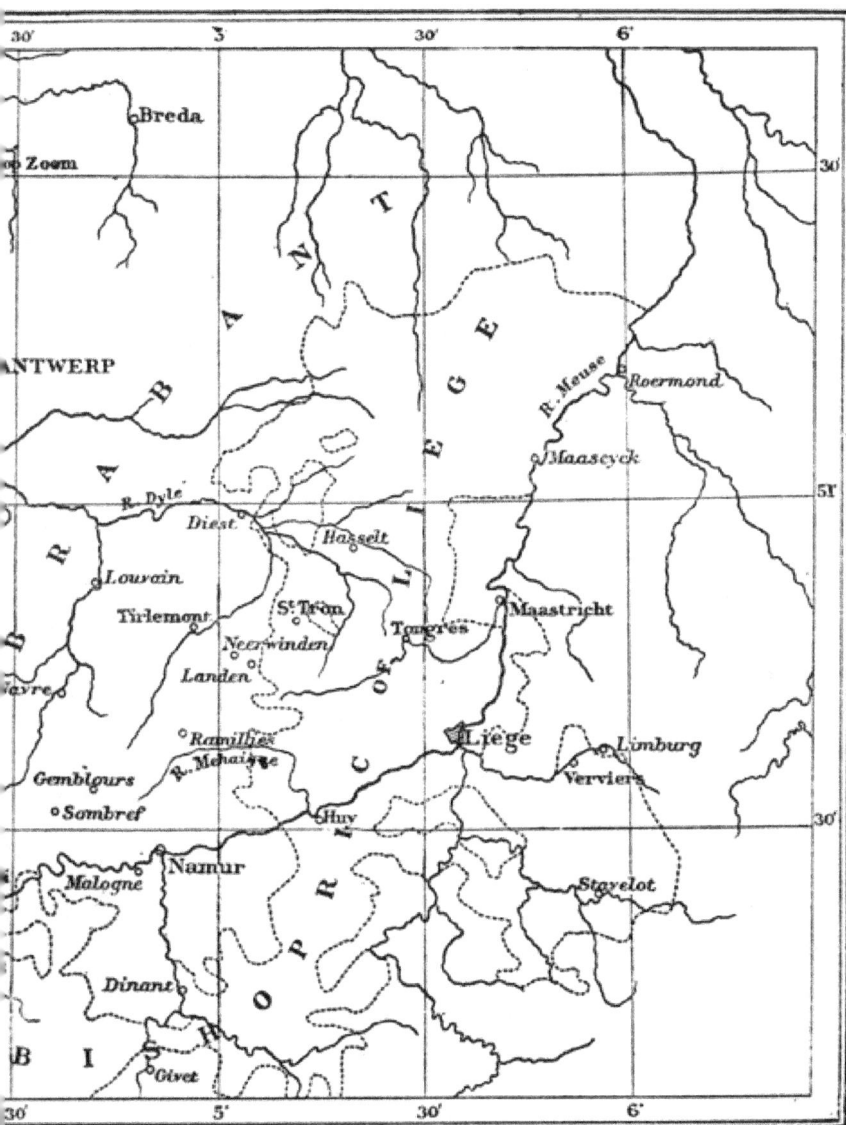

for it is certain that I never turned it to him." He died before the Campaign of 1695 opened.

With regard to the bloodless nature of the campaign, D'Auvergne, writing of an attack by the French on some bread wagons, says the officer commanding had the misfortune to be mortally wounded;

> ... which is the only officer of our army I have heard of, that has been killed this campaign by the enemy.

Each year of the war had been hitherto one continued success to the French, and a series of discouragements and disasters to the Allies, but the turning point had at length been reached. The operations of the French had been offensive; but several reasons combined to deprive them now of this advantage, and to reduce them to the defensive. Not only was the great General de Luxemburg dead, and a comparatively untried general, the Maréchal de Villeroi, invested with the command, but the drain on the French resources was becoming more and more felt each year. Added to this, the Allies had at length learned the importance of beginning the campaign in good time, and with an adequate force. They had determined to concentrate their whole efforts upon Flanders for this campaign, and no endeavours were spared to assemble as large an army as possible, and to get into the field as early as the season would permit.

The French Lines now comprehended all the country within one long stretch of defence from Namur to Furnes. From Namur they ran to Charleroi: from the Sambre to the Haisne at Mons and Condé, thence to the Espierre, whence they were carried to the Lys and on to Ypres: and on from Ypres to Dunkirk *via* the Knoque Fort and Furnes. During the winter 20,000 navvies, covered by a *corps d'armée*, had been employed in renewing and strengthening the lines, the whole of which was connected along its length by forts and redoubts at intervals, while, where a natural frontier such as the Haisne and the Dunkirk canal was wanting, entrenchments had been run up. But the maintenance of this great extent of frontier within an enemy's territory compelled the French general to keep to the defensive.

During April a letter was sent to Brigadier Wynne to supply three men to guard the king's yacht at the Hague.

In April both armies began to assemble. The main army of the Allies under King William, with the Prince de Vaudemont and Duc de Würtemberg as second in command, assembled at Deinse on the left bank of the Lys: and a force under the Elector of Bavaria encamped at Assche with its left towards Brussels. The king's army consisted of about 11,000 cavalry and 42,000 infantry, and included all the English regiments except about a dozen that were with the Elector, whose force numbered some 15,000 cavalry and 20,000 infantry.

The following is a list of the British Contingent:—

CAVALRY

Lieut.-Generals. M. D'Auverquerque.
                   The Duke of Ormond.
Major-Generals. Earl Rivers.
                   Eppinger.

Brigade	Regiments	Squadrons
L'Etang.	Life Guards. 1st Troop	1
	„ 2nd „	1
	„ 3rd „	1
	Horse Grenadiers.	1
Lumley	Lumley (1 D.G.)	3
	Langston (4 D.G.)	2
	Wyndham (6 D.G.)	2
	Schomberg (7 D.G.)	2
Coy	Wood (3 D.G.)	2
	Coy (5 D.G.)	2
	Leveson (2 D.G.)	2
	Galway's Horse.	3
Mathews	Livingstone's (Scots Greys)	4
WYNNE	Essex (4 D. and Hussars)	4
	WYNNE (5 D. and Lancers)	4
	Cunningham (7 D. and Hussars)	4

D'Auvergne in his line of battle at the Arseel Camp shows Wynne's brigade, consisting of his own and Essex's Dragoons, as being in the first line of the left wing. A squadron of dragoons at this time consisted of one hundred men.

FOOT.

General. Duke of Würtemberg.
Lieut.-Generals. Count Nassau.
                   Count Noyelles.
                   Sir Henry Bellasyse.
Major-Generals. Churchill.
                   La Melonière.
                   Ramsay.

Brigade.	Regiments.	Battalions.
Guards	1st Foot Guards	2
	2nd „ (Coldstream)	1
	3rd „ (Scots)	2
Erle	Hamilton (1st Royals)	1
	Selwyn's (Queens)	1
	Churchill (Buffs)	1
	Trelawny (4th)	1
	Stanley (16th)	1
	Erle (19th)	1
Fitzpatrick	Fairfax (5th)	1
	Fitzpatrick (7th Fus.)	1
	Fred Hamilton (18th)	1
	Ingoldsby (23rd)	1
	Collingwood's	1
	La Melonière	1
Collier	Hamilton (1st Royals)	1
	Columbine, Rada (6th)	1
	Granville (10th)	1
	Seymour	1
	Saunderson	1
	Collier	1
O'Ffarrel	O'Ffarrel (21st)	1
	Lauder	1
	Mackay	1
	Morton	1
	Strathnaver	1
	Geo. Hamilton	1

WITH THE ELECTOR'S FORCE.

General. The Earl of Athlone.

CAVALRY.

Brigade.	Regiment.	Battalions.
Lloyd	Mathews' (1 D.)	4
	Lloyds' (4 D. and Hussars)	4

FOOT.

Brigade.	Regiments.	Squadrons.
	Brewer (12th)	1
	Tidcombe (14th)	1
	Leslie (15th)	1
	St. George (17th)	1
	Maitland (25th)	1
	Ferguson (26th)	1
	Tiffeney (27th)	1
	Graham	1
	Lorne	1
	Buchan	1

The total of the British Contingent was 29,100 men, of whom 5700 were cavalry. Besides the two armies under William and the Elector, the Allies had the following:—

Ellenberg's corps of 13,000 men at Dixmude.

Brandenburg Contingent of 16,000 men at Liége.

Count de Tilly with about 4000 men also near Liége. These brought the total Allied Army in the field up to about 124,000 men.

On the morning of the 31st May the king reviewed the army at the camp of Arseele.

> Our English Cavalry..... which made a very gallant show, the horses being in very good order, and the men very well clothed and armed.

The French assembled in three bodies: the first under de Ville-roi near Menin; the second under de Boufflers, between the Lys and the Scheldt: the third under M. de Montal, in the neighbourhood of Furnes.

On the 2nd of June William marched from Arseele to Rousselaer, and on the next day to Becelaer. On this march D'Auvergne writes:

> We made detachments of 4000 dragoons towards Menin, which was not far from our left, to cover our march. They met with a party of the enemy's dragoons, which they pursued to the very palisades of Menin, and brought back 23 prisoners.

At the camp the dragoons of the left faced to Moorsleede, covering the king's horse.

The whole of the French forces, with the exception of a small flying column under the Marquis d'Harcourt, were between the Scheldt and the sea. D'Harcourt was on the Meuse in observation of the Brandenburg and Liége contingents, which had now been joined at Liege by a large body of cavalry from the main armies.

During the winter the French had much facilitated the defence of their lines by cutting what were termed "*routes royales*" for purposes of speedy communication: these "*routes royales*" were perfectly direct, nothing being allowed to interfere with their course; trees, houses, walls and villages were ruthlessly demolished if they stood in the way.

William now detached the Duc de Würtemberg with eight battalions under Churchill, together with some artillery and a pontoon train, to join Ellenberg and threaten Knoque Fort. From the 8th to the 16th June de Würtemberg operated against Knoque, finally withdrawing in silence to Dixmude. At the same time the Elector made feints of attacks on the lines of the Lys and Scheldt.

When de Würtemberg marched to Knoque, William returned to Rousselaer; and then pushed speedily on towards the Meuse, escorted only by the Life Guards and some Dutch cavalry, leaving de Vaudemont with the army of observation, and instructing de Würtemberg and the Elector to march on Namur.

The design was, to draw all the French forces westwards, and then suddenly to invest Namur. To this end an immense quantity of siege material had been collected at Maestricht, and all the boats on the Meuse had been pressed. De Tilly, with the Liége and Brandenburg contingents, had gone to Falaise on the Mehaigne; and on the 18th the Earl of Athlone, with the cavalry from the Elector's Army, went to Tirlemont *en route* to join them. On the 20th de Vaudemont moved to Grammen on the Lys, and there remained. The Elector's corps left Tieghem on the 18th, and marched to St. Livens, and thence to Ninove, to Halle, to Genappe, and to Le Masy, each stage being a day's march.

In the meantime the Earl of Athlone, leaving some cavalry at La Falaise, (which lies a little north of Namur), marched towards Charleroi, crossed the Meuse at Castelet, and then doubled back and marched straight towards Namur, sweeping the river of boats as he went: the effect of this feint on Charleroi was to deceive d'Harcourt, and to induce him to weaken his forces by throwing a body of dragoons into Charleroi. Athlone, on arrival in front of Namur, occupied posts on the North stretching from Floreff on the Sambre across to the Meuse. The Elector meanwhile crossed the river to Malogne, where he arrived on the 23rd. The same day the Brandenburg contingent closed in on the South. This last move was, however, a day too late; for de Boufflers, who had made forced marches by Solre and Phillipsville, was able to reach the town a few hours later with seven regiments of dragoons, some artillery and sappers. The king arrived in camp the same day, and on the 23rd the investment of Namur was complete.

Namur was one of the most formidable strongholds in the world: and this strength it owed partly to nature, and partly to its strong defences. Its garrison consisted, (after de Boufflers reinforcement), of nineteen battalions of foot, eight regiments of dragoons, a company of miners, and a company of gunners, in all about twelve or fourteen thousand men: and of artillery there were 120 guns and 8 mortars: and ample stores of munitions, money and provisions. The Comte de

Guiscard was the governor, and de Boufflers took the general command of the troops.

Immediately after the investment, Lord Athlone was detached with the cavalry to consume the forage between Mons and the Sambre, while the investing army awaited the arrival of reinforcements and of the guns and siege material. By the 28th of June these had arrived and the trenches were opened.

With the siege of Namur we have little to do, as the cavalry were not employed in the investment. We note that on the 6th of July there was an assault in which the Brigade of Guards bore the brunt of the attack, and greatly distinguished themselves. The result of the affair was that the Allies were left masters of the whole of the heights of Bouge, with a loss of not fewer than 4000 men killed and wounded in the evening's work. Another assault took place on the afternoon of the 17th, and from that date to the surrender of the town on August the 27th there was continuous fighting, in which the British regiments bore the lion's share.

To return to the operations which had in the meantime taken place in the neighbourhood of the Scheldt and Lys.

We left de Vaudemont at Grammen on the Lys, whither he had marched on June the 20th, and where he was joined by the Duc de Würtemberg.

On June the 18th, when William marched from Becelaer to Rousselaer, de Villeroi crossed the Lys and encamped at Harlebeck, and shortly afterwards marched to Pottes beyond the Scheldt, at the same time detaching bodies of cavalry towards the Sambre to harass the convoys of the Allies.

At Rousselaer on the 14th June:

> The king had notice the enemy were sending a party of dragoons to attack our bread wagons commanded from Ghent. Immediately a detachment of dragoons was ordered to wait for them at Moorsleede by which they were to march under the command of Brigadeer Wynne, they mett the party, which had . . . . . our hands, had we not attacked them too. In the action Brigadeer Wynne was wounded in the Legg, Lieut. Webb and 10 private men killed. Of the enemy one hussar captain and eight men made prisoners, what was killed of the enemy is uncertain by reason this action happened in the dark, (Add. MS. 18,776, fol. 4.)

The following account of this affair is taken from D'Auvergne:—
The dragoons under Wynne were "advised they (the enemy) were to pass that evening (on the 14th) by Moorsleede." The dragoons overtook them and had orders to dismount and attack them, "which they did with a great deal of courage." The enemy were commanded by a lieutenant-colonel and were about four hundred strong; and:

> They made some barricades of wagons, which they defended no longer than to gain time to make their escape; but notwithstanding, a captain and thirty men remained prisoners, and they had several killed and wounded. The fire was very hot for half-an-hour. Brigadier Wynne was wounded in the knee, which though it was not esteemed very dangerous at first, yet he died afterwards of this wound at Ghent, being generally regretted. The king has since given his regiment of dragoons to Colonel Ross, lieutenant-colonel of the regiment, who has been one of the king's *aides-de-camp* the three last campaigns. Captains Collins and Holdgate likewise wounded, both officers of dragoons. Lieutenant Webb was killed.

The next day the convoy came safe to camp.

On the 3rd of July, de Villeroi marched to attack de Vaudemont, whose presence on the Lys prevented him leaving the Lines for the relief of Namur. Leaving Pottes at ten o'clock at night, he arrived at Rosebeck at nine the next morning, having during the night marched some four and twenty miles, and crossed the Scheldt and the Lys, besides two smaller streams.

The Allies, with their usual neglect of scouting precautions, were only aware of de Villeroi's approach when some of their advanced posts had been made prisoners by the French.

De Vaudemont's numbers were not much more than half of his opponent's. He despatched his baggage to Ghent and awaited the French general's attack. Three English regiments were ordered up from Deinse, the right was thrown back so as to occupy the higher ground about Arseele, and the front was entrenched. The British position extended from the right at Arseele to the left at Gothem, where the Mandel River joins the Lys. The Mandel protected the left flank, while in the front were numerous ravines, streams and woods.

De Villeroi halted at the village of Denterghem on the morning of the 4th, while his troops effected some sort of clearance of the ground between themselves and the Allies: and the design was formed of surrounding de Vaudemont under cover of the very obstacles on which he was relying for protection from attack. A large body of French cavalry under de Montal and Berwick, got on to the high road at Thielt and so round the right flank of the Allies: the infantry meanwhile extended along the front, and at intervals little explosions were made along the line to maintain communication and regulate the advance.

De Vaudemont, however, perceived the intentions of his adversary. His situation was critical; to retire might prove even more disastrous than the attempt to hold on to his position, but he finally saved the situation by an extremely clever retirement. Giving orders for the troops in front to continue at work on the entrenchments, and directing the artillery on his left to keep up a perpetual cannonade, he caused a number of houses along his front to be set on fire, and then with the greatest possible caution and silence withdrew his Artillery from the front and from the right, and despatched it to Deinse. At the same time he moved the cavalry of the right wing, alternated with the infantry regiments of Collier's brigade, to his right rear between Arseele and Vinckt, as if to check de Montal's approaching attack on that flank; but suddenly M. d'Auverquerque marched off with the cavalry straight upon Ghent by a narrow road through the woods, while the infantry, with their pikes and colours trailed, took the road along the rear to Deinse. During this movement the Prince de Vaudemont, the Due de Würtemberg and a number of English staff officers remained formed in line, in order to keep up an appearance of the presence of cavalry. Lastly, the cavalry of the left, together with the Dutch infantry, drew off towards Deinse.

So silently was the withdrawal carried out that two companies of Tiffeney's (27th) Foot who had been left at their post in the front near Arseele to keep up the deception to the last, had not a notion of their abandoned situation, until an *aide-de-camp* brought them the order to withdraw.

The French generals nearest the Allies, on discovering what was being done, sent off word to de Villeroi, but not one of them would take the responsibility of acting without orders. By the time de Villeroi received the news, only the rearguard of the Allies was to be seen retiring in the distance. The French pursued, but the rearguard contested every point of vantage and so gained time for the retreat of their main body, while cavalry trumpeters were sent to the rear of the main body and sounded repeatedly, as if the force were drawing up for battle, thereby causing the pursuers to halt and form for attack. These constant delays, together with the advent of nightfall, put an end to the pursuit.

Ross' Dragoons were apparently engaged in this action. D'Auvergne writes that:

> This great and renowned retreat is as fine a piece of the art of war as can be read of in history, and which can hardly be paralleled in it; which has showed more the art conduct, and prudence of a general, than if the prince had gained a considerable victory.

The next day de Vaudemont reunited his forces at Ghent, and de Villeroi returned to his camp between Rosebeck and Rousselaer.

On July the 6th de Vaudemont, with the smallest portion of his force, camped at Oostaker near Ghent, while Bellasyse and de Würtemberg marched through Bruges to Placendael, where the Nieuport and Ostend canals join.

With Sir Henry Bellasyse's force of twelve battalions marched Ross' and Cunningham's dragoons. On the 7th he halted his infantry to refresh near Bruges, but sent his dragoons on to Placendael, whence, on being joined by the infantry, the whole force marched *via* Newendam to Nieuport.

De Vaudemont's aim was now the defence of the line of the Nieuport, Ostend, Bruges and Ghent canals, and the guarding of the country to Brussels.

Bellasyse reached Nieuport on the 8th, and de Würtemberg following him, the defence of the canal from that place to Placendael was provided for; and de Villeroi, who had advanced a body of troops beyond Dixmude with intentions against Nieuport, was forestalled. De Würtemberg still further confined the movements of the French by opening the sluices about Nieuport, and putting the whole country under water.

Baulked at Nieuport, de Villeroi detached a force under de Montal to invest Dixmude. Major-General Ellenberg (a Danish officer) was in command of that place, and had a sufficient force of Danish and English troops for its defence, and plentiful supplies and munitions. Not twenty-four hours had elapsed, however, after the trenches were opened, before Ellenberg beat a parley, and, in spite of the opposition of some of the officers, and to the great disgust of the soldiers, next day surrendered the place. Numbers of the men broke their weapons, and Lord Lorne's Scotsmen tore their colours to pieces rather than give them up.

The French met with equally good fortune at Deinse, where O'Ffarrel surrendered without a shot being fired.

Ellenberg was subsequently beheaded, and O'Ffarrel broke with ignominy and imprisoned, and many of the other officers cashiered by sentence of a court martial.

Finding it hopeless to compel William to raise the siege of Namur by attempting the capture of the large fortresses between the Scheldt and the coast, de Villeroi marched eastwards. Leaving the Comte de Montal with 6000 men to protect the lines, he moved on the 25th July to Avelghem on the Scheldt; and the next day with a large portion of his army to Enghien *via* Renaix; whereupon, de Vaudemont marched by way of Dendermonde to Dieghem, just N. of Brussels, "having twenty-six battalions with him and all the English horse and dragoons, except the dragoons of Ross and Cunningham, which remained with Lieut.-General Bellasyse," whose force now marched to Bruges, and on the 30th to Ghent, and subsequently joined the army at Brussels.

De Würtemberg joined de Vaudemont at Dieghem on the 30th with twelve battalions, having first provided for the safety of the Western fortresses by inundations and reinforcements.

On the 1st of August de Villeroi marched to Halle, and next day camped between Gaesbeck and Anderlecht; but he found his intentions on Brussels anticipated, for de Vaudemont had inundated the front of the town from the Senne to Monterey, and had entrenched along the river and canals from Monterey to Vilvorde; the Earl of Athlone was also approaching with a large body of troops from Namur, while William himself had left Namur with a further reinforcement, leaving the Elector to carry on the siege. De Villeroi was forced to content himself with the barbarous satisfaction of bombarding the town of Brussels.

The shelling began on the 3rd August, and about it Parker writes:

Five days the bombardment continued, and with such fury that the centre of that noble city was quite laid in rubbish. Most of the time of bombarding I was on the counterscarp, where I could best see and distinguish; and I have often counted in the air at one time, more than twenty bombs; for they shot whole bombs out of their mortars all together. This, as it must needs be terrible, threw the inhabitants into the utmost confusion. Cartloads of nuns, that for many years before had never been out of the cloisters, were now hurried about from place to place to find retreats of some security. In short the groves and parts remote were all crowded: and the most spacious streets had hardly a spectator left to view the ruins.

All this time the siege of Namur was being carried on. On August the 7th de Villeroi desisted from the wanton bombardment of Brussels and marched to Enghien, and on the 9th to Soignies, where he halted some days to receive orders from Paris, detaching d'Harcourt to Solre on the Sambre to get together any troops available on that frontier.

The moment de Villeroi retired from Brussels, de Vaudemont effected a junction between Waterloo and Genappe with Athlone, and on the 10th he joined the army before Namur.

De Villeroi, on receiving his orders from the Court, marched to Nivelles; and on the 16th proceeding towards Ornlau, he encamped between St. Amand and Sombref. On the 18th August he continued his march to Gemblours, where he took up a position with the Bois de Grand-Lez on his left, the river along his front, and his right near Tougrines.

King William had returned to Namur, and on hearing of de Villeroi's movements took command of the covering army, secured de Vaudemont's junction with him, and camped behind the village of St. Denis, with his left entrenched as far as Isne-les-dames.

De Villeroi arrived in front of this camp on the 18th, and made every sign of intending to remain for at least a day; but at 11 o'clock the same night he struck camp in the profoundest silence, crossed the Orneau, and arrived at dawn in the thick woods which alone now separated him from the Allied Camp. Here he found every precaution for defence had been made, and he was reluctantly forced to return to the other side of the Orneau.

On the 20th de Villeroi moved to the Mehaigne, and halted with the village of Grand Rosiere in his rear. He had found the Allied position too formidable for attack, and was obliged to remain an inactive witness of the calamity he was powerless to prevent. This catastrophe was not long in arriving. At noon on August the 20th an exploded barrel of powder flashed from the British quarters at Salsines, the signal for a general assault on the fortress of Namur.

From the first line of trenches towards the Terra Nova marched four English sergeants, each with fifteen men. Immediately behind them came the grenadiers of the Guards under Colonel Evans, and closely following them were the grenadiers of the other regiments. Lord Cutts commanded and personally led the attack. St. George's (17th) and Mackay's foot supported the attack, and Fred Hamilton's (18th) and Buchan's regiments were in reserve.

At the same time 3000 Bavarians marched out of the second parallel towards the breach of the Coehorne. Two thousand Brandenburgers assailed the point of the Coehorne, and were in touch with the attack of two thousand Dutch on the Cassotte. Six hundred men were also detailed to assault the *basse-ville* which lay below the castle.

The breach assigned to the English was more exposed to fire than the others, and the access to it was more difficult; while between it and the besiegers' trenches was an open space of more than half a mile. Across this valley of death the British grenadiers marched exposed to a terrible fire from front and flank. They mounted the breach supported only by St. George's foot; the other three regiments having been delayed. Nearly every officer of the grenadiers was killed or wounded, and Lord Cutts himself was severely wounded in the head.

When the three supporting regiments at length came up, the men were dispirited, and all the *élan* of the first attack had evaporated; but the troops again advanced, and again made their way on to the breach. Fred Hamilton's regiment got quite within the breach, and planted their colours on the ramparts. But now for the first time it was discovered that the enemy had erected within the breach an interior entrenchment which was untouched and unassailable. The English troops retired; and, as they went, a large body of French foot and dragoons came down between the Coehorne and Terra Nova and fell upon them, while a cross-fire was poured upon them from both fortresses. Lord Cutts, returning so soon as his wound was dressed, saw it was suicidal to remain, and gave the order to retreat. The British attack had failed.

Meanwhile, the Bavarians got into difficulties in their attack on the breach in the Coehorne, and after two hours' fighting found themselves on the point of being beaten back, although they still held their ground upon the glacis. It was at this critical moment that Lord Cutts, as he retreated from the Terra Nova, perceived the state of affairs: calling for two hundred volunteers to form a forlorn hope, he was promptly answered, and Lieutenant Cockle of Mackay's was selected to lead them. This officer's instructions were to attack the face of the salient angle next the breach, without firing a shot; and, if he could master the palisades, to lodge himself in the covered way. Mackay's regiment was next to the front, with the Ensigns bearing their colours at their head.

Liberal promises of promotion and rewards were made, and the soldiers were encouraged by handfuls of gold being given to those who particularly distinguished themselves.

Cockle succeeded in surmounting the palisade; and, beating the enemy back on the covered way, he turned their own guns on to them. He was ably supported by the four English regiments, and the Ensigns of Mackay's marched boldly up and planted their colours on the ramparts, which so fired the men that not only was the covered way gained, but held.

The Brandenburgers and Dutch were also successful in their efforts, and by 5 o'clock in the afternoon the fighting was over, and the Allies remained effectually lodged within the enemy's works.

King William had watched the whole affair with the greatest anxiety, and having assigned to the British troops the post of most danger, he especially observed their conduct. He marked his approbation of the bravery of Fred Hamilton's (18th) regiment in the second, and almost hopeless, attack on the Terra Nova, by conferring upon it the title of "The Royal Regiment of Ireland," together with its present badge and motto. Lieutenant Cockle was shortly rewarded with money and promotion.

The loss on this day amongst the British force alone, consisting of four regiments and seven hundred grenadiers, was:—

	Killed	Wounded
Officers	29	55
Men	275	790

On the 26th of August the garrison surrendered and filed out between two long lines of the Allied troops with all the honours of war, colours flying, arms carried, bullet in mouth, and matches lighted, and six guns following with the baggage. The garrison began the siege with 13,000 troops, and marched out under 5,000 strong, and when the victors entered the place they found it absolutely reeking with the putrid stench of dead men and horses.

The Allied Army before Namur next marched towards Brussels, whereupon, de Villeroi, detaching a force to take care of Dinant, marched by way of Charleroi and Mons towards the lines.

Bellasyse's force marched to Ghent upon the capitulation of Namur.

Nothing, however, came of these movements, and the Allies commenced to move into winter quarters, the dragoons being quartered in the villages between Ghent and Sans van Ghent, except the dragoons of Ross, who were quartered in the villages between Bruges and Damme.

During the winter the French king expended his resources in preparation for an invasion of England. This abortive design had no effect on the Allied Army in Flanders beyond causing the recall home of some twenty battalions, ten of which, however, returned without even landing in England. Two regiments, Erle's (19th) and Bellasyse's (22nd), were captured by the French during the passage home and carried into Dunkirk. While the Allies were thus compelled to weaken their army, the French on the other hand were reinforced by their forces from the Duchy of Savoy, peace having been concluded with that State.

On the 4th March, in a raid made on Givet by a body of Cavalry under the Earl of Athlone, joined by a detachment from the garrison of Namur, an immense quantity of forage accumulated by the French was destroyed.

During the first week in May the opposing armies began to assemble.

Ross' Dragoons, with those of Livingstone, were the dragoons of the 2nd Line of the right wing, the brigadier being Mathews.

De Villeroi with his main army was between Menin and the Scheldt, while de Bouffler's corps was collected about the Orneau. Also, two flying columns were assembled, under de la Mothe and de Montal, towards the sea; another in Luxembourg under d'Harcourt, and a fourth about Dinant under the Comte de Guiscard. In all, the French forces reckoned 173 battalions and 223 squadrons, or about 120,000 men. These numbers were so overwhelming that the Allies contented themselves with forming two corps of observation, one at Tirlemont under Prince Nassau-Saarbruck, and the other at Affleghem near Alost, under the Prince de Vaudemont.

On May the 9th de Villeroi, marching along the Lys from Courtrai reached Deinse, and at the same time de Boufflers encamped at Fleurus; whereupon Prince Nassau-Saarbruck retreated from Tirlemont to Parck Camp.

De Villeroi contented himself at Deinse with foraging and consuming the country, but none the less every measure was taken by the

Allies to secure the line of canals against him.

On May the 27th William arrived in camp and took command of the Army of the West. By this time Nassau-Saarbruck had been joined by the Brandenburg, Cologne, and Liége contingents, and had advanced as far as Wavre, while de Boufflers had retired to Charleroi.

On June the 1st William marched with a strong force from Ghent to Wavre.

On June the 9th the king marched from Wavre to Conroy (halfway between Wavre and Gemblours), but de Boufflers' attitude all along the Sambre was such, that William hesitated before making any fresh move. On the 27th, however, he advanced to Gemblours, and there awaited the arrival of the contingent under the Landgrave of Hesse. On the 15th July the Landgrave with 15,000 men arrived at Namur, and William advanced to Sombref to meet him.

De Boufflers' fears at this time were that the Allies would either force the Sambre, and thus make their way on to French territory towards Dinant and in rear by Charleroi, or else, repeating their tactics of 1694, make a sudden rush against the lines of Espierre or for the siege of Mons.

The following moves of the two armies need not be gone into at length. The attitude of both sides was simply that of waiting for something to turn up. The French Army was the stronger. The aggressive therefore lay with them, while the Allies could not initiate any action of decision. On August the 16th William left the army. De Vaudemont and de Villeroi had meanwhile remained observing each other on the canals of Ostend and Bruges, contenting themselves with foraging and reconnaissance.

On the 20th of August:

The enemies beat the 'General' very early in their camp, which we could hear very easily from ours; the Prince Vaudemont thought that it was in order to march, and accordingly ordered the 'General' to beat on our side, and the army marched forthwith towards Bruges. . . . . . The same day that we marched up so near to Bruges, the prince ordered a detachment of horse and dragoons to march on the other side of the canal, to observe the enemies, whom we expected to be on the march too. Captain Cornwallis of Ross' Regiment commanded the dragoons, who fell in at Oostcamp with a party of the enemies posted in a defile; and though this was a considerable disadvantage, yet

Captain Cornwallis charged them with his dragoons sword in hand so vigorously that he killed several of the enemies, and brought off all his detachment safe out of the defile (except for two killed) and a prisoner that was wounded in the action: the Dutch horse being informed that several of the enemy's squadrons lay between Oostcamp and Lophem to cover the foragers, would not venture in to the dragoons' assistance, else we might have taken the whole party.

Another extract from D'Auvergne, under date 31st August:—

The prince, having advice that all the French troops under Villeroi were now upon their march towards Torhout, ordered the infantry of his army, with the dragoons of Eppinger, Ross, and Mirmont, to pass the canal. The infantry, having passed the canal, encamped in two lines, two and twenty battalions in the first line and sixteen in the second, with the right near the canal of Ostend, and the left at St. Michael; the dragoons of Eppinger and Mirmont encamped upon the right of the first line, while those of Ross upon the left at St. Michael near the canal of Bruges.

About the 29th September the firing of the enemy's guns created a stir in the prince's camp, upon which:

Eppinger and Mirmont's dragoons on the right and Ross' on the left were ordered to mount and pass the canal of Ostend, to march towards Placendael.

It was found, however, to be a foraging party, and that there was no danger to Placendael, and the prince "countermanded the dragoons."

Meanwhile the army was beginning to go into winter quarters, the campaign having been got through without loss, though at the end of July Huy had an exceedingly narrow escape of capture.

The dragoons of Ross and Livingstone were quartered for the winter in the Palis de Nort, beyond Bruges.

The campaign of 1697 was almost as devoid of incident as that of the previous year.

During April the Allies occupied themselves in making a line of defence from Ostend by Bruges and Brussels to Namur; for the protection of this work the Elector of Bavaria assembled a force at Deinse, while the rendezvous of the main army was at Bois-Seigneur-Isaac.

On the French side de Villeroi took command of an army of observation, while Maréchal de Catinat undertook the siege of Ath; and de Boufflers assembled a corps on the Meuse.

The strength of the French force was as follows:—

De Villeroi	60,000
De Boufflers	56,000
Catinat	40,000

On May the 16th both the Allied armies united at St. Quintin-Lenneck, under the command of the king, who had arrived on the 14th,

De Boufflers had approached de Villeroi, who now had under his hand in case of a general action some one hundred and twenty thousand men besides those engaged in the siege, while William had some fifteen or twenty thousand fewer.

With this preponderance of force, and with dispositions so much in favour of de Villeroi, William regarded it impracticable to relieve Ath, and on the 22nd marched to Genappe *via* Oudenarde, while the Elector returned to Deinse.

On the 28th of May Ath surrendered with all the honours of war.

On June the 12th de Villeroi marched to Gammerage and de Boufflers to Enghien, and both made ready to march conjointly on Brussels. If the French could start from Enghien before William became aware of it, they were sure to reach Brussels before him; in which case they would be able to proceed to cut off all communication between the Eastern and Western portions of the Allied line of defence.

But fortunately for the Allies, they for once had scouts on the look-out, and these movements were known to William the same afternoon. The King, grasping the situation, marched by the one road open to him. Starting three brigades of infantry between four and five o'clock, he despatched the artillery two hours later, the baggage at ten, and the rest of the infantry at eleven. He personally superintended the despatch of the troops, and at midnight he rode with four regiments of the dragoons to the front to reconnoitre, and to be ready for the army on its arrival. The main body of the cavalry left Genappe at daylight, and so covered the rear.

Before ten next morning the Allies had occupied the camp of Anderlecht; and when de Villeroi and de Boufflers appeared presently on the heights of Anderlecht and on the Assche road, they saw the Dutch and English flags waving over the coveted ground, and knew that they were foiled. Besides providing against an attack on the camp, the Allies placed Brussels in readiness for a siege. The failure of the design upon the Capital was the concluding act of the War in Flanders.

For some months negotiations had been proceeding, and on the 11th of September peace was signed at Ryswick.

After the Peace of Ryswick steps were taken by Parliament to reduce the strength of the Standing Army, and to make matters worse the government failed to find the money necessary to wipe off the arrears of pay due to the troops. Discontent and insubordination became rife, and the effect of disbanding such a large body of men was disastrous. The country was flooded with gangs of unemployed men rendered desperate by the refusal of government to settle their just dues.

A new Parliament met in December, and William urged the necessity of maintaining an army sufficient for the needs of England, and the imperative duty of settling the arrears of pay.

The House thereupon passed an act fixing the army to be maintained in England at 7,000 men, and that in Ireland at 12,000, Ireland bearing the cost of her own troops. The army was to consist entirely of British subjects, thereby excluding William's Dutch soldiers.

With the exception of the regiments specially named, all corps were to be disbanded by the next 25th of March.

To complicate matters, the Mutiny Act, which had expired in the previous April, was not re-enacted, and the military authorities were powerless to enforce discipline.

The following is a list of the regiments of the British Army continued in force by the proclamation.

IN ENGLAND.

HORSE.

3 troops of Guards.
1 troop Horse Grenadiers.
Oxford's Regt. (Blues).
Lumley's (1 D.G.)
Wood's (3 D.G.)
Arran's (5 D.G.)
Wyndham's (6 D.G.)
Schomberg's (7 D.G.)
Marchfield's.

DRAGOONS.

Raby's (1 D.)
Lloyd's (3 Hrs.)
Essex's (4 Hrs.)

FOOT.

1st Regt. Foot Guards.
2nd   „   „   „
Selwyn's (Queen's).
Churchill's (Buffs).
Trelawny's (King's Own).

IN IRELAND.

HORSE.

Harvey's (2 D.G.)
Langston (4 D.G.)

DRAGOONS.

Ross (5 Lancers.)
Echerin (6 D.)
Conyngham (8 H.)

FOOT.

Orkney (R. Scots).
Columbine (6th).
Fairfax (5th).
Webb (8th).
Stewart (9th).
Granville (10th).
Hanmer (11th).
Brewer (12th).
Jacob (13th).
Tidcombe (14th).
Howe (15th).

Stanley (16th).
Bridges (17th).
Fred Hamilton (18th).
Erle (19th).
Geo. Hamilton (20th).
Bellasyse (22nd).
Ingoldsby (23rd).
De Tinzar (24th).
Tiffan (27th).

IN SCOTLAND.

HORSE.

1 troop guards (afterwards disbanded).

DRAGOONS.

Royal Regiment (Scots Greys).
Jedburgh's (7 H.).

FOOT.

Scots Guards.
Colyear's.
Scots Fusiliers (21st).
Maitland's (25th).
Geo. Hamilton's.
Strathnavar's.

IN CHANNEL ISLANDS.

O'Hara's (7th Fusiliers).

Ross' Dragoons to consist of 8 troops, making a total of 362 men.

The dragoons disbanded out of the regiment received a total sum of £272. 19. 2¾ amongst them.

Soon after the Peace of Ryswick Ross' Dragoons had returned to Ireland where they enjoyed a term of home service until March, 1702.

Quarters of the Army, 27th June, 1698. Colonel Ross' Dragoons are quartered as follows:—

1 Troop at Mullingar and Ballynalackbridge.
1   „   Longford and Castleforbes.
1   „   Castlebar and Foxford.
1   „   Birr, Ballyboy and Ballyloghuane and the adjacent villages.
1   „   Roscommon, Athleage and Castlereagh.
1   „   Loughrea.
1   „   Boyle and Elphin.
1   „   Sligo.

Warrant of six months' allowance of powder to the Army.

Dragoons.
{
Colonel Ross'.
"   Echlin's.
"   Conyngham's.
Marquis de Mirmont's.
}

The allowance for each troop being half a barrel of powder. Establishment of the regiment.

34 Officers.
8 Sergeants.
16 Corporals.

8 Drums.
8 Trumpeters and Hautbois.
288 Private men.

———————

362 Total.

———————

The following confirmation of a court martial dated in Dublin on the 2nd of December 1698 is interesting as showing the cruel methods of punishment in vogue in the army at the time. Six of Ross' Dragoons were convicted of mutiny and were sentenced "to run and be whipped three several times by an entire regiment of foot drawn out for that purpose on three several days on St. Stephen's Green."

This punishment was termed the gatloup. The troops ordered to carry it out were paraded with open ranks, each man being furnished with a stout switch; the ranks were faced inwards, and the prisoner, stripped to the waist, was marched up and down the lanes of men, each man striking him on the "naked back, breast, arms, or where his cudgel should light" as he passed; and in order to drown the cries of the "patient," drums were beaten during the punishment.

At the same court martial sixteen more men of Ross' Dragoons suffered the gatloup, while another ten were to be present "stripped of their clothes."

This latter was a common punishment of the time, the lesser offenders having to be present to witness the punishment of the more guilty, undergoing all the disgrace short of the actual infliction.

While on the subject of Military Law, we notice that on the 15th of March 1698 a petition was presented to the House of Commons by soldiers of Ross' Dragoons against the major, among other things, for beating a soldier for remonstrating about his accounts, with a thick cane, to such a degree as to damage him for life. Evidently the officer could not be amenable to ordinary martial law for this. The allegation was considered proven by the House.

"Drumming out," too, was a punishment of the time, for in the same year sixteen of Ross' Dragoons were to lose their horses, clothes, etc. and:

To be declared broken and disbanded and for ever incapable to serve His Majesty, and then to be trooped out of the garrison with drums, (Dublin State papers).

Quarters of the Army, 4th June, 1700.

Colonel Ross' Dragoons quartered at:—

1 troop at Mallow.
2   „   Clonmel.
1   „   Rosse and Rossebarcan.
1   „   Cashell.
1   „   Carrickneshure.
1   „   Cappoquin and Lismore.
1   „   Thurles.

Quarters of the Army, 1701.

Colonel Ross' Dragoons quartered at:—

1 troop at Colooney.
1   „   Boyle
1   „   Athlone
1   „   Longford
1   „   Longhrea
1   „   Castlebar
1   „   Roscommon
1   „   Castlereagh
1   „   Headfoed

UNIFORMS OF THE REGIMENT AT DIFFERENT PERIODS OF ITS HISTORY

CHAPTER 3

Campaigns of 1702-1703

On the last day of the year 1701 the king, in a masterly speech to Parliament, pointed out the position in which the nation found itself by the action of the French king in violating the treaties and accepting the Crown of Spain on behalf of his grandson; and Parliament was at last aroused when Louis XIV proclaimed James's son as King of England, thus ignoring the Treaty of Ryswick, by which William's claim to the Crown had been recognised.

The regiments of the army were brought up to war strength, orders were given for a force to be sent to the Low Countries, and for nine additional regiments of foot to be raised.

War became inevitable, and an address was presented by the Commons to the king:

> That no peace shall be made with France until His Majesty and the nation have reparation for the great indignity offered by the French king in owning and declaring the pretended Prince of Wales King of England, Scotland and Ireland.

William at this time was in an enfeebled state of health, and falling from his horse at Hampton Court on February the 20th, broke his collarbone. The shock was fatal, and he gradually sank and expired on the 8th of March. He was succeeded by the Princess Anne, daughter of James II.

Marlborough, who had been appointed Commander-in-Chief of the Allied Forces, arrived at the Hague in the middle of May.

The general plan of operations was as follows:—

A German Army on the upper Rhine was to threaten Eastern France, the Prussians and Dutch were to besiege Kaiserwerth.

The main army, 35,000 strong, under the Earl of Athlone, was to hold the frontier of Holland from the Rhine to the Meuse, at the same time covering the siege of Kaiserwerth. A fourth army, collected near the mouth of the Scheldt, threatened the country round Bruges, (Knight).

The main French Army of 60,000 men was in the neighbourhood of Liége. Tallard with 13,000 men was detached on the Upper Rhine to raise the siege of Kaiserwerth, while another French force was to oppose the fourth allied army in the neighbourhood of Bruges.

Kaiserwerth capitulated on the 15th of June.

Boufflers, on the 10th of June, made a sudden dash to cut off Athlone, who was encamped twenty miles away near Cleve with 25,000 men, from Nimeguen.

By a forced march, accompanied by a running fight, the Allies were able to forestall the French design. Athlone next withdrew across the Waal.

On July the 2nd Marlborough joined the army, accompanied by two Dutch deputies. These, throughout the long war now commencing, except during 1704, frequently used their influence to obstruct the operations of the British commander who was also much troubled by the jealousies of the various Allied commanders.

On arrival at Nimeguen Marlborough concentrated 60,000 men, 12,000 of whom were British troops, the British contingent consisting of seven regiments of horse and dragoons, fourteen battalions of foot, and fifty six guns.

Marlborough then crossed the Waal and encamped at Ober-Hasselt, about six miles from the French camp, where he was delayed until the 26th of July.

Meanwhile Brigadier Ross had received an order that six troops of the regiment under his command were to be employed beyond the seas, the remaining two to remain in Ireland. The regiment of eight troops at this time consisted of 362 officers and men.

Ross' Dragoons embarked at Dublin on March the 16th, and the ships being dispersed at sea, presumably by a storm, they were landed at different ports in England.

The regiment assembled at Northampton at the end of April, and soon after left England for Holland.

The pay of the two troops left behind in Ireland was fixed at the following rates for each troop:—

	s	d	
Captain	10.	0	per diem
Lieutenant	5.	0	„
Cornet	4.	0	„
Quarter Master	3.	0	„
1 Sergeant	2.	6	„
2 Corporals, each	1.	6	„
1 Drummer	1.	6	„
1 Hautboye	1.	6	„
36 Dragoons, each	1.	2	„

The following entry is found in the *Marlborough Despatches* dated 24th July:—

The English train, with the three regiments of dragoons commanded by Colonel Ross, will arrive from Breda tomorrow night at Bois-le-Duc; an express was sent them yesterday to halt at that place until further orders.

On the 27th:—

The ways were so bad on Tuesday by the continued rains, that the generals thought fit to defer the march of the army from Ober-Hasselt for that day; however, most part of the baggage went over the Meuse in the afternoon upon three bridges just below the Grave, and yesterday the whole army followed.
Some squadrons of the enemy appeared yesterday morning at a good distance while the army was going over the Meuse, but did not advance so as to interrupt our passage, (Marlborough's Despatches).

In five marches Marlborough arrived at Hamont, threatening Brabant. This move caused Boufflers to fall back hurriedly towards the Demer, calling Tallard from the Rhine to join him.

On the 2nd August the French Army, exhausted and worn out by forced marches, was encamped in a very unfavourable position at Lonovur, and lay practically at Marlborough's mercy, but the Dutch deputies forbade an attack, and the French were enabled to cross the Demer at Diest unmolested, (Knight).

On the 10th August:—

This night a thousand men were commanded to make the roads,

and all the horse and dragoons are commanded to make each a fascine to fill up a bog which lies between us and the French; and tomorrow as soon as the roads are made, the army will march towards the enemy to oblige them to decamp, (Marlborough's Despatches).

Marlborough was now making preparations for the siege of Venloo.

The French Army again escaped the possibilities of a defeat on two occasions. On the first, the Dutch General Opdam deliberately refused to carry out his orders to attack, and then when Marlborough proposed attacking Boufflers, the deputies insisted on further delay, and the French Army got away.

On the 24th both armies were in camp near Helchteren, and during the afternoon their artillery were engaged. All night long both camps remained under arms, and on the night of the 26th the Allies prepared to attack the French. During the night, however, the enemy retired:

> In great disorder, whereupon at daylight Marlborough followed them with twenty squadrons of the right, as the Earl of Athlone did with the same number from the left; but only Brigadier Wood with some squadrons of the right managed to catch up the French rear guard of three or four squadrons which he entirely broke, (Marlborough's Despatches).

Meanwhile the siege of Venloo had been going on, and on the 18th of September the castle was carried by storm; Lord Cutts and the English grenadiers, behaving with the greatest gallantry, were the first to enter.

Stevenswaert was not invested, and on the night of the 1st of October:

> The besieged having abandoned the counterscarp, and our men being ready to mount the breach, they beat the *chamade*, and desired to capitulate, (Marlborough's Despatches).

Maeseyk and Ruremond next fell into the hands of the Allies. Boufflers, anxious for the safety of Cologne and Bonn, despatched Tallard back to the Rhine, remaining himself in the vicinity of Tongres. Becoming anxious about Liége, the French general marched for that place about the 9th of October. He, however, found himself anticipated by Marlborough, for on arrival in front of the town he found the Allied Army drawn up on the very ground he had intended occupying. Again the Dutch deputies interfered, and prevented Marlborough from throwing himself on the enemy, who during the night made good their retreat to within the lines of Landon.

The town of Liége at once surrendered to the Allies, and on October the 23rd the citadel was stormed and taken, the British troops again figuring conspicuously in the assault.

The capture of Liége brought the campaign of 1702 to an end, and Marlborough set out for the Hague. At Maestricht he embarked on a boat with an escort of twenty five men, while a party of fifty horse rode along the banks of the river. These latter contrived to lose themselves, and at midnight an ambuscade of the enemy surrounded and seized the duke's boat. Marlborough luckily was not recognised, and after the baggage had been looted the party was allowed to proceed. He was in a great degree indebted for his escape to the presence of mind of one of his attendants named Gill, who, happening to have in his possession a passport which had been granted by the French general for the use of General Churchill, who had not employed it, put it into Lord Marlborough's hands, who thus passed for his brother. Marlborough afterwards rewarded Gill with an annual pension of fifty pounds.

On his return to England the queen conferred a dukedom on Marlborough.

In the early spring of 1703 the British contingent in Flanders was reinforced by four regiments of foot.

Knight in his *History of the Buffs*, obtaining his appreciation from Allison's *Life of Marlborough,* finds the situation in Flanders at the end of April to be as follows:—

> The French King instead of confining the war to one of posts and sieges in Flanders and Italy . . . . resolved to throw the bulk of his forces into Bavaria and operate against Austria from the heart of Germany, by pouring down the valley of the Danube. The advanced post held there by the Elector of Bavaria in front, forming a salient angle, penetrating as it were into the Imperial dominions, and the menacing aspect of the Hungarian insurrection in rear, promised the most successful issue to this decisive operation. For this purpose Marshall Tallard, with the French Army on the Upper Rhine, received orders to cross the Black Forest and advance into Swabia and unite with the

Elector of Bavaria.

Marshal Villeroi, with 40 battalions and 29 squadrons, was to break off from the army in Flanders and support its advance by a movement on the Moselle, so as to be in a condition to join the main army on the Danube, of which it would form, as it were, the left wing; while Vendomme, with the army of Italy, was to penetrate into the Tyrol and advance by Innsbruck or Salzburg. The united armies, which, it was calculated, after deducting all the losses of the campaign, would muster 80,000 combatants, were then to move direct by Lintz and the valley of the Danube on Vienna, while a large detachment penetrated into Hungary to support the already formidable insurrection in that Kingdom. The plan was grandly conceived; it extended from Verona to Brussels, and brought the forces over that vast extent, to converge to the decisive points in the valley of the Danube."

But if the plan was ably conceived on the part of the French Cabinet, it presented from the multiplicity of its combinations serious difficulties in execution, and it required to insure success a larger force than was at their disposal. . . . . . Marlborough, by means of secret information which he obtained from the French headquarters, had got full intelligence of it, and its danger to the Allies if it succeeded struck him, as much as the chances of great advantage to them, if it could be baffled. Louis had contemplated offensive operations in the Low Countries as well as in other quarters; and Marshal Villeroi. . . . . . even flattered himself he would be able to regain possession of the fortresses on the Meuse before the Allies were in a condition to take the field.

Marlborough's force was stronger than that of the enemy.

With these, however, he meditated offensive operations of the most important kind. His design was to make a grand attack on Antwerp, and after taking it to reduce Ostend, which would have opened up a ready communication with England. . . . . But he could not prevail on the States to adopt so vigorous a plan, and by them he was compelled, much against his will, to begin his operations with the siege of Bonn, a considerable fortified town on the Lower Rhine.

Having been obliged to adopt this secondary plan of operations,

Marlborough set about its execution with his usual vigour and activity. He landed at the Hague on the 17th March; and having completed his arrangements there, he set out for Bonn at the head of forty battalions and sixty squadrons, with one hundred guns, leaving Auverquerque with the remainder of the army to form a corps of observation between Liége and Bonn." Marlborough arrived in the vicinity of Bonn on the 20th April, but thanks to the dilatoriness of the Dutch, it was not until the 3rd May that the trenches could be opened.

Meanwhile the following British troops, under Lieutenant-Generals Lumley and Charles Churchill, assembled at Aerschot, whence they marched to Ruremond on the Meuse, arriving at Maesyck by the 7th of May:—

Lumley's Horse	(1 D.G.)
Wood's ,,	(3 D.G.)
Cadogan's ,,	(5 D.G.)
Wyndham's ,,	(6 D.G.)
Schomberg's ,,	(7 D.G.)
Raby's Dragoons	(1st D)
Teviot's ,,	(2 D)
Ross' ,,	(5th Lancers)
1st Battn. (1st Guards)	
Orkney's (R. Scots)	
*Portmore's (2nd Queen's)	
Churchill's (Buffs)	
Webb's (8th King's)	
*Stewart's (9th)	
North and Grey's (10th)	
*Stanhope's (11th)	
*Barrimore's (13th)	
Howe's (15th)	
Stanley's (16th)	
*Bridge's (17th)	
Fred Hamilton's (18th)	
Rowe's (21st)	
Ingoldsby's (23rd)	
Marlborough's (24th)	
Ferguson's (26th)	
Huntingdon's (33rd)	
Meredyth's (37th)	

* Sent to Portugal at the end of this year.

103

In order to raise the siege of Bonn, Villeroi determined to suddenly threaten Maestricht and to then turn on Liége and to endeavour to carry that place before Marlborough could arrive to its assistance.

The French Army on the 8th of May invested Tongres with 3000 men. The garrison consisted of only two regiments of foot, a British and a Dutch, and after a gallant resistance for 28 hours they were compelled to surrender.

Meanwhile Lumley and Churchill made a forced march of 35 miles and effected a junction with Auverquerque at Maestricht on the 9th.

On the 15th of May Villeroi appeared before Maestricht with the intention of attacking the Allies, but not liking the look of things, he retired to Tongres.

Meanwhile Bonn had surrendered to Marlborough, and the duke hastened to join Auverquerque's army at Maestricht, six battalions of foot and three regiments of English dragoons following him from Bonn.

Upon his Grace's coming out of Maestricht (to the camp), the cannon was discharged round the town and in the evening the army and artillery was drawn out, and a triple discharge made of all the cannon and small arms for the taking of Bonn.

The following letter, dated the 27th May, 1703, from Marlborough to the Duke of Queensberry, showing the arrears of pay etc. due to a regiment of this time, is interesting:—

My Lord,
Having read the enclosed memorial from Colonel Rowe, who produces a certificate from the treasury that there is upwards of £5500 due to his regiment . . . . ., I could not refuse recommending his request to your Grace, since it must needs be a very great hardship to the regiment to have so great an arrear, and that it would much contribute to the service if some parts of it were paid, to enable the colonel to better clothe his regiment, and the officers to support themselves in the army.
> I am. My Lord,
> > Yours Grace's etc.
> > > M.

On the 25th of May the army under Marlborough marched to Hannut, and the enemy, remaining on the defensive, and conforming their movements to Marlborough's, gradually fell back on Huy. Marlborough now contemplated the capture of Antwerp as well as Huy, but the noncompliance with his orders on the part of the Dutch General Cohorn, caused delay, and forced him to change his plans and to attack Antwerp forthwith.

The Allies struck their camp at Hannut on the 20th June, and, repassing the Jecker, crossed the Demer at Hasselt. The French, on discovering what was happening, marched by Diest on Antwerp. The success of Marlborough's plans unfortunately depended on the co-operation of several distinct corps advancing from opposite directions. The Dutch generals Cohorn, Spaar and Opdam again failed to carry out their orders, the latter allowing himself to be surprised and surrounded, with a loss of 4000 killed and wounded, 600 prisoners and eight guns; which disaster completely upset Marlborough's plans for the capture of Antwerp. But in spite of this he conceived a fresh attack on the place.

Marlborough's main army was at Bavin on the 6th of July, and on the 20th advanced to Hoogstraeten. The French, however, declined the battle. Next morning the Allies again advanced in order of battle, but once more the French declined to fight, and fell back into the lines covering the town, Marlborough with 400 horse following them right up to the entrenchments. He was eager to attack, but his propositions were, as usual, vetoed by the Dutch deputies.

In a letter to Mr Stepney, dated 11th of August, Marlborough writes about:

> The disappointment we have met with in our designs on Flanders and against Antwerp; this is partly owing to M. de Cohorn's stubbornness and the dissensions among those generals, which has obliged us to return towards the Meuse, where we are now making all necessary preparations for attacking Huy.

On the 15th of August the duke's army was encamped at Val-Notre-Dame, within half a league of Huy, and the next day the siege was commenced by the Prince of Anhalt and Brigadier Hamilton.

Ross' Dragoons in the brigade commanded by Brigadier Ross, and fifteen battalions under Lieutenant-General Somerfeldt, on the 16th crossed the Mehaigne, and encamped near the Meuse to secure the bridge, and to preserve the communication between the main army and the troops carrying on the siege on the other side.

Huy surrendered after a fourteen days' siege, and on the following day, at a Council of War, Marlborough strongly urged the attacking of the French lines. The Dutch, however, would not hear of this course, but insisted on the siege of Limburg.

Marlborough having to give way, the 5th of September found the Allied Army encamped at Hannut, less than two leagues from the French grand camp.

The Allied cavalry were set to collect and make fascines, as if an assault were about to be made on the lines, while Marlborough reconnoitred the position. The French, expecting an immediate attack, manned the defence, and Marlborough was able to perceive that the position was too strong. The following day the Allies fell back to St. Trond, to cover the attack on Limburg, which fell into their hands on the 27th.

The Duke of Marlborough shortly after left the army for the Hague and England. The troops went into winter quarters at the end of October.

Marlborough was so disgusted at the perversity and obstruction of the Dutch authorities, that on his arrival in England he was determined to resign the appointment of commander-in-chief, and it was only the personal intervention of Queen Anne that induced him to reconsider his decision.

In the Order of Battle for the campaign of 1703, Ross' brigade of dragoons were in the right wing of the 1st Line and consisted of the following regiments.

Raby's Dragoons   **(1 R. D.)**
Tuviot's   „   **(Scots Greys)**
Ross'   „   **(5th Lancers)**
A Foreign regiment.

CHAPTER 4

Campaign of 1704

It will be remembered that Ross' Dragoons landed in the Low Countries in 1702 with six troops only, two being left behind in Ireland. In letters to the Duke of Ormond and to Lieutenant-General Earle, dated St. James', 6th of January, 1704, these two troops are ordered by Marlborough to "be forthwith put into the best condition that may be, and sent to the sea coast in order to be embarked." Every effort was made in England during the winter to bring the regiments in the Low Countries up to strength.

We now come to the granting of a special title to the regiment by Queen Anne. Since its formation it had been known by the names of its commanding officers—the dragoons of the gallant Wynne and of Ross. The latter officer petitioned that his regiment should be known as The Royal Dragoons of Ireland, and in a letter dated Whitehall, 22nd February, 1704, Marlborough writes to the Duke of Ormond:—

> Brigadier Ross acquaints me that your Grace has given your consent to his regiment's having the title of Royal Dragoons of Ireland, wherein, however, I shall not venture to do anything until I have it from you.

And in a subsequent letter dated the 9th March, Marlborough writes:—

> Brigadier Ross is sensibly obliged to your Grace for your readiness in gratifying him in his request.

For the coming campaign the French plans were to follow up the successes of the previous year in Germany. Villeroi was to remain in the Low Countries while Tallard with 45,000 men was to join the Elector of Bavaria, who had some 45,000 Bavarians and French, at

Ulm. In addition the French had 10,000 men on the Moselle, available to reinforce either Villeroi or Tallard.

Marlborough, foreseeing the French strategy, determined to carry the war into the heart of Germany, leaving the defence of the Low Countries to the Dutch,

These plans he confided only to those whom he could implicitly trust.

In April Marlborough, who had already visited the Hague during this year, again set out for the Continent, accompanied by his brother Churchill, who had been promoted general to command the British contingent.

It was only with the greatest difficulty that he persuaded the Dutch to consent to his marching on the Moselle.

Indeed, it was only on his threatening to proceed with the British troops alone that they gave way.

The following is a list of the British contingent of the 1704 campaign:—

Lumley's Horse	(1 D. G.)
Wood's do.	(3 D. G.)
Cadogan's do.	(5 D. G.)
Wyndham's do.	(6 D. G.)
Schomberg's do.	(7 D. G.)
Hay's Dragoons	(Scots' Grays).
Royal Dragoons of Ireland	(5 Lancers).
1st. Battn.	(1st. Foot Guards).
Lt. Gen. Hamilton's Foot.	
Churchill's	(Buffs).
Webb's	(8 th.)
Lord North & Grey's	(10 th.)
Howe's	(15 th.)
Stanley's	(16 th.)
Hamilton's	(18 th.)
Rowe's	(21 st.)
Ingoldsby's	(23 rd.)
Marlborough's	(24 th.)
Ferguson's	(26 th.)
Meredith's	(37 th.)

Also 34 guns, 4 howitzers and 21 pontoons.

Having no Dutch troops with him, Marlborough was not troubled with the Dutch deputies, who had impeded him so much in 1703; and by appointing his brother to command the contingent, he silenced the pretensions of Foreign commanders.

During the middle of March the Dutch Army of 60 battalions and 100 squadrons, made Maestricht their rendezvous, and remained in that neighbourhood under the command of Auverquerque throughout the campaign.

On the 8th of May the British troops commenced their famous march into Germany.

From Maestricht Marlborough writes on the 11th of May to Mr. St. John:

> I may venture to tell you (though I would not have it public as yet) I design to march a great deal higher into Germany.

On the 17th May the British contingent crossed the Maes at Ruremond. The infantry and artillery under Churchill continued their march by Sinzig and Andernach, arriving at Neuendorf close to Coblentz on the 26th; while, on the same day Marlborough, having gone with the mounted troops to inspect Bonn, crossed the Moselle and Rhine at Coblentz.

On the 21st, Marlborough, writing to Sir Charles Hedges says:—

> We have certain advice today that the Maréchal de Villeroi passed the Meuse on Monday last with thirty battalions and forty five squadrons of the best troops in the Low Countries, with orders, as I am informed, to observe me wheresoever I march.

In addition to these troops Tallard had succeeded in sending a reinforcement of 10,000 men to the Elector of Bavaria.

Churchill's force of infantry and artillery marched from Neuendorf to Branbach; the duke with the cavalry marched to Schwalbach and thence to Castel, opposite Maintz.

Churchill resumed his march on the 30th, and on the 3rd of June encamped at Castel, where they were:

> Inspected by the Elector and the various allied generals present, and their appearance, discipline, and excellent equipment, and the remarkably orderly manner in which the march had been conducted, excited universal surprise and admiration.

Marlborough with his horse and dragoons had meanwhile crossed the Maine on May the 30th, and marched *via* Zwingenberg and Weinheim, to Ladenburg, where they crossed the Neckar and encamped.

The infantry and artillery, resuming their march, encamped a little below Heidelberg on the 8th of June, having marched by Zwingenberg, Weinheim and the Neckar.

Marlborough and the cavalry left Ladenburg on June the 6th, and marched *via* Wisloch, Eppingen and Gross Gartach, crossing the Neckar on the 9th, and arriving at Mondesheim the following day. On June the 11th the cavalry marched to Gross Heppach, where they were reviewed by the duke in the presence of the Prince Eugene, "who was loud in his praise of their remarkable efficiency." "Their good order and fine appearance after so long and rapid a march, and the excellent condition of their clothing, accoutrements, and horses" especially struck him with admiration.

The Prince Eugene is reported to have said:

My Lord, I never saw better horses, better cloaths, finer belts, and accoutrements; yet all these may be had for money, but there is a spirit in the looks of your men, which I never yet saw in any in my life.

Marlborough was not to be outdone in politeness and is said to have replied:

Sir, if it be as you say, that spirit is inspired in them by your presence, (*The Field of Mars*).

The cavalry with Marlborough next marched to Ebersbach, and on the 16th of June reached Gross Saxenheim, and thence on the 21st "to a point between Lannsheim and Urspring." "The next day he formed a junction with the army of Prince Louis of Baden near Westerstetten," and on the 24th the combined force encamped with their right at Elchingen and their left at Langenau, where they halted to allow Churchill's columns to join them, which they did on the 27th of June.

The enemy, under the Elector of Bavaria, continued in camp at Dillingen and Lavingen, two leagues away.

The relative strength of the two forces was as follows:—

Allies, under Marlborough and Prince Louis of Baden:—

96 battalions.

202 squadrons.

44 field guns.

4 howitzers.

24 pontoons.

Elector of Bavaria (including the garrison of Donawert):—

88 battalions.

160 squadrons.

90 cannons.

40 howitzers and mortars.

30 pontoons

The object of Marlborough's recent movements had been to obtain the fortified town of Donawert, at the junction of the River Wernitz and the Danube, the possession of which place would give the allies a bridge over the Danube and afford them a place of arms for the invasion of Bavaria, the road into which country it covered. "

The recent northerly movements of the Allies, however, betrayed the duke's intentions to the Elector of Bavaria, who, to secure the passage leading through Donawert, detached a force of 10,000 infantry and 2,500 cavalry, under General Count d'Arco, to occupy the hill of Schellenberg, which commanded the town from the north bank of the Danube.

Marlborough at once urged Prince Louis to consent to an advance upon Donawert before reinforcements from France could reach the Elector.

On the 30th of June the Allied camp at Giengen was struck, and the army marched to Lauthausen and Balmershofen, and on the following day to Amerdingen and Onderingen. These movements left no doubt in the Elector's mind as to the object of the Allies, and he sent a strong force to the aid of d'Arco on the Schellenberg, which position was now strongly entrenched.

Marlborough and Prince Louis on alternate days assumed supreme command of the army, and on July the 2nd it was Marlborough's turn. He saw the necessity of attacking the position on this day at all risks, and not leaving it for his colleague to attempt the following day. For Prince Louis would probably waste the day, and allow the enemy to receive reinforcements and complete their defences.

Having established a field hospital at Nordlingen for the wounded, Marlborough detailed a force of 35 squadrons and 130 men out of each battalion of the left wing to form the van of the attack.

Preceded by a mounted force of several squadrons under Quarter-

Master-General Cadogan to mark out a camp, and by the pioneers and a pontoon train, the detachment marched off at 3 a.m. on the 2nd of July. The foot, 5850 strong, was commanded by Lieut.-General Goor. The 35 squadrons were commanded by Lieut.-Generals Lumley and Hompesch, and under them Major Generals Schuylemberg, Wood, Count Erbach, Vittinghoof, and Brigadiers the Prince of Saxe Heibourg and Bothmar.

The remainder of the army followed at 5 a.m. under the command of Prince Louis in two columns, the objective being a height that was between Ebermergen and Wernizstein, while the artillery, also in two columns, marched to Harburg with instructions to wait there, for further orders, without unharnessing their teams. All the baggage followed the artillery, and strict orders were given that no baggage whatever should interfere with the march of the columns.

About 8 a.m. Cadogan with the advanced party arrived within two miles of Donawert, driving in the enemy's "grand guard" divided into three squadrons, while the Quartermasters of the regiments marked out a camp by Ebermergen.

At 9 a.m. Marlborough came up, and reconnoitring with the advanced party towards Donawert, discovered that the enemy had made two fronts, as if they expected to be attacked in two different places. Prince Louis, Lumley and Goor joined the duke in this reconnaissance:

> And they were now so near the enemy that they were exposed to their great shot, which began to pour upon them very plentifully from several of their great works.

However, this did not prevent them from making a careful reconnaissance of the ground and entrenchments, and they also discovered a camp in preparation on the other side of Donawert.

At 12 noon Goor's detachment arrived at the Wernitz, and soon after the whole army came up, when Goor's force was ordered to cross the river by a stone bridge and to form up on the other side, and the pontoons were immediately placed for the whole army to follow.

The duke having judged it absolutely necessary to attack the enemy at once, before reinforcements could arrive, ordered the 35 squadrons to go into the adjoining woods to get fascines for the infantry.

From a hill called Boschberg, Goor's detachment, supported by eight entire battalions under Major-Generals Withers and Beinheim, and with eight more battalions under Count Horn, as a reserve, were ordered to the attack.

About 4 p.m. these troops reached the bottom of the Schellenberg, where they made a short halt to receive the fascines from the horse.

To describe the situation:—The Schellenberg hill was about two English miles in circumference at the base, and had generally a gradual ascent. At the top was a plateau, half a mile across, where the enemy were encamped in several lines. The entrenchments began at Donawert on the south, and ran round the top of the hill to a point where it joined the Danube on the other side. The hill was more accessible on the northern side and there were also the Nieuburg woods; the entrenchments on this side were consequently stronger.

At 6 p.m. Marlborough ordered Goor to commence the attack. The detachment then moved up the rising ground in six lines, four being of foot and two of horse, "the English being on the left and close to the wood"

The fascines were then distributed to officers and soldiers alike, who were ordered to carry them until they could throw them down in the enemy's entrenchments, and to move on steadily and reserve their fire. In spite of the enemy's heavy artillery fire, the foot advanced resolutely and calmly to within eighty paces of the entrenchments, and were gallantly sustained by the horse and dragoons; Lumley keeping close with eighteen squadrons in the first line, and Hompesch bringing up the other seventeen in the second. The enemy now used case shot, doing great execution. Goor was killed, and a great many other officers. The troops, however, kept gallantly on, and the enemy essaying a bayonet charge, were driven back by Her Majesty's Guards. The enemy, finding they were not attacked elsewhere, now threw all their strength against the English attack. Some of the attacking infantry showing signs of retiring:

Lieutenant-General Lumley and Major-General Wood with the first line of horse and dragoons moved up, and stood so close, and animated the foot so much by their brave example, that they rallied and went on again."

The horse were now, however, so near a mark for the enemy's shot, that a great many fell or were disabled." "Major-General Wood received a wound in his breast from a musket shot, as did Colonel Palmer in his body. Count Erbach and Colonel Cadogan had their horses shot under them. The Hereditary Prince of Hesse was shot in the breast, and so was the Prince of Saxe

Heidelberg. Brigadier Bothmar and a great many other horse officers were likewise wounded. But for all this, both the lines of horse continued firm, and encouraged the infantry to keep their ground and to press the attack with renewed vigour.

And so the battle raged. Lumley eventually ordered Lord John Hay's Dragoons to dismount and charge on foot, which they were preparing to do when the enemy gave way and the infantry entered the trenches. The cavalry now pursued, and putting the enemy to flight, killed a great many and captured thirteen colours.

In writing his despatch of the Battle of Schellenberg to Mr Secretary Harley under date 3rd of July, Marlborough says:—

> All our troops in general behaved themselves with great gallantry, and the English in particular have gained a great deal of honour in this action, which I believe was the warmest that has been known for many years, the horse and dragoons appointed to sustain the foot standing within musket shot of the enemy's trenches most of the time.

Milner puts the British losses during this action at 32 officers and 420 men killed, and 83 officers and 1001 men wounded, which was about one-third of the losses of the Allies. Amongst the casualties of the Allies were 8 general officers killed and 9 wounded.

In this action Major Caldwell and Cornet Hamilton of the Royal Irish Dragoons were wounded, and four men of the Regiment were killed and nineteen wounded.

The French Armies in the Low Countries meanwhile had crossed the Rhine, and hearing of the Elector's defeat at Schellenberg, Tallard hurried on and joined hands with the Bavarians.

On August the 9th Prince Louis of Baden, much to the relief of Marlborough, left the Allied camp with 1 5,000 men for the siege of Ingolstadt.

Marlborough now decided to give Tallard battle. The dangers of attacking a superior force were pointed out to him, and he replied that he knew the difficulties, but a battle was absolutely necessary: "and," he said, "I rely on the discipline of my troops."

Alison, in his *Life of John, Duke of Marlborough* gives the strength of the Allies before the Battle of Blenheim as 66 battalions, 164 squadrons and 66 guns, in all 56,000 men. The French and Bavarians he gives as 84 battalions, 147 squadrons, a total of 60,000 men.

The two hostile camps lay some five miles apart. The intervening ground was a plain of varying breadth bordered by a line of woods and the Danube.

This plain is cut by a succession of streams running down at right angles to the Danube, no fewer than three crossing the line of march between the Kessel and the French position. The first of these, the Reichen, cuts a ravine through which the road passed close to the village of Dapfheim; and Marlborough, seeing that at this point the enemy could greatly embarrass his advance, sent forward pioneers to level the ravine, and occupied the village with two brigades of British and Hessian infantry.

At two o'clock on the morning of August the 13th the Allied Army passed the Kessel in a dense white mist. They marched in eight columns, the two outer ones on each flank consisting of cavalry, and the inner ones of infantry. At Dapfheim the army halted, and the two outlying brigades, reinforced by eleven more British battalions, formed a ninth column under Lord Cutts, whose orders were to cover the march of the artillery along the great road on the extreme left, and in due time to attack Blenheim. With this column went Major-General Wood and Brigadier-General Ross "with fifteen squadrons of dragoons to sustain them," the first line of cavalry being formed by Ross' Dragoons, and the second by part of Wood's brigade.

Marlborough, on the left, occupied the ground from the Danube to Oberglau, while Eugene prolonged the line to Lutzingen. At 6 a.m. the French advanced posts were driven back, and at 7 o'clock the Allies were on the Nebel, and in full view of the enemy's camp.

Marlborough in writing home his despatch says that the enemy "we found did not expect so early a visit." In truth they did not. Their cavalry had dispersed to gather forage, and no precautions had been taken against attack. The French outposts came hurrying back and all was confusion. Tallard with his defective eyesight was able to make out the red coats of Cutts' British soldiers, and he knew that there on his right the heaviest fighting was to be expected. He therefore lost no time in occupying Blenheim.

The story of Blenheim has been told so often that but a slight account will suffice here.

Amongst his dispositions, Tallard had barricaded with wagons that side of Blenheim next the Danube, as being the most open against the British horse. From the village of Blenheim to that of Oberglau were posted 80 squadrons of French cavalry and two brigades of infantry. The last named village was also occupied by fourteen of the enemy's battalions, among which were three regiments of Irishmen commanded by the Marquis de Blainville.

On the side of the Allies, Lord Cutts with his twenty battalions still continued on the left of all towards Blenheim, drawn up in four lines; and Wood and Ross, with their fifteen squadrons, were in two lines behind that body of foot. As before mentioned, Ross' brigade of dragoons were in the first line of cavalry while Wood's formed the second line.

About eight o'clock, Tallard's guns opened fire, whereupon Eugene hurried off to his command on the right, and Marlborough personally superintended the posting of his batteries.

> The chaplains came forward to the heads of regiments and read prayers; and then the duke mounted and rode down the whole length of his line. As he passed, a round shot struck the ground under his horse and covered him with dust. For a moment every man held his breath, but in a few seconds the calm figure with the red coat and the broad blue ribbon reappeared, the horse moving slowly and quietly as before, and the handsome face unchangeably serene.

At last, at about half past twelve, an *aide-de-camp* galloped up from Eugene to say that all was ready. Marlborough at once directed Cutts to commence his attack on Blenheim, and ordered all the lines to cross the Nebel.

It was nearly one o'clock when Cutts' leading brigade, with Brigadier Rowe at the head, advanced across the stream to Blenheim. At thirty paces' distance they were received by a murderous fire, but Rowe had given orders that no shot was to be fired until he struck the palisades, and that the village was to be carried by cold steel. The British, without firing, reached the palisades which Rowe struck with his sword, and the troops, pouring in a volley, rushed forward and endeavoured to drag down the timbers and force an entrance. In a few minutes the gallant Rowe fell mortally wounded; his lieutenant-colonel and major were killed in the attempt to bring him off, and the brigade, shattered to pieces, fell back in disorder. As they retired they were charged in flank by several squadrons of gendarmes, who captured the colours of Rowe's regiment, but, pursuing too far, were stopped by a terrific fire poured into them by the Hessian Foot, and driven back pell-mell by a charge of five British squadrons (apparently of Ross' brigade) . These were, however, attacked in turn by a superior force of fresh cavalry and forced across the rivulet. Again the Hessian infantry poured a tremendous fire into the pursuing cavalry, and utterly routing them, retook the lost colours of Rowe's regiment.

Marlborough, to avoid a useless sacrifice of life, ordered the infantry regiments to remain under cover and to keep the defenders of Blenheim occupied, while Wood's and Ross' brigades were directed to join the centre, where he intended to make his main effort.

As soon as the first line of infantry had formed on the far side of the Nebel, Marlborough ordered the cavalry over. They reached the stream in good order, but got into difficulties in the morass between the two branches of the stream. The British squadrons had the most difficult place on the left, and in addition were heavily shelled by the enemy's guns near Blenheim. However, the horse struggled on, and with the aid of fascines, got over, and formed up in front of the infantry. The cavalry now met with an extremely warm reception, the enemy's infantry and artillery firing heavily into their left flank from Blenheim, while the French cavalry thundering down the slope of the hill, charged them in front.

The English squadrons were overwhelmed, and driven back nearly to the banks of the stream, where the infantry fire checked the victorious French. Then the Prussian general Bothmar fell upon the disordered French with the second line cavalry, and drove them in confusion behind the Maulweyer, where for some time they held their own, but were penned in behind the stream, the head of which they dared not pass for fear of being charged in flank.

The Duke of Marlborough sent for five more squadrons from Major-General Wood to strengthen the British cavalry, and these on coming up with Brigadier Ross, passed the Nebel. The rest of the cavalry was meanwhile crossing the rivulet with some difficulty; for on its far side was an enemy already formed and supported by several guns. Yet, by the brave example and the diligence of the officers, and the eagerness of the men, all passed over by degrees and held their ground. The English cavalry got over on the left under Lumley; that of the Dutch was in the centre, and the Danes on the right. Bulow with the second line of cavalry followed, and stretched away towards Oberglau.

On the right, the Danish and Hanoverian cavalry were now engaged in a severe struggle near Oberglau, and the Prince of Holstein-Beck commenced his attack on that village. He was met by a fierce

counter-attack from the famous Irish Brigade, and things would have gone ill with him had not Marlborough hastened up with fresh infantry and artillery, and forced the enemy back into Oberglau, thus securing the passage for the centre of the Allied Cavalry.

It was now three o'clock; and the duke sent Lord Tunbridge to Prince Eugene's wing for news. From his A.D.C. he learnt that the prince was holding his own and no more.

By four o'clock Marlborough had got the whole of his left wing of the Allied Army across the Nebel, his cavalry being drawn up in two lines in front of the infantry, the latter being ranged at intervals to allow of the cavalry passing through, in case of repulse.

On the opposing side the French had intermingled nine battalions of foot from the second line amongst their horse, and against these Marlborough sent three Hanoverian battalions and a battery of artillery.

For a long time the young French infantry stood the storm of shot. To relieve them, Tallard ordered the squadrons on their left to charge, but they refused, and fled before a charge of the Allied Cavalry, who rode into the hapless battalions of infantry and swept them out of existence. At the same time, a wide gap was left in the French line by the cavalry on Marsin's right, who, having seen their flank exposed, fell back on his centre. About five o'clock Marlborough ordered the "charge," and placing himself at the head of the Allied cavalry, the two lines of cavalry pressed up the slope, sword in hand, to the attack. The French, firing a feeble volley from the saddle, broke, and falling back on their supports, carried all away with them in confusion, and fled wildly in the direction of Hochstadt and the Danube, pursued by Hompesch's division of horse, who drove them into the river, where hundreds were drowned, hundreds cut down, and a vast number taken prisoners.

Meanwhile, Marsin and the Elector on the French left, seeing the collapse of Tallard's army, set fire to Oberglau and retreated, followed by Eugene.

All this while the village of Blenheim still held out and gave employment to the English infantry. Directly the Allied Cavalry had beaten and cleared the field of that of the enemy. General Churchill had marched the foot upon the village and surrounded it. The finest troops of France were locked up in Blenheim without orders of any kind. At last they tried to break out to the rear of the village, but were headed back by the Royal Scots Dragoons. They made a final attempt

Battle of Blenheim

to cut their way out towards Oberglau, but here they were checked by the Royal Irish Dragoons—who had been sent from the pursuit to Blenheim—and were compelled to seek cover behind the houses and enclosures. Churchill now ordered Cutts to make another attack on the side of the Nebel, while Orkney assailed the churchyard on the west with eight battalions, and Ingoldsby with four more, and the Royal Irish Dragoons endeavoured to force their way into the village by the opening opposite Oberglau. Supported by artillery fire they succeeded in entering; but the French made such a determined resistance that they had to retire. The attack was about to be renewed when the French called a parley, and after some demur, surrendered at about eight o'clock in the evening, twelve squadrons of dragoons and twenty four battalions laying down their arms.

The field now being entirely cleared of the enemy, the Allied army was drawn up with the left to Sondersheim and the right towards Morselingen; "and the soldiers were to lie all night upon their arms on the field of battle," though as a matter of fact, several regiments quickly possessed themselves of the enemy's tents and the food they contained, while a hundred fat oxen, killed and skinned (apparently the day's rations for the French Army) proved a boon to the famished soldiers.

The total loss of the Allies amounted to four thousand five hundred killed, and seven thousand five hundred wounded, of which number the British lost six hundred and seventy killed, and some fifteen hundred wounded.

The day was closing on the field of Blenheim "when Marlborough borrowed a leaf from a commissary's pocket-book and wrote a note in pencil to his wife, the message and the handwriting both those of a man who is quite tired out."

13 August 1704.

I have not time to say more, but to beg you will give my duty to the queen, and let her know her army has had a glorious victory, Monsr. Tallard and two other generals are in my coach, and I am following the rest. The bearer, my *aide-de-camp*, Colonel Parke, will give her an account of what has passed. I shall do it in a day or two by another more at large.

Marlborough.

The day after the battle the whole of the victorious army marched by Hochstadt and camped between Steinheim and Wittislingen. No regimental lists of the casualties amongst the rank and file appear to exist.

In the Blenheim Roll Call, the following officers of the Royal Irish Dragoons, are shown as having been wounded:—

Captain Hugh Caldwell
Cornet Jno. Hunter
Cornet Edw. Hamilton
Quarter-Master Jno. Skelston
Adjutant David Ross.

In the *Annals of Queen Anne*, the following evidently inaccurate statement appears: "the dragoons suffered so little, that only the adjutant of Ross' regiment was much wounded."

In his letter to Mr. Secretary Harley, dated at Hochstadt 14th August 1704, giving a report of the battle, Marlborough writes:

And in the village of Blenheim, which the enemy had entrenched and fortified, and where they made the greatest opposition, we obliged twenty-six battalions and twelve squadrons of dragoons to surrender themselves prisoners at discretion. We took likewise all their tents standing, with their cannon and ammunition, as also a great number of standards, kettle-drums, and colours in action, so that I reckon the greatest part of M. Tallard's army is taken or destroyed. The bravery of all our troops on this occasion cannot be expressed; the generals as well as the officers and soldiers behaving themselves with the greatest courage and resolution, the horse and dragoons having been obliged to charge four or five several times.

Grose, in his *Military Antiquities*, writing of the Royal Irish Dragoons, says:

In consequence of the marked good behaviour of this regiment at the Battle of Hochstet (Blenheim), in August 1704, three additional troops were put upon the establishment, making its strength to consist of nine troops. The three kettle-drums which were captured from the French by the regiment at this memorable engagement, were directed by the Duke of Marlborough to be carried at the head of the Royal Dragoons of Ireland.

The following list of officers of the Royal Dragoons of Ireland, and the bounties they received after the campaign, is from the *Blenheim Bounty Roll*. It is to be noted that officers and men who were wounded received double the amount allowed to their rank.

122

MARLBOROUGH AT BLENHEIM

COLONEL

Charles Ross . . . . . £105. 0. 0. Bounty

LIEUT: COL: COMMANDING

Owen Wynne . . . . . £ 78. 10. 0. „

MAJOR

Robert Hunter . . . . . £ 61. 10. 0. „

CAPTAINS

Jno. Hill. . . . . £ 46. 10. 0. „
Ric. Gore . . . . . £ 46. 10. 0. „
Hugh Caldwell (Wounded) . . . £ 93. 0. 0. „

CAPTAIN LIEUTENANT

Robt. Drury . . . . . £ 27. 0. 0. „

LIEUTENANTS

Chas. Beatty . . . . . £ 27. 0. 0. „
Jno. Johnston . . . . . £ 27. 0. 0. „
Mat. Watts . . . . . £ 27. 0. 0. „
Danl. Boisragon . . . . . £ 27. 0. 0. „

CORNETS

Jno. Dunbar . . . . . £ 24. 0. 0. „
(Alex) Abercromby . . . . £ 24. 0. 0. „
Jas. Hamilton . . . . . £ 24. 0. 0. „
Jas. Poé . . . . . £ 24. 0. 0. „
Jno. Hunter (Wounted) . . . £ 48. 0. 0. „
Edwd. Hamilton (Wounded) . . . £ 48. 0. 0. „

QUARTER-MASTERS

...... Brown . . . . . £ 16. 10. 0. „
(Geo.) Mackean . . . . . £ 16. 10. 0. „
(Ric.) Johnston . . . . . £ 16. 10. 0. „
Ric. Dunbar . . . . . £ 16. 10. 0. „
Jno. Skelston (Wounded) . . . £ 33. 0. 0. „
David Ross (Wounded) . . . £ 33. 0. 0. „

CHAPLAIN

Simon Babe . . . . . £ 20. 0. 0. „

ADJUTANT

David Ross (Wounded) . . . £ 30. 0. 0. „

SURGEON

Wm. Cocksedge . . . . . £ 18. 0. 0. „

NON-COMMISSIONED OFFICERS AND MEN

12 Sergeants each . . . . £ 2. 10. 0. „
18 Corporals „ . . . . £ 2. 0. 0. „
268 Dragoons „ . . . . £ 1. 10. 0. „
(Including drummers and hautboys).

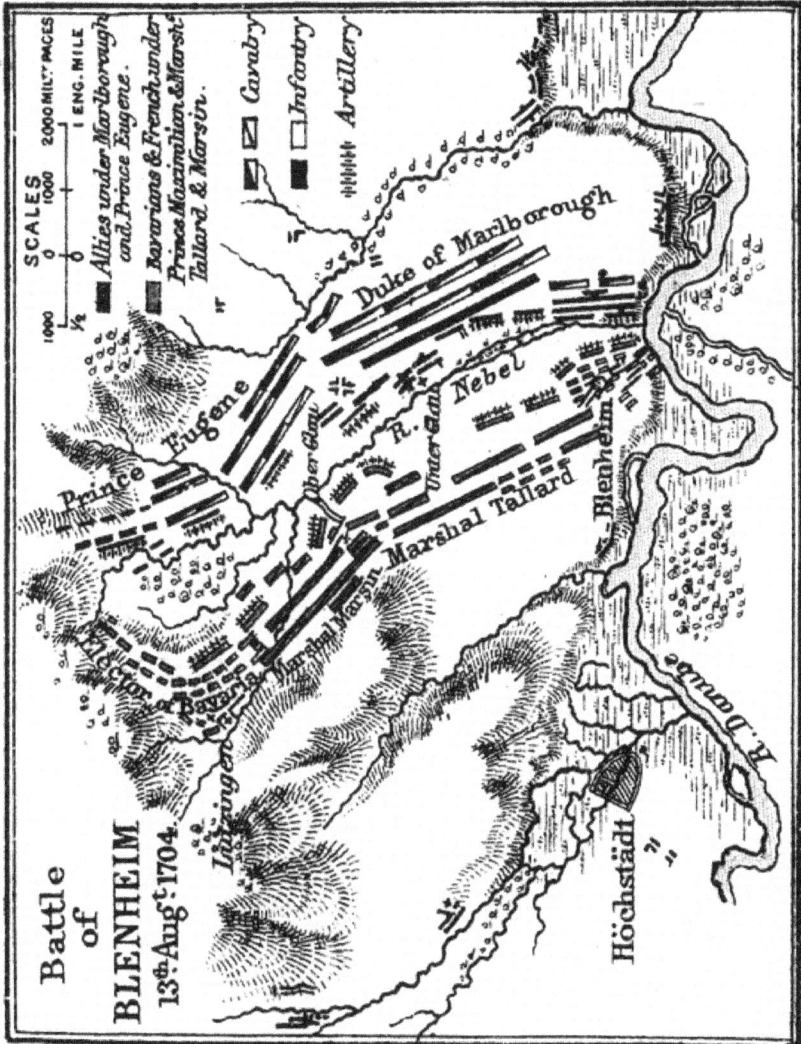

Battle
of
BLENHEIM
13th Augt 1704.

SCALES
1000   0   1000   2000 MILY PACES
½   0   1 ENG. MILE

■ Allies under Marlborough
   and Prince Eugene.
▨ Bavarians & French under
   Prince Maximilian & Marshl.
   Tallard & Marsin.

▨ Cavalry
☐ Infantry
▦ Artillery

Duke of Marlborough

Prince Eugene

Ober Glau

R. Nebel

Unter Glau

Nebel

Blenheim

Marshal Tallard

Elector of Bavaria Marshal Marsin

Lützingen

R. Danube

Höchstädt

In connection with the Battle of Blenheim it is to be noted that the French call it Hochstet, after the village (Hochstadt) near Blenheim. There is an old print now in the possession of the officers of the regiment, published in 1800, and dedicated to General Lord Rossmore, who was at the head of the regiment from 1787 to 1799, in which is depicted a 5th Royal Irish Dragoon bearing in a corner a green standard with the Harp and Crown and the word Hochstet.

It is unnecessary to follow the events of this year any further, suffice it to say that in November the English troops were sent into Winter Quarters for the rest they had earned so well.

The result of the famous campaign of Blenheim, rightly grouped with Creçy, Poitiers, Agincourt and Waterloo, was a crushing blow to the French. For well nigh forty years had their armies triumphed in every quarter of Europe. But now an English general had administered a decisive and humiliating defeat. Marlborough had outwitted the Marshals of France by his march to the Danube, had twice attacked a vastly superior force, and had utterly destroyed one army, and driven the other in a headlong flight to the Rhine.

"Blenheim" is born on the Standards, colours and appointments of the following regiments which fought in that battle and are still existent in the British Army:—

1st Dragoon Guards	The Buffs.
3rd ,, ,,	Liverpool Regiment.
5th ,, ,,	Lincolnshire ,,
6th ,, ,,	E. Yorkshire Regiment.
7th ,, ,,	Bedfordshire Regiment.
R. Scots Greys	R. Irish Regiment.
5th Lancers	R. Scots Fusiliers.
Royal Artillery	R. Welsh Fusiliers.
Royal Engineers	South Wales Borderers.
Grenadier Guards	1st Scottish Rifles.
Royal Scots	1st Hampshire Regiment.

The order of Battle for the Campaign of 1704 places the British Cavalry in the 1st Line of the left wing, the Irish Dragoons being brigaded with the Scots Dragoons.

The following is an extract from a letter to Mr. St. John from Marlborough, dated 22nd October, 1704, at Weissemburg:—

But I must observe to you, in reference to our English Horse and Dragoons, that having clothed entirely new this year, and

CAVLRY IN ACTION AT BLENHEIM

lost a great many men with all their accoutrements in the two actions, the officers of horse humbly hope Her Majesty will be pleased to allow them twenty pounds a horse, and the dragoons fifteen, towards enabling them to repair this great loss.

The Campaign of 1705 does not call for much note.

In the order of battle of the Allied Armies for this campaign, the British contingent under Marlborough were in the first line of the right wing. The Royal Irish Dragoons with the Scots Dragoons, each regiment consisting of three squadrons, were brigaded together on its extreme right. Ross was now a major-general.

The regiment was engaged in the forcing of the French lines on the 18th of July.

For this expedition Marlborough made up a force of some eight thousand men, divided into two columns. One column was placed under the command of the Count of Noyelles, and consisted of twelve battalions (four of which were English), and the first line cavalry of the right wing, the whole of which were British squadrons belonging to the:—

Royal Scots Dragoons.
Royal Irish Dragoons.
The present 1st Dragoon Guards.
3rd   ,,   ,,   ,,
5th   ,,   ,,   ,,
6th   ,,   ,,   ,,
7th   ,,   ,,   ,,
and six fieldpieces and workmen, and materials for making bridges.

Lieutenant-General Scholten commanded the other column, and had with him the 2nd Line Cavalry of the Right Wing, and also workmen and materials for bridging.

The utmost secrecy was observed in the preparations, even the corps composing the force knowing nothing of each other or of the work before them.

At 9 o'clock on the night of July the 17th, the two columns moved off in the strictest silence. Noyelles marched towards the castle of Wanghe before Elixheim, while Scholten marched on the village of Neerhespen. The instructions given to both commanders were to seize the barriers in the openings in the French Lines opposite the points they were marching on, and with as little noise as possible to overpower the guards defending them. If the columns should not succeed in surprising the enemy, and should find the French prepared for them, they were to advance in full force without waiting for orders, and attack with all the vigour they could. Marlborough with the main army marched an hour after the two leading detachments in support of them. The distance to be covered was about ten miles.

It was an extremely dark night, and Noyelles' guides missed their way, which resulted in a delay of two hours or more, so that his column did not arrive near Wanghe until between three and four o'clock in the morning. He, however, immediately ordered a captain with sixty grenadiers, supported by a colonel with all the other grenadiers of the twelve battalions, to cross the River Geete and capture the barrier. As the grenadiers approached the castle, the garrison of thirty men abandoned it and retreated within the lines. The grenadiers gained the castle and at once pushed on over the river to the barrier at the opening in the lines; but this the enemy also abandoned on the approach of the grenadiers. The infantry, following, forded the river and scrambled over the ramparts into the French lines with such determination and celerity, that three regiments of French dragoons, camped near by, had not time to oppose them, but hastily retired to Leau. Meanwhile, the opening in the lines having been enlarged, bridges were quickly thrown over the Geete, and the cavalry, who had apparently found the banks of the river too steep for fording, crossed with all haste.

Marlborough arrived on the scene during the passage of the cavalry. But meanwhile, the alarm had been given, and the enemy got together a force of forty or fifty squadrons and eight guns, which they drew up in two lines; and some twenty battalions of infantry were coming up quickly to support their horsemen.

Marlborough took in the whole situation at a glance, and having got over nearly the whole of the cavalry of both columns, he formed them in two lines, and with the British cavalry leading in the first line, amongst them being the Irish Dragoons, he led them personally against the enemy, sword in hand. The French fired a feeble volley from their saddles and broke in confusion. But soon after they managed to rally, and rode a counter attack against the flank of the British squadrons and broke them in their turn. Marlborough, who was riding on a flank, was cut off with his trumpeter. A Frenchman, apparently famed for neither good horsemanship nor swordmanship, galloped furiously at the duke, and, striking a blow at his head, missed his mark, lost his balance, and was captured by the duke's trumpeter. The fighting for a

MARLBOROUGH CHARGING WITH HIS CAVALRY

little while was fast and furious, but the allied squadrons rallied, and once more charging the French, rode them down and broke them past all reforming, also overthrowing part of the infantry who were coming up in support, and capturing the guns.

Marlborough at once sent on a detachment of dragoons, the Irish Dragoons being amongst them, to pursue the enemy: and they had the good fortune to overtake and capture a good part of their baggage.

Marlborough with the allied army now followed the enemy in his retreat.

The lines were of a most formidable description, and Marlborough's capture of them was due firstly to his drawing the main body of the French towards the Mehaigne, whither for that purpose he had sent d'Auverquerque with his army, while with the remainder of the Allies he suddenly, and at night, fell upon the two most unguarded posts; and secondly to the bravery of his cavalry.

The French losses were some two thousand men, amongst the prisoners being two lieutenant-generals, two major-generals, and the entire regiment of Monlve. The Allies also captured eighteen pieces of cannon,—eight of which were triple-barrelled, and were sent to England to be copied.

CHAPTER 5

Campaigns of 1706 and 1707

Marlborough, who had been home to England during the winter, returned to the Hague in April, and found a most discouraging state of affairs. The Dutch were backward in their preparations; the contingents of Prussia and Hanover were apparently not forthcoming; Prince Lewis of Baden was sulking; everybody was ready with a separate plan of campaign; and there had been great difficulty in providing the British force with horses to replace the large numbers which had died from sickness.

Villeroy lay safely entrenched with a French Army behind the River Dyle. He knew that the Prussian and Hanoverian contingents had not yet joined Marlborough, and that the Danish cavalry had refused to march to him until their wages were paid; and he resolved to risk a general action. On May the 19th he left his lines for Tirlemont, on the Great Geete.

Marlborough hastily made arrangements for the payment of the Danish troops, and, concentrating the British and Dutch at Bilsen on the Upper Demer, moved south to Borchloen, at which place the Danes joined him, swelling his force to sixty thousand men, an army but little inferior to that of the enemy. On the same day came the news that Villeroy had crossed the Great Geete and was moving on Judoigne. Marlborough decided to attack him.

At 1 a.m. on Whitsunday the 23rd of May, Quartermaster-General Cadogan, with six hundred cavalry and all the quartermasters and camp colours of the army, was dispatched to the Great Geete to mark out a camp for the army by the village of Ramillies; and some two hours later Marlborough followed with the army divided into eight columns. About 8 a.m. on a foggy morning Cadogan's force rode up the heights of Merdop, whence they dimly descried troops moving in front of them. A message was sent to Marlborough, who hastened up and ordered the cavalry on through the mist.

Shortly after 10 o'clock the fog rolled away, and the whole of the French Army was seen marching towards them.

Marlborough had appeared to the French a day before he was expected. Villeroy, however, promptly drew up his army on the line of the villages of Taviers, Ramillies, Offus and Autréglise, in two lines facing due East, the line being somewhat over four miles in length.

Villeroy's left, extending from Autréglise (Anderkirch) to Offus, consisted of infantry backed by cavalry. His centre, composed of infantry, stretched from Offus to Ramillies: while on his right, on the plain between the Geete and the Mehaigne, were massed more than one hundred and twenty squadrons of cavalry, with some battalions of infantry. The village of Ramillies covered the left of this expanse, and was defended by twenty battalions and twenty guns, the village being surrounded by a ditch. On the right, the villages were defended by detachments of infantry, and in Taviers were guns. It appeared to Marlborough that Taviers was too far from Ramillies for the maintenance of a cross-fire of artillery, and the cavalry of the French, left secure against attack behind the marshes of the Geete, was for that same reason incapable of aggressive action. Marlborough determined to turn the French right, and, to prevent its being reinforced, opened the action by a demonstration against the French left.

The British Force was once more in the right wing of the confederate army. The following regiments being in the First Line:—

Scots Greys Dragoons.
The Royal Irish Dragoons.
The present 1st Dragoon Guards.
    ,,   5th   ,,   ,,
    ,,   7th   ,,   ,,
    ,,   6th   ,,   ,,
Eighteen Dutch Squadrons.
The present 1st Battalion, 1st Guards.
    ,,   1st   ,,   Royal Scots.
    ,,   16th Foot.
    ,,   26th Cameronians.
    ,,   28th Foot.
The present 23rd Royal Welsh.
    ,,   8th Foot.

BATTLE OF
RAMILLIES
23rd May 1706
Statute Mile
½

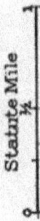

British and Allies
French

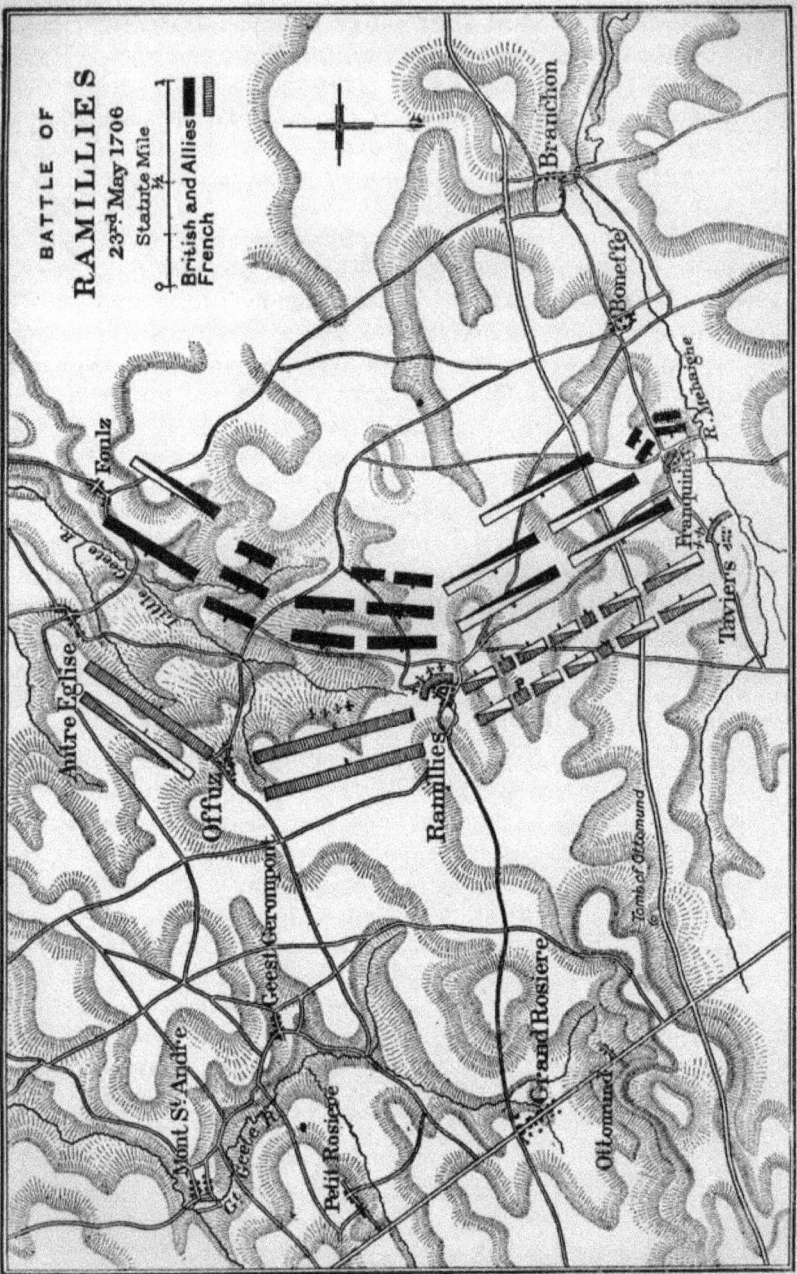

Branchon
Boneffe
Foulz
R. Mehaigne
Franquins
Taviers
Autre Eglise
Offuz
Ramillies
Geest Geromport
Tomb of Ottomund
Mont St Andre
Grand Rosiere
Ottomund
Petit Rosiere

„   3rd Buffs.

„   21st Royal Scots Fusrs.

„   Evans' Foot.

„   Macartney's Foot.

„   Stringer's   „

„   15th Foot.

Second Line:—

The present 2nd Battalion Royal Scots.

„   18th Royal Irish.

„   29th Foot.

„   37th   „

„   24th   „

„   10th   „

and Foreign Cavalry and Infantry.

The infantry of the Allied Right now moved in two lines towards Offus and Autréglise, with all the pomp of war. At the river they halted, and appeared to be busy with pontoons.

The mass of British scarlet appeared to indicate to Villeroy where Marlborough was about to launch his attack. He accordingly strengthened his left with several battalions from his right and centre. The duke, seeing the white coats of these battalions streaming away to the French left, ordered the infantry of his right to fall back to some heights in their rear. The second line halted on the crest, and facing about, covered the ground with the well known scarlet, while the first line marched on until out of sight, and then, covered by the hill from the view of the French, hurried with all possible speed to the opposite flank.

Many British battalions stood on that height all day without moving a step or firing a shot, but none the less paralysing the French left wing.

About 1.30 p.m. the guns of both armies opened fire, and soon after four Dutch battalions carried Taviers and Franquinay. Twelve more battalions were ordered to attack Ramillies, while the cavalry of the left slowly advanced. Franquinay, a village on the Mehaigne, had been galling the left wing cavalry with a flanking fire, and this annoyance having been disposed of, Auverquerque led on his horse and charged.

The Dutch after routing the first French line, were driven back by the second; but some fresh squadrons under Marlborough himself

HORSE AT RAMILLIES

checked the advance of the French. Marlborough then ordered up every squadron of the Right wing, except those of the British cavalry. The duke was now in the thick of the fight, and being thrown from his horse, which escaped, was furiously attacked by some French dragoons, and in imminent danger of capture. His *aide-de-camp*, Captain Molesworth,[1] dismounted at once and gave his horse to the duke, enabled him to escape, and remained to face the enemy alone. The French, however, were so intent upon pursuing the duke that Molesworth escaped with a few sabre-cuts. He then recovered the duke's horse and rejoined him. While Marlborough mounted, the equerry who was holding his stirrup had his head carried away by a round shot.

Meanwhile the infantry attack on Ramillies had fully developed; and the fresh horse ordered up from the right by Marlborough came along at top speed and formed up in rear of the re-forming lines. Before they could get into action, however, the Danish horse and Dutch guards were getting round the French right flank. Then the rest of the Allied horse rode against the French front and a fierce fight ensued. The famous French Household Cavalry (the *Maison du Roi*) were cut to pieces, and in spite of Villeroy's efforts, the whole of the French horse were driven in headlong flight off the field, leaving the infantry to their fate. Villeroy now endeavoured to use his cavalry of the left to cover the retreat of the infantry, in which he only partially succeeded, as the horsemen were much obstructed by the baggage which encumbered the ground.

The French troops in Ramillies now gave way, and the battle was won. The British dragoons, amongst them being the Royal Irish Dragoons pushed their way into the village of Autréglise, and made "a terrible slaughter of them," while the Dutch and the Danes pursued those that fled to the left "and made an abundance of prisoners," and "those that fled to the right were chased by the regiments of Lumley, Hay, and Ross." The last two regiments, the Scots Dragoons and the Irish Dragoons fell in with, and captured the entire King's Regiment (*Regiment du Roi*): "of whom having killed many, the rest threw down their arms and begged quarter, which was generously granted."

The French Army now broke up in panic and fled in all directions. The British cavalry, practically fresh, took up the pursuit, and the redcoated troopers pressed on, playing havoc with the beaten enemy. Not till two o'clock in the morning did they pause, having by that time

---

1. Molesworth was in 1737 the Colonel of The Royal Irish Dragoons.

reached Meldert, fifteen miles from the battlefield. The loss of the French during the battle and pursuit of Ramillies was some fifteen thousand men in killed, wounded and prisoners; eighty standards and colours, fifty guns, and an enormous quantity of baggage. The loss of the Allies was between four and five thousand killed and wounded. This loss was chiefly amongst the Dutch and the Danes, for excepting in the pursuit by their cavalry, the British contingent was but little engaged.

The following were the casualties amongst the Allied Cavalry at Ramillies:—

	Killed.	Wounded.
Colonels.	2	3
Lt.-Colonels.	—	3
Majors.	4	3
Captains.	10	24
Lieutenants.	6	27
Cornets.	4	28
Subalterns.	8	18
Troopers and Dragoons.	343	695
Horses.	990	351

Writing of the Royal Irish Dragoons at Ramillies, in his *Military Antiquities*, Grose says:

In consequence of this regiment (5th Dragoons), assisted by the Scots Greys, making two battalions of the regiment of Picardie prisoners of war, and cutting a third to pieces, before it could secure a retreat behind a line of horse that were galloping to bring it off, both corps were distinguished from other cavalry regiments by being permitted to wear grenadier caps.

In this action, Mr. Ellis of the regiment, captured Count Horn, a French lieutenant-general.

The main army, having slept for two or three hours, started after the pursuing cavalry at 3 a.m., and steadily followed the demoralised French troops until the 27th May, when Marlborough gave his weary troops a halt at Grimbergen; the French retiring into Ghent.

"Ramillies" is borne on the standards, colours and appointments of the following regiments of the British Army:—

1st Dragoon Guards. Liverpool Regiment.
3rd   „   „   Lincolnshire Regiment.

5th	„	„	E. Yorkshire Regiment.
6th	„	„	Bedfordshire Regiment.
7th	„	„	R. Irish Regiment.
R. Scots Greys.		R. Scots Fusiliers.
5th Lancers.		R. Welsh Fusiliers.
Royal Artillery.		S. Wales Borderers.
Royal Engineers.		1st Scottish Rifles.
Grenadier Guards.		1st Gloucester Regiment.
Royal Scots.		1st Worcester Regiment.
The Buffs.		1st Hampshire Regiment.

On the 1st June, from the camp at Meerlebeck, Marlborough despatched Major-General Ross with 600 of his dragoons to Bruges, with letters inviting the magistrates of that city and of the Franc to submit themselves to the obedience of their lawful sovereign, King Charles III of Spain. On his approaching Bruges, the French battalion there retired, and the magistrates expressed their desire to submit themselves to Charles III.

The enemy also having quitted Damme, fifty of Ross' Dragoons took possession of that place. The dragoons remained in both these places until relieved by Dutch regiments.

Marlborough sent the following letter to Major-General Ross, dated 3rd June, 1706, from Meerlebeck:

I received your letter early this morning: the magistrates both of the Franc and the city of Bruges have been with me since, and made their submission to King Charles. . . . Upon the encouragement you give me, we have ventured to write to the Governor of Ostend. You will find enclosed two letters for him, both under flying seals; that signed by myself alone is only by way of summons. You will march that way with your whole detachment, or such part as you think fit, and send him in that letter. If you find he is inclined to surrender, you may then send him in the other letter as a security likewise from the States. Since the writing of these letters, Oudenarde has likewise surrendered. A French battalion that was in garrison has leave to retire, but the governor, with two Spanish battalions, have declared for King Charles. This you may make use of as an argument to induce the Governor of Ostend to follow so good an example.

I find the people of Bruges are apprehensive those of Ostend should let the sea in upon them; this you should endeavour to prevent either by fair means or by threats.

I am, etc.   M.

P. S. We shall march tomorrow, and pass both the Scheldt and the Lys to take the camp of Deynse and Nivelle, and be so much nearer. You need not hasten your return to the army as long as you can be victualled where you are.

On June the 4th Marlborough wrote from Nivelle to Major-General Ross:—

I have received your letter of this day with the account of the stores and ammunition which the enemy left at Damme, which are sufficient marks of a precipitate retreat. I am glad you give me hopes of Ostend, and shall expect the success of your summons with great impatience. We shall be at Aerzeele tomorrow, which is a good deal nearer to you; it may be, our approach may influence those parts.

I am, etc.   M.

The Governor of Ostend, however, refused to surrender, and Marlborough decided to besiege the place. He was delayed in this by his artillery being five or six days behind him. The troops destined for the siege, under Auverquerque, arrived before Ostend on June the 17th, and a British squadron, under Sir Stafford Fairborn, which had been sent by Her Majesty to lie off Ostend and Nieuport to help in reducing the garrisons of those places, was already on the coasts; but it was not until the last day of June that Auverquerque was able to commence his attack. After a week's hard fighting Ostend surrendered, the garrison marching out on the 8th of July.

After this followed the siege and capture of Menin by British battalions, and the capture of Ath, and with the latter ended the campaign of Ramillies, "one of the most brilliant in the annals of war, wherein Marlborough in a single month carried his arms triumphant from the Meuse to the sea."

The year 1707 was barren of any great military operations in the Netherlands, and proved a great disappointment after the glories of Ramillies. Owing to numerous complications on the part of the Allies, Marlborough spent the greater portion of the season in camp before a superior French force at Meldert.

For this campaign the 5th Dragoons were again brigaded with the Scots Dragoons; the Brigadier being Stairs.

Towards the end of the summer Marlborough was twice within

an ace of surprising the French who had withdrawn some of their forces towards Provence. On August the 12th the Confederate Army marched to Nivelle to attack the French, who, at midnight, had moved from Gosseliers to Seneff. It was ordered that the attack should be made in the early morning. Lest the enemy should endeavour to get away during the night to their camp at Cambron, Count de Tilly, with forty squadrons of horse and dragoons, commanded by Albemarle, d'Erbach and Ross, with a strong detachment of grenadiers, was ordered to watch the French, and in the event of their decamping, to fall upon their rear and endeavour to keep them employed until the main army could come up.

The enemy moved during the night, and in spite of all Tilly could do, even with strong reinforcements from Marlborough, it was found impossible to bring them to an engagement. The following extract of a letter written by Marlborough to the Earl of Cardigan, on December the 19th, in reply to his Lordship's request that the son of the late Major-General Brudenell should be given a company in a regiment on service in Spain, is interesting as indicating the manner in which commissions were given in the army at this time. The duke writes:

I have so just a sense of the father's good services that I shall be always glad to embrace any opportunity of showing it to his family; but your Lordship tells me he is not above five years old. This giving him a command in the army would be directly contrary to the rules the queen has prescribed to herself in that matter; besides that the enquiry the Parliament is making of the officers absent from their commands in Spain makes it yet the more difficult.

CHAPTER 6

Campaign of 1708

For the campaign of 1708 Parliament voted money for an additional ten thousand men, and of the new battalions raised three were sent to Flanders.

It is interesting to note that all regiments took the field this year with their new colours, bearing the cross of St. Andrew blended with that of St. George; the Union of England and Scotland having taken place the previous year.

Early in the year Charles Ross was promoted to be a Lieutenant-General, and another troop was added to his regiment under the following order:—

Anne R. January 12th, Whitehall.
It is our will and pleasure that a troop shall be raised and added to our dragoons whereof our well beloved Lieutenant-General Charles Ross is commander. To consist of two drums and 60 privates and 3 corporalls.

St. John

This order apparently brought the regiment up to the nine troops as mentioned by Grose in his *Memoirs*, for which it was so long conspicuous. Ross was also commanded to fill up the regiment from 54 to 60 men in each troop. For this purpose £1500 was paid under the head of:

Some extraordinary charges of War incurred and not provided for by Parliament. Buying one hundred horses and accoutrements to augment the regiment of dragoons commanded by Lieutenant-General Ross.

An over abundance of unnecessary transport was evidently as much of a nightmare to general officers of this time as it is today, for we find Marlborough writing from St. James' in January to Mr. (Lieutenant-General) Lumley, in command of troops in Flanders, on the subject of the approaching campaign:

> As to what you mention in your last relating to the wheel carriages, I am very sensible of the great embarras and trouble they are to us upon all occasions, and therefore desire you would earnestly recommend it from me to all the officers to have as few as possible.

The French, who in the early spring had made a futile endeavour to land a force in Scotland, marched at the end of May from their rendezvous south of the Haine, North, to the Forest of Soignies. Marlborough had landed in April, and promptly concentrated his army at Hal and summoned Eugene to him.

Marlborough's army numbered but eighty thousand men, while that of the French main army in Flanders under the Duke of Burgundy and Vendôme was little under a hundred thousand. Ever since the Ramillies campaign the French had been drawing troops from all quarters to Flanders.

From Soignies the French manoeuvred towards Waterloo, as if to threaten Louvain. Marlborough met this move by a forced march to the river Dyle, where he remained inactive for a month, waiting for Eugene. On the night of the 4th of July the French marched Westward and crossed the Senne at Hal, whence they detached small forces to Bruges and Ghent, and within twenty four hours they were in possession of both towns; the result of bribing the authorities in these places.

At 2 a.m. during the same night, Marlborough moved his army and crossed the Senne at Anderlecht, and after a most trying march was almost within reach of the French. During the night of July the 6th a report reached the duke that the enemy were approaching to attack him. This report was false, and before the truth could be ascertained, the French had crossed the Dender, in great haste to get away from the Confederate Army. Marlborough's cavalry was soon in pursuit, but failed to do more than capture some prisoners and baggage. The French army now encamped at Alost, where it threatened Brussels. Marlborough thereupon moved to Assche, midway between Alost and Brussels, in order to allay the panic in the capital. Here Eugene's force joined the army.

The French meditated a descent upon Oudenarde, for the recovery of the line of the Scheldt, and were already across the Dender and had destroyed the bridges, having had a start of Marlborough. The duke, however, being unable to leave Brussels exposed, remained perforce where he was, but ordered the Governor of Ath to collect what troops he could and garrison Oudenarde, which was promptly done.

On the 9th of July Vendôme sent a force to invest Oudenarde, and with the main army moved to Lessines, to cover the siege. Meanwhile, however, Marlborough had started at 2 a.m. on the 9th, and, by a splendid march *via* Herfelingen, was in occupation of Lessines on the arrival of the French. Baulked in their plans, the French wheeled about, and moved North West towards Gavre on the Scheldt.

At dawn on the 11th, Marlborough sent Cadogan with 30 squadrons and 16 battalions and 24 guns, to prepare and cover the passage of the Scheldt below Oudenarde for the army. By 10.30 a.m. Cadogan had reached the river. Presently parties of French horse appeared to the North. Their advanced guard had leisurely crossed the river at Gavre, six miles further down the river, and were marching in happy ignorance of the presence of an enemy, which however, was quickly dispelled by a dash of Cadogan's squadrons. Vendôme, on receiving the report, and seeing that the mass of the Allied Army was on the wrong side of the Scheldt, gave orders to take up a position parallel to the river. The Duke of Burgundy objected to the line ordered by Vendôme, and ordered a position to be taken up on the heights of Huysse, in rear of the river Norken, from Asper to Wannegem, and some two miles from the Scheldt. Unfortunately, seven battalions ordered by Vendôme to occupy the village of Heurne, in ignorance of the change of orders, marched down to the village of Eyne instead of Heurne, in the centre of Vendôme's proposed line, where they remained backed by a few squadrons.

Marlborough, who had early arrived on the scene, meanwhile sent orders hurrying up the main body, and at 2 p.m. the head of the infantry had reached the Scheldt. The march of the seven French battalions into Eyne had been marked by Cadogan, who got the whole of his advanced guard across to the left bank. His British infantry brigade, supported by the other two, moved against Eyne, while the Hanoverian cavalry rode to the rear of the village and cut off all hope of retreat.

The British were soon hotly engaged, and the French, making a poor resistance, had three of their battalions captured entire, and the remaining four killed or taken piecemeal in their flight. The cavalry under Prince George of Hanover, afterwards King George II of England, now charged the few French squadrons in rear of the village, routed them, and drove them across the Norken. The prince gallantly led the charge and had his horse shot under him, and ever after maintained that Oudenarde was the hottest thing of his life.

The Duke of Burgundy now made every preparation for the defence of his position behind the Norken, but when four o'clock had arrived and the Allied army was not yet in order of battle, he changed his mind; he advanced the whole of his centre and right, pushing his right cavalry across the stream. Marlborough judged the attack would be against his left, and against Cadogan's isolated battalions about Eyne. Two Prussian regiments of this force had been pushed forward half a mile beyond Eyne to Groenewald, and were promptly reinforced by twelve more from the advanced guard. The British cavalry were formed up on the left, on the heights of Bevere, and the Prussian horse on the right near Heurne; and the rest of the army were gradually crossing the Scheldt.

At about 5 p.m. thirty French battalions advanced on Groenewald, which was only held by Cadogan's two advanced regiments of Prussians. They, however, gallantly held their own among the hedges until reinforced by twenty battalions under the Duke of Argyle. The fresh battalions formed in succession on the left of the Prussians, and the fighting became most severe. The ground was so enclosed that the struggle became a duel between battalions. At one time the French, outflanking the left of the Allies, drove them back, but Marlborough's fresh infantry kept arriving on the scene, and, by prolonging the line on the left to the South, defeated the movement.

Eugene was now given eighteen battalions, and entrusted with the command of the right. With this accession of strength, he was able to relieve Cadogan's corps, and even to pierce the first line of the enemy's infantry; whereupon the Prussian cavalry charged the second line, only to be driven back by the French Household Cavalry with heavy loss.

Marlborough, meanwhile, was slowly pressing on with the Hanoverian and Dutch infantry on the left. The French, contesting every inch of ground, were gradually forced back to Diepenbeck, where they stood fast, and all the efforts of the Dutch and Hanoverians could not shift them. Marlborough now directed the gallant old Dutch cavalry leader, Auverquerque, to take the cavalry of the left undercover round the French right, and take them in their rear. Auverquerque carried out his orders, and fell upon the rear of the unsuspecting French, and although some of their Household Cavalry and dragoons made a short stand, he rode them down, and pressing rapidly, the French right was fairly surrounded.

During all this time the French left, for some unaccountable reason, had remained motionless and inactive on the far side of the Norken. The Duke of Burgundy now tried to bring them forward, but it was too late. Vendôme himself, at the head of the infantry, failed to make the slightest impression, and the cavalry dared not advance, for the ground in front of them was bad, and the whole of the British cavalry, who had been withdrawn from their first position, stood watching, ready to swoop down on them should they begin to move.

Darkness came on, and the Allies wormed themselves closer and closer round the French right. At nine o'clock, fearful lest his own troops should engage each other in the darkness, Marlborough ordered a halt, and to cease firing. Many of the French seized the moment to escape, but presently all the drums of the Allies began to beat the French retreat, and the Huguenot officers, shouting *"A moi, Picardie! A moi, Roussillon!"* gathered the relics of the scattered French regiments around them, and so captured several thousands of prisoners. Vendôme endeavoured to keep the army together, but, Burgundy having ordered a retreat, the French ran off in confusion and disorder towards Ghent. Another hour of daylight, Marlborough always declared, would have enabled him to finish the war.

The total loss of the Allies was about three thousand killed and wounded. The British contingent suffered little, losing only 4 officers and 49 men killed, and 17 officers and 1 60 men wounded; for the infantry, though early engaged, suffered slightly, while the cavalry, being employed to watch the inactive French left, scarcely suffered at all.

The French lost six thousand in killed and wounded, and nine thousand prisoners, and their army was completely shaken and demoralised for the remainder of the campaign.

The Allies lay on their arms on the field for the night, and at dawn forty squadrons, mostly British, started in pursuit.

Of the Battle of Oudenarde, Fortescue says it was undoubtedly the most hazardous action that Marlborough ever fought. His troops had started at two o'clock on Monday morning, and had covered fifty miles, including the passage of two rivers, when they came into action at two o'clock on Wednesday afternoon. This march of eighty thousand men over fifty miles of the bad roads of those days, and with heavy packs, in sixty hours, was no mean performance. Finally, the army had to pass the Scheldt in the face of the enemy, and ran no small risk of being destroyed in detail.

"Oudenarde" is borne on the standards, colours and appointments of the following regiments of the British Army:—

1st Dragoon Guards
3rd   ,,   ,,
5th   ,,   ,,
6th   ,,   ,,
7th   ,,   ,,
Royal Scots Greys
5th Lancers
Royal Artillery
Royal Engineers
Grenadier Guards
Coldstream   ,,
Royal Scots
The Buffs
Liverpool Rgt.
Lincolnshire Rgt.
E. Yorkshire Regt.
Bedfordshire Rgt.
R. Irish Rgt.
R. Scots Fusiliers
R. Welsh Fusiliers
S. Wales Borderers
1st Scottish Rifles
1st Hampshire Rgt

The army halted to rest for a couple of days where it lay, during which time news was received that the French Army on the Moselle was marching, with all haste, to occupy the lines constructed by the French to cover their frontier from Ypres to the Lys. At midnight of the 13th of July, Marlborough despatched Count Lottum, a distinguished Prussian officer, with fifty squadrons and thirty battalions, to capture these lines. The news that Lottum had carried out his orders reached the duke when following with the main army. The next day, the 14th of July, Marlborough's army was encamped along the Lys between Menin and Commines, and actually on French territory. The

Allies next undertook the siege of Lille. Their preparations at last being complete, a huge convoy left Brussels on its seventy-five mile march to Lille, arriving there on the 12th of August without the loss of a single wagon.

The garrison of Lille amounted to fifteen thousand men, commanded by the brave old Marshal Boufflers. Vendôme at Ghent in the North, and Berwick at Douay in the South, with their enormous army of one hundred and ten thousand men, failed to prevent Marlborough, with his inferior strength of eighty four thousand men, from prosecuting a successful investment. This long and famous siege lasted to the 9th of December, when the gallant commander and his heroic garrison marched out with all the honours of war, having lost eight thousand men, or more than half its number, and having cost the Allies no fewer than fourteen thousand.

There were but five British battalions regularly employed in the trenches, and it is worthy of note that the first advance to attack was opened by a single English soldier. Sergeant Littler, of the first Guards, who swam across the Marquette to a French post which commanded the passage of the stream, and let down the drawbridge.

During the siege Marlborough's covering army was engaged in watching the armies of Vendôme and Berwick, who employed themselves in harassing the Allies' convoys proceeding to the siege. On the evening of August the 29th, we find that Ross and his dragoons were ordered to cover the march of a convoy of seven hundred and fifty wagons of provisions and ammunition from Ath to the Army and the siege, which duty they successfully performed, the convoy arriving before Lille on the morning of the 30th. The covering army on the 18th of September defeated the French at the action of Wynendale.

After the fall of Lille followed the capitulation of Ghent and Bruges, and therewith the end of the campaign, and Marlborough and Eugene at last sent their troops into winter quarters.

For the campaign of 1709 the French had greatly strengthened their army by withdrawing troops from all quarters to Flanders, and had placed in command "their only fortunate general, that very able soldier and incomparable liar. Marshal Villars." To cover Arras, "the north-western gate of France," Villars had thrown up the strong lines of La Bassée, extending from Douay to the Lys, behind which he lay "entrenched to the teeth." By June, Marlborough and Eugene, with an army of one hundred and ten thousand men, lay encamped near Lille. From there, the Allies moving South, made Villars anticipate a direct attack upon his Lines for the purpose of a march into France. On the evening of the 26th of June the Allies struck their camp, and marched towards the French Lines, before which the army expected a bloody action at dawn.

After advancing for some time, to the general surprise, the columns were ordered to change their direction to the left, and, marching eastward, the soldiers at dawn saw "the grey walls and the four spires of Tournay before them," and found they were about to invest one of the strongest fortresses of France. The garrison of Tournay had, unfortunately for the French, been weakened by Villars, for that unsuspecting general had, upon Marlborough's apparent move against his Lines from Lille, summoned the greater part of it to his assistance at the Lines. On the 7th of July the trenches were opened, and by September the 3rd, in spite of Villars' demonstrations, the town and citadel were in the hands of the Allies. Only seven battalions of the British contingent were employed in the investment.

Before the close of the siege, Marlborough and Eugene[1], leaving the besieging force before Tournay, had marched the main army towards the Lines at Douay. The French lines being too formidable to be forced, Marlborough sent Lord Orkney, with twenty squadrons and all the grenadiers of the army, silently eastward towards St. Ghislain. Three days later a force under the Prince of Hessen-Cassel followed; a few hours later Cadogan, with forty squadrons; and at midnight the remainder of the army. Twenty-six battalions were left before Tournay with orders to watch Villars, and not to move until he did.

Too late, Villars discovered that he had again been duped, and that Marlborough, instead of ramming his head against the formidable French Lines, proposed an easier entry into France round their eastern end, across the Trouille. He at once sent a detachment to Jemappes, the nearer entrance across a natural barrier of forest which cut him off from the weakly garrisoned fortress of Mons; but the detachment came too late, for the Allies were before them. The Allied Army had invested Mons, and on September the 7th Villars and his whole army had arrived on the scene, and encamped a couple of miles to the west of the forest barrier, between Montreuil and Athis. Here he was joined by the veteran Marshal Boufflers, whose arrival caused such a tumult of rejoicing in the French camp that the Allies, not knowing what the clamour might portend, advanced westward into the plain of Mons,

---

1. *Eugene of Savoy* by Prince Eugene and Alexander Innes Shand is also published by Leonaur.

and bivouacked in order of battle between Ciply and Quévy, leaving only a small investing force before Mons.

The French, however, did not move, but remained threatening both the passages of the forest. We have seen that the Northern crossing was at Jemappes, while the southern one was at Malplaquet. That night Villars sent detachments to occupy the southern crossing, and by midday of September the 9th the whole of his army was taking up its position across this opening. Marlborough immediately moved forward, but at a Council of War, for some extraordinary reason, it was decided not to attack. Villars at once prepared his position for defence, and next morning Marlborough proposed to attack him, but was again obstructed by the Dutch Deputies. The attack was fixed for the morrow, which delay Villars did not fail to turn to account in the way of entrenching.

Villars' position was on the high ground about a mile in advance of the villages of Campe du Hamlet and Malplaquet. His extreme right occupied the forest of Laignières, the natural obstacles of a thick and tangled cover being strengthened by abattis. From the edge of the wood he constructed a triple line of entrenchments, which ran a third of its way across the passage, where the defence was continued by a line of nine redans. From these redans stretched a swamp, backed by more entrenchments, to the wood of Taisnières. Several cannon were mounted on the entrenchments, and twenty guns were before the redans. The woods of Taisnières and Sart projected beyond the French front, and formed a salient and re-entering angle on Villars' left, and here entrenchments and abattis were constructed, and guns placed at various points to enfilade an advancing enemy. In rear of all, the French cavalry was drawn up in several lines. Ninety-five thousand men was the strength of the French, and the Allies numbered about the same.

The dawn of the 11th of September broke in a dense heavy mist. At three o'clock prayers were said in the Allied camp, and shortly after the artillery moved into position.

Marlborough and Eugene had decided to feint against the French right, and to force home a true attack against their left front and flank, for the reason that the wood of Sart ran out some distance beyond the fortified angle, and would serve to conceal the movements of troops against the extreme left flank.

The French cavalry, being massed behind the entrenchments, could not take any part in the action until the defences were forced.

The Allies massed forty guns against the French left, and covered them from enfilade fire by an epaulment; twenty-eight pieces were placed against the French right, and the remainder distributed amongst the brigades. Count Lottum was directed against the eastern face of the salient angle of the Taisnières wood with twenty-eight battalions supported by the British and Hanoverian cavalry. Forty battalions under General Schulemberg moved against the northern face of the wood, and were backed by Eugene's cavalry, while a little to Schulemberg's right. General Gauvain with two thousand men was to press on the French left flank in rear of their entrenchments. In rear of Schulemberg, Lord Orkney had fifteen British battalions drawn up in a single line, ready to advance against the centre as soon as Schulemberg and Lottum had done their work, and thirty squadrons under Auvergne.

Far away to the right was General Withers, with five British and fourteen foreign battalions, and six squadrons, ready to turn the extreme left of the French at the village of La Folie. The Prince of Orange, with thirty-one battalions, chiefly Dutch, and twenty-one Dutch squadrons under the Prince of Hesse, stood ready behind the small wood of Tiry to make his feint against the French right.

The cavalry was ordered to sustain the foot, but to keep out of the range of grape shot, and, on the central entrenchments being forced, they were to press forward, form on the other side of the entrenchments, and "drive the French Army from the field." Eugene was to command the right, and Marlborough the left of the army.

At half past seven the fog lifted, and the guns of both armies opened fire. The Allied advance began by the divisions of Orange and Lottum moving in two dense columns up the glade. The Prince of Orange's men halted just out of range of grape shot, while Lottum's column pushed on under heavy fire to the rear of the forty gun battery, and deployed to the right in three lines. About nine o'clock a salvo of the forty guns gave the signal for the attack, Lottum's and Schulemberg's divisions, each in three lines, advanced perpendicularly to each other, and Gauvain's force moved into the wood unperceived, while Orkney extended his scarlet battalions across the glade. Both Schulemberg's and Lottum's attacks were repulsed with very heavy losses. The former then resumed the attack with his second line, but unsuccessfully, for the French regiment of Picardie stubbornly held its own.

Orkney sent three British battalions to reinforce Lottum, who attacked again. The Englishmen moved on Lottum's left, and scrambled on through a swamp in spite of being threatened by twelve French battalions on their left, who, however, retired on catching sight of Auvergne's supporting squadrons led by Marlborough himself.[2] Lottum's men attacked the entrenchments in front, while the British brigade succeeded in turning the flank, and after desperate fighting and heavy losses, the French were forced back into the wood. Then the Picardie regiment, exposed to the double attack of Lottum and Schulemberg, fell back on to the regiment of Champagne, and these two gallant corps made yet another stand behind an abbatis. Eventually they had to give way in disorder, and, owing to the denseness of the wood, the struggle resolved itself into a succession of small parties fighting desperately from tree to tree. The entrenchments on the French left had been won.

The Prince of Orange, who had been waiting for orders to commence his feint, lost patience, and without orders, opened, not a false, but a real attack against the French right. Orange himself led the attack, and at the head of the famous Blue Guards, and the Highlanders in the Dutch service, advanced under a most appalling fire of grape and musketry. His horse being shot dead, he continued on foot, and the gallant Highlanders and Dutchmen pressed on, and, in spite of whole ranks being swept away by the fire of a French battery on their left flank, they carried the first entrenchment with a rush. While they halted to deploy, the French rallied, and charging down on the prince, drove him and his force headlong back. This impatience of the Prince of Orange had cost the Dutch a loss of some six thousand men killed and wounded, and the Blue guards had been annihilated, while the supporting battalions had suffered little less severely.

Meanwhile Schulemberg and Lottum continued to push their attack, and now, on the extreme Allied right, Withers was advancing. Villars, seeing this danger on his left flank, called up his Irish brigade, and other regiments from the centre, and launched them upon the British and Prussians. Wither's battalions were forced back some way by the impetuous Irish, whose formation was eventually broken by the density of the forest.

Then up came Withers, just when he was wanted. The Eighteenth Royal Irish of the British Army met the French Royal Regiment of Ireland, crushed it with two volleys by sheer superiority of fire, drove it back in disorder, and pressed on.

---

2. *Marlborough's Wars* Volumes 1 & 2 by Frank Taylor, and *Marlborough's Cameronians* by Andrew Chrichton and James Ferguson, are also published by Leonaur.

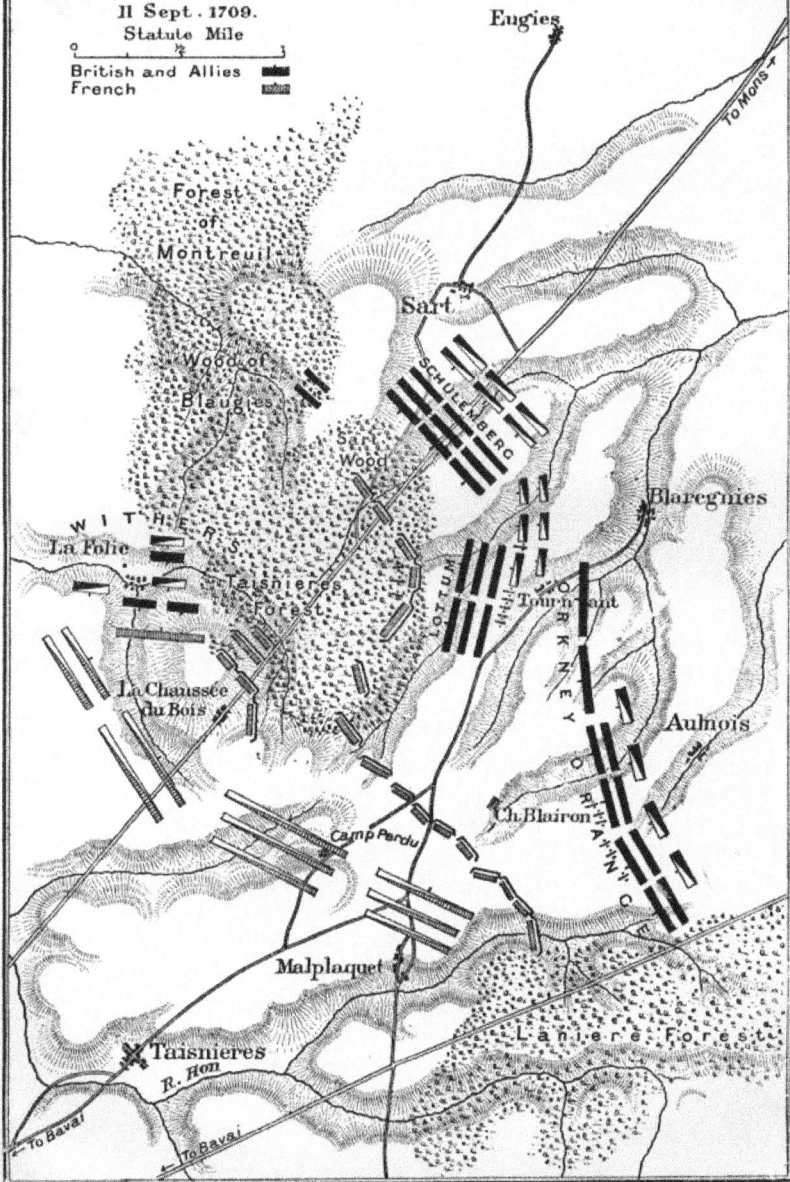

BATTLE OF
MALPLAQUET
11 Sept. 1709.
Statute Mile
British and Allies
French

Eugies

To Mons

Forest
of
Montreuil

Sart

Wood of
Blaugies

SCHULEMBERG

Wood

Blaregnies

WITHERS

La Folie

Taisnieres
Forest

LOTTUM

TOURNANT

Tournant

ORKNEY

La Chaussée
du Bois

Aulnois

O R K N E Y

Camp Perdu

Ch. Blairon

R T H I A N O

Malplaquet

Lanier's Forest

Taisnieres

R. Hon

To Bavai

To Bavai

Villars was badly wounded and carried insensible from the field, but notwithstanding his fall, and the fact that they had been driven from their entrenchments and from the wood on their left, the French still barred the advance of the Allies; but Marlborough's time had now come.

The forty-gun battery was moved forward, and Lord Orkney led his British battalions against the redans, which, after a severe fight, he captured; and on the left of the British, the Prince of Orange again advanced, and cleared the whole of the defences in the glade. Now came the turn of the Allied cavalry. The Dutch squadrons were first past the entrenchments, but were driven back to their edge by the veteran Boufflers at the head of the French Gendarmerie. Here, however, Orkney's British infantry lining the parapet, three times forced the *gendarmerie* to retire. Meanwhile, the central battery of guns advanced and supported the infantry by a cross fire, and Marlborough at the head of the British and Prussian cavalry, fell upon the *gendarmerie*. Boufflers now came along with fresh squadrons, and leading the French Household Cavalry, crashed into Marlborough, and threw his horsemen into disorder. Then Eugene, coming up with fresh squadrons, threw the Imperial Horse into the *mêlée*, and drove the French back. Simultaneously the Prince of Hesse charged the infantry of the French right, and with the help of the Dutch foot, kept it isolated from the bloody fight raging in the centre. Then Boufflers saw that the day was lost and sounded the retreat, which was carried out in admirable order, for the Allies were too exhausted to pursue.

Thus ended the Battle of Malplaquet, one of the bloodiest ever fought by mortal men

The loss of the French was some twelve thousand men, and five hundred prisoners, fifty standards and colours, and sixteen guns. The Allies lost not less than twenty thousand in killed and wounded, due chiefly to the mad attack of the Prince of Orange. The British contingent out of their twenty battalions lost nineteen hundred men. The Royal Irish Dragoons were again brigaded with the Scots Greys during this campaign.

The Regiments of the British Army who now bear "Malplaquet" on their colours and appointments are:—

1st Dragoon Guards	The Buffs
3rd ,, ,,	Liverpool Regiment
5th ,, ,,	Lincolnshire ,,

6th ,, ,,	E. Yorkshire ,,
7th ,, ,,	Bedfordshire ,,
2nd Dragoons	R. Irish Regiment
5th Lancers	Yorkshire ,,
Royal Artillery	R. Scots Fusiliers
Royal Engineers	R. Welsh
Grenadier Guards	S. Wales Borderers
Coldstream ,,	Scottish Rifles
Royal Scots	Hampshire Regiment

Malplaquet has been described as a grand action. The French were equal in numbers to the Allies, and occupied a position which was described at the time as a fortified citadel. They were commanded by an able general, and yet they were driven back, and forced to leave Mons to its fate.

On the third day after the fight the Allies returned to the investment of Mons, which capitulated on the 9th of October, and the campaign came to an end.

The following is a list of the officers of Her Majesty's Royal Regiment of Dragoons of Ireland present of Malplaquet:—

Captains.
Lieutenant-General Chas. Ross. Colonel-Staff.
Brevet-Col. Jno. Hill. Lt.-Col. Commanding.
Brevet-Major Ric. Gore.
Robert Drury.
Bt.-Major Jno. Warre.
Jno. Usher.
Jno. Johnston.
    Lieutenants.
Chas. Beatty—Captain-Lieutenant.
Jno. Mann.
Jas. Poé.
Ed. Hamilton—Staff A.D.C.
Beverley Newcomen.
Jas. Hamilton.
Michael Parker
Alex. Abercromby.
Jno Hunter.
    Cornets.
Wm. Cocksedge

Robt. Barker.
Jno. Skelston.
Geo. McKean.
Fras. Bogges.
Edw. Hill.
Wm. Ross.
Jno. Gough.
> *Quartermasters.*

Jas. Knox.
Jer. Balfour.
Rich. Dunbar.
Mor. White.
Jas. Welsh.
Jno. Evans.
Ric. Johnston.
> *Adjutant*

Wm. Ross.
> *Chaplain.*

Simon Babe.
> *Surgeon.*

Jas. Scott.

CHAPTER 7

Campaigns of 1710-1711

Negotiations for peace coming to naught, Marlborough opened the campaign of 1710 by a rapid movement over the lines of La Bassée and the capture of Douay, the siege of which place lasted from the 22nd of April to the 26th of June.

He next turned to the siege of Bethune, and the generals of that siege being under some apprehensions from the detachments the enemy had sent towards St. Omer, Lieutenant-General Ross with twenty one squadrons (amongst them being his own regiment), and nine battalions, was ordered on the 21st of August to march and encamp between the Allied main army at Viar Brudin and the siege; where he would be at hand to prevent any design the enemy might have "to give us a disturbance."

The next day Marlborough wrote to Ross that he was very well satisfied with his having thrown bridges over the stream in his front; and that he had taken every care that Ross' force should be supplied regularly with bread.

General Schulemberg being somewhat retarded in his attack during the siege by want of fascines, Marlborough writes to Ross to help that general to make fascines, adding that "the service will be no great fatigue to your men, I need not tell you they will be paid for it."

Bethune surrendered on the 28th of August, and after that Ross' force joined the army on its march towards Aire, camping between Teroneune and Lillers on the 4th of September.

The capture of Aire and St. Venant on the Upper Lys, after a desperate resistance, closed the campaign for the year.

On the 20th of December Marlborough wrote to Mr Sweet:—

The village of Steesch in the *mairie* of Bois-le-duc complains of exactions committed by Ross' regiment of Dragoons in their march to winter quarters in November 1709, amounting to 1122 odd *gilders*; whereof 236 *gilders* they allege to have been obliged to pay in money, to be exempted from further quarters. The regiment having neglected the repeated directions to satisfy the same.

Mr. Sweet is authorised to pay to the village the sum of 720 *gilders* and "to place it to the account of the regiment, they having neglected the repeated directions."

With regard to the opening of the campaign of 1711, Fortescue says:—

> The French, fully aware of the political changes in England, had during the winter made extraordinary exertions to prolong the war for yet one more campaign, and to that end had covered the northern frontier with a fortified barrier on a gigantic scale. Starting from the coast of Picardy the lines followed the course of the River Canche almost to its source. From thence across to the Gy or southern fork of the Upper Scarpe ran a line of earthworks, extending from Oppy to Montenancourt. From the latter point the Gy and the Scarpe were dammed so as to form inundations as far as Biache, at which place a canal led the line of defence from the Scarpe to the Sensée. Here more inundations between the two rivers carried the barrier to Bouchain, whence it followed the Scheldt to Valenciennes. From thence more earthworks prolonged the lines to the Sambre, which carried them at last to their end at Namur.

Beyond a couple of moves, the rival armies were inactive during May and June. The French, safe behind their formidable lines, would not come out and fight; and the Allied Army, which had been greatly reduced from one cause and another, was not strong enough to attempt an attack. To pass the lines Marlborough therefore had to resort to stratagem.

> The inundation on the Sensée between Arras and Bouchain could be traversed only by two causeways, the larger of which was defended by a strong fort at Arleux, the other being defended by a redoubt at Aubigny half a mile below it.

> The Arleux fort Marlborough knew he could take and demolish, but he also knew that so soon as he had left it Villars would cer-

tainly retake it and rebuild it. He therefore schemed to induce Villars to demolish it himself. With this view a strong force under General Rantzau was detached to capture the fort, and the general successfully carrying out his orders on the 6th of July, the duke ordered that the captured works should be greatly strengthened, while a large force under the Prussian general Hompesch was posted three miles away on the glacis of Douay, as a further protection.

Two days later Villars surprised and made a determined attack on Hompesch's force, and was only repulsed with considerable difficulty, whereupon the duke reinforced Hompesch as if to show his regard for the safety of Arleux, and pushed forward the new works there with renewed vigour. When these new works were completed, Marlborough left but a weak garrison in the fort, and on the 21st of July led the rest of the army away two marches to the west, encamping opposite the lines between the Canche and the Scarpe. Villars moved west parallel with the Allies, but before starting, detached a force to attack Arleux. The commander of the fort sent an urgent message to the duke for help, whereupon Cadogan was sent with a strong force to its relief; before, however, he had gone half way, he returned with the news that Arleux had surrendered.

Villars was elated beyond measure—and Marlborough correspondingly cast down. He declared in public, with much passion, that he would be even with Villars. The duke's ill temper was not appeased by the news that Villars had razed the whole of the works of Arleux to the ground. All the time and trouble Marlborough had spent over the new works had been wasted, and he angrily vowed he would avenge the insult to his army; and declared his intention of a direct attack on the French entrenchments. Villars, on the 26th of July, detached a force to make a diversion in Brabant. This step seemed to drive Marlborough distracted. He sent a force of ten thousand men under Lord Albermarle to Bethune to check its march, and the whole of his heavy artillery and baggage to Douay; and so weakened an army already greatly inferior to the French. With his weakened forces he repaired the roads that led to the enemy's entrenchments, and with much display of sulkiness and temper advanced a day's march nearer to the lines.

His own troops could not understand such proceedings from Corporal John; and while they watched him with amazement, Villars was in a transport of delight. "He drew every man not only from all parts of the lines but also from the neighbouring garrisons towards the

DRAGOONS IN ACTION

threatened point," and asked nothing better than that Marlborough should be mad enough to attack him.

On the 2nd of August the duke was within a league of the lines, and during that day and the next set the whole of the cavalry to work to collect fascines. The quote from Fortescue:—

At nightfall of the 3rd he sent away all his light artillery, together with every wheeled vehicle, under escort of a strong detachment, and next morning rode forward with most of his generals to reconnoitre the lines. . . . . He had now thrown off all his ill-temper and was calm and cool as usual, indicating this point and that to his officers. 'Your brigade, general, will attack here, such and such brigades will be on your right and left, such another in support, and you will be careful of this, that, and other.' The generals listened and stared; they understood the instructions clearly enough, but they could not help regarding them as madness.

But none of them noticed General Cadogan slip away from the crowd and gallop off to camp at top speed. The orders for the morrow's attack were issued, and not a man in the army could fail to see how hopeless the enterprise was. A direct attack on the lines itself was an over bold venture, and to attempt it with an army half depleted, and in the absence of all the artillery, appeared insane.

Again Marlborough's violent and unprecedented outburst of surliness and ill temper was difficult to explain; and the only possible explanation was that the duke, rendered desperate by failure and misfortunes, had thrown prudence to the winds and did not care what he did.

A few there were, however, who clung to the hope that the chief who had so often led them to victory, might still have some surprise in store.

But meanwhile, Cadogan, with forty cavalry soldiers, had left the camp for Douay, five leagues away.

There he found Hompesch ready with his garrison, now strengthened by detachments from Bethune and elsewhere to twelve thousand foot and two thousand horse, and told him the time was come. Hompesch thereupon issued his orders for the troops to be ready to march that night. Still the main army under Marlborough knew nothing of this, and passed the day in

161

dismal apprehension till the sun went down, and the drummers came forward to beat the tattoo. Then a column of cavalry trotted out towards the Allied right, attracting every French eye and stirring every French brain with curiosity as to the purport of the movement. Then the drums began to roll; and the order ran quietly down the line to strike tents and make ready to march immediately.

The cavalry having distracted the French vigilance to the wrong quarter, returned unseen by the enemy.

At nine o'clock the whole army faced to its left and marched off eastwards in utter silence, with Marlborough himself at the head of the vanguard.

Hour after hour did the army march on this memorable night of the 4th of August, and by 5 a.m. had reached the Scarpe, There they found pontoon bridges already laid for them, and on the further bank were waiting the field artillery; and soon after a despatch arrived for Marlborough. A message was passed down the columns of weary soldiers:

Generals Cadogan and Hompesch crossed the causeway at Arleux unopposed at three o'clock this morning, and are in possession of the enemy's lines. The duke desires that the infantry will step out.

The infantry responded to a man; the right wing of horse halted to form the rearguard, while the duke at the head of fifty squadrons pushed on at a trot.

Villars heard of Marlborough's march only two hours after he had started, but was so bewildered by the Duke's intricate manoeuvres that he did not awaken to the true position for another three hours. He then at the head of the Household Cavalry rode away so hard to the east, that he finished near Oisy with but one hundred of his troopers, who were captured by Marlborough's outposts, Villars himself only escaping the same fate by a miracle. Meanwhile, Marlborough's infantry were pressing forward desperately; hundreds dropped under the severity of the march, but the survivors were still ahead of the French when they turned off the Arleux causeway, and by five o'clock in the afternoon the whole force was drawn up between Oisy and the Scheldt, and within striking distance of Arras, Cambrai and Bouchain. They had covered some forty miles in eighteen hours, and Villars was defeated; a warning to generals who put their faith in fortified lines. So ended what is perhaps "the most remarkable, and certainly the most entertaining feat of the duke during the whole war."

Marlborough's succeeding manoeuvre was the capture of Bouchain, which place surrendered under the very eyes of Villars on the 23rd of September, and "the last and not the least of Marlborough's campaigns came, always victoriously, to an end."

The duke at this time was out of favour at home. To quote from Fortescue:

> The most brilliant manifestation of military skill was, however, powerless to help him against the virulence of faction in England. The passage of the lines was described as the crossing of the kennel, and the siege of Bouchain as a waste of lives. In May the House of Commons had addressed the queen for inquiry into abuses in the public expenditure, and when the duke arrived at the Hague in November, he found himself charged with fraud, extortion, and embezzlement. The ground of the accusation was that he had received in regular payment from the bread contractors during his command sums amounting to £63,000. Marlborough proved conclusively that this was a perquisite regularly allowed to the commander-in-chief in Flanders as a fund for secret service, and he added of his own accord that he had also received a deduction of two and a half per cent from the pay of the foreign troops, which had been applied to the same object. But this defence, though absolutely valid and sound, could avail him little. His reasons were disregarded, and on the 31st of December he was dismissed from all public employment.

The Duke of Ormonde was now appointed commander-in-chief in Marlborough's place, and to him the Ministry in England confirmed the very perquisites which the House had just declared to be unwarrantable and illegal.

Fortescue writes:

> Effrontery and folly such as this arc nothing new in representative assemblies, but it is significant of the general attitude of English civilians towards English soldiers, that not one of Harley's gang seems to have realised that this vindictive persecution of Marlborough was an insult to a brave army as well as a shameful injustice to a great man.

It is not necessary to dwell on the operations, if such they may be called, of the Duke of Ormonde. He did indeed take the field with Eugene, but under instructions to engage neither in a battle nor a siege, but virtually to open communications with Villars. . . Ormonde was directed to suspend hostilities for two months, and to withdraw his forces from Eugene. Then the troubles began. The auxiliary troops in the pay of England flatly refused to obey the order to leave Eugene, and Ormonde was compelled to march away with the British troops only The British and the Auxiliaries were not permitted to speak to each other . . . The parting was one of the most remarkable scenes ever witnessed. The British fell in, silent, shamefaced, and miserable; the auxiliaries gathered in knots opposite to them, and both parties gazed at each other mournfully without saying a word. Then the drums beat the march and regiment after regiment "tramped" away with full hearts and downcast eyes, till at length the whole column was under way, and the mass of scarlet grew slowly less and less till it vanished out of sight.

At the end of the first day's march Ormonde announced the suspension of hostilities with France at the head of each regiment. He had expected the news to be received with cheers: to his infinite disgust it was greeted with one continuous storm of hisses and groans. Finally, when the men were dismissed they lost all self-control. . . . They cursed Ormonde with an energy only possible in an army that had learned to swear in the heat of fifty actions. The officers retired to their tents, ashamed to show themselves to their men. Many transferred themselves to foreign regiments, many more resigned their commissions; and it is said, doubtless with truth, that they fairly cried when they thought of Corporal John.

We will not follow the sad and troublesome march of the British through the Dutch towns.

Early in this year the queen thought fit to nominate and appoint the following general officers to serve in Flanders under the command of the Duke of Ormonde.

Henry Lumley Esq—General of the Horse.
Earl of Orkney—General of the Foot
Lieut.-Generals of Horse.
Cornelius Wood Esq.,

Charles Ross Esq—General of the Dragoons.
Earl of Stain &c.

Fortescue says:

> The negociations so infamously begun with King Lewis shortly after found as infamous an end in the Peace of Utrecht, which not only sacrificed every object for which the war had been fought, but branded England with indelible disgrace.

With the death of Queen Anne in the following year, and the accession of King George I, Marlborough returned to power, but in his after operations the Irish Dragoons took no part, being quartered in Ireland.

In June General Ross was informed that:

> The regiment under your command is to be put on the Establishment of Ireland and to be paid for by the revenues of that country.

In September of this year Charles Ross Esq, Colonel-General of the Dragoons, and Lieut.-General, was appointed Envoy Extraordinary to the Court of France.

CHAPTER 8

Miscellanea 1728-1790

PAY LIST OF ROYAL IRISH DRAGOONS.

1 Colonel, as Colonel 12/- and 6 servants 7/- . . .	19. 0.	diem 1728
1 Lt.-Colonel as Lt.-Colonel	7. 0.	" Add. MS
1 Major as Major	5. 0.	" 21,188
1 Chaplain	6. 8.	"
1 Surgeon	4. 0.	"

ONE TROOP.

1 Captain 10/- 2 Servants 2/4.	12. 4.	"
1 Lieutenant 5/- 1 Servant 1/2	6. 4.	"
1 Cornet 4/- 1 Servant 1/2	5. 2.	"
1 Quarter Master 3/-	3. 0.	"
1 Sergeant	2. 6.	"
2 Corporals	1. 8.	"
1 Drummer	1. 6.	"
1 Hautboy [1]	1. 6.	"
25 Dragoons 1/4	1. 13. 4.	"

Eight more troops at a like pay.

A detachment of the Regiment, together with others from regiments 1744
of Dragoons in Ireland was reviewed on Hounslow Heath at 9 a.m. on Add. MS
12th April. 20,005

The Army List of 1752 gives to all regiments of the Army 1752
the numbers they are known by. The Royal Dragoons of Ireland MS Army
are shewn as the 5th Royal Irish Dragoons. List

ESTABLISHMENT OF 5 DRAGOONS, TROOPS.

1 Colonel and Captain.	1763 to
1 Lieut. Colonel and Captain.	1777
1 Major and Captain.	Add. MS
6 Captains.	33,048

1 The Hautbois was a wooden musical instrument carried in all dragoon regiments.

166

```
 9 Lieutenants.
 9 Cornets.
 9 Quarter Masters.
 1 Chaplain.
 1 Adjutant.
 1 Surgeon.
 9 Sergeants.
18 Corporals.
 9 Trumpets.
 9 Hautbois.
180 Privates.
```

1764
Sec. of
State's Letters for
Ireland.

August. Alteration in the clothing of the regiments of cavalry in Ireland ;

The Officers and men of the 5th Royal Irish Dragoons are to have epaulettes on the left shoulder instead of shoulder knots and are to wear light boots.

Height of men from 5 feet 8½ inches to 5 feet 10½ inches.
Height of horses 15 hands to 15 hands 1 inch.

1770
and
1771
Muster
Rolls

The 5th Dragoons were stationed at Athlone (head quarters), Navan, Belturbert, Roscommon.

1772
Muster
Rolls

The 5th Dragoons were stationed at Athlone, Dublin, Donaghmore, Roscommon, Belturbet, Cappoquin.

1775
and
1776
Muster
Rolls

The 5th Dragoons were stationed at Clonmel, Clogheen, Kilkenny, Carrick, Casheel, Tallow.

In January, 1776, a whole troop was drafted to the Infantry, and in the December of the same year a whole troop deserted.

1777-8-9
Muster
Rolls

The Stations of the Regiment were Roscommon, Athlone, Ballyraget, Kilkenny, Longford, Fermoy, Carlow, Carrickfergus and Belfast.

At the "Man of War" Oct. 22nd, 1782.

Sir,

I have the honour to acquaint you, that agreeable to my instructions, I was proceeding with the three troops to Drogheda, and was within half a mile of the town stopped by the mayor and recorder of that city, informing me that everything was perfectly quiet and that if the troops were to go into the town they had reason to fear very disagreeable consequences might arise. They therefore directed me to return with the troops to this place and I arrived here at 5 o'clock this morning, where I shall remain for further orders. Enclosed I have the honour to send you the mayor and recorder's order for my returning here. The accommodation here is extremely bad and insufficient for both men and horses.

(Sgd)

James Allen,
Capt. 5th Dragoons.

To
The Right Honble,
The Commander-in-chief.

Soldiering in Ireland about the year 1784 was of a pleasing nature to the individual soldier, and is thus described by John Francis Smet, Surgeon of the 8th Light Dragoons:—

Cavalry Corps in Ireland were extremely select, as from the very low establishment, it was in the power of the Colonels of choosing among a number of young gentlemen of distinction who might wish to get a commission, and who all could easily afford to add a hundred pounds a year to their pay. The warrants were also purchased at a high price, often by the sons or gentlemen for as much as five hundred guineas. The privates were always young men well recommended and whose connections were known. Indeed, the dragoon service was at that time extremely easy and pleasant, so much so, that when a vacancy happened, several desirable recruits always offered, and the man selected in general, got no more than one shilling bounty. Two thirds of the officers had in general leave of absence for the greater part of the year.

Many of the dragoons were often on furlough, who were sometimes allowed to take their horses with them to their parents' houses, and generally wore their own clothes while with their friends. The horses were a considerable time of the year at grass, when the proportion of furlough men was usually greater than at other times; but the whole corps assembled at headquarters once a year and were kept together for a couple of months to perfect themselves in its evolutions preparatory to its being reviewed, after which most of the officers were again indulged in leave of absence, many of the men allowed to go on furlough and several troops detached to out quarters. Such a service had many attractions. While detached, everybody had an opportunity of amusing himself; the officers with the gentlemen whose estates were in the neighbourhood, and the men among the farmers, having hardly any duty to do; but when the regiments prepared to be reviewed, then was fashionable dissipation carried to a great length.

And even some scenes and theatrical decorations, concerts, private plays, balls, dinners, and suppers in the evening, which gave the country towns where headquarters happened to be, an air of life and gaiety which they only possessed in an inferior degree at other times. The officers now meeting again, after such long separation from each other, in affluent circumstances, which they had improved while they had lived with their friends, justly looked on the time of the year they were to be reviewed in as the pleasantest season. The mornings were spent at exercise and the remainder of the time in festivity, (Smet's *Historical Record of the 8th Hussars*).

A pleasant enough time, no doubt, but scarcely soldiering. From 1784 to 1798 is not a long cry, and we are yet to read of the Rebellion in Ireland, of the state of insubordination and licentiousness of the Army in Ireland, of a regiment of Dragoon Guards behaving infamously in the face of the attack of a French force, of four regiments of Dragoon Guards removed to England to relearn the discipline they had lost in Ireland, and finally, and that which cuts us most to the heart, of the disbanding of the 5th Dragoons. Through small fault of their own were these gallant and well tried regiments brought into disrepute. The foregoing account of dragoon soldiering by Surgeon Smet tells the tale, and in spite of the cavalry in Ireland in 1784 and 1786, the British Government took no heed; and the natural consequence was the appalling occurrences which have been mentioned and of which we are yet to read.

Clonmel. 16 June, 1785.

That your Memorialist took a field of exercise for the 5th Dragoons Military during their assembly and review at Cashell, in the last and present Memorials months, as there was no common ground near that town. That he was Dublin, obliged to pay 13 guineas for that field, as he could not get a proper place for less money. Praying to be allowed to charge the said sum to the contingent bill of said Regiment in the usual manner.

(Signed)   James Stewart,
Lt.-Col. 5 Dragoons and
Colonel in the Army.

Robert Cunningham's troop at Tullamore. Earl of Errol's „ „ Tipperary.	1787 Muster Rolls

The Regiment was in Dublin.	1790

CHAPTER 9

Disbandment of the 5th Dragoons
1799

With the origin and causes of the disaffection in Ireland which led up to the rebellion of 1798 we have nothing to do; and as regards the rebellion itself, we confine ourselves to the part played by the 5th Dragoons in its suppression. The barbarous murders and massacres enacted during its course will not be related here.

We have no thrilling charges or hard fought battles against an honourable or foreign foe to read of, but merely the heroic struggles of detached parties of the regiment for the cause of Law and Order in the midst of appalling brutality and crime, and finally, the last sad scenes in the disbandment of the 5th Dragoons. The story is more than a hundred years old, and cannot be read of in this history but with regret. Our regret, however, is greatly tempered by being told of a few of the instances of the loyal part taken by the gallant soldiers of the Royal Irish Dragoons throughout the rebellion, up to the unfortunate circumstances which brought to an untimely end the life of a famous regiment.

At the commencement of 1798 the army in Ireland was undisciplined and demoralised. Even the few regular troops in the country were tainted by the appalling state of insubordination, in their case the result of having for years been scattered in small parties throughout the country for the protection of small towns and the estates of country gentlemen, with but little supervision or control.

It was a trial which would have corrupted the Ironsides under Cromwell himself.

The French were meditating a descent upon Ireland, and so great

5TH (ROYAL IRISH) DRAGOONS ABOUT 1780

was the danger all round, that Sir Ralph Abercromby was sent over from England to the command of the troops.

Abercromby found the state of the army to be so bad, that one of his first acts towards reform was the publishing of the following General Order, dated the 26th of February 1798:—

> The very disgraceful frequency of courts-martial and the many complaints of irregularities in the conduct of the troops in this kingdom, have too unfortunately proved the army to be in a state of licentiousness which must render it formidable to everyone but the enemy.

The situation he found himself in was, however, impossible. The lord lieutenant was adverse to many of his measures for reform, and he obtained but little support from the English Government. Declining to be a cipher or a tool in the hands of the party that governed the country, he resigned his post. The government found a difficulty in appointing a successor, and were obliged to place the command temporarily in the hands of the senior officer, General Lake. Fearing that he too might perchance actively endeavour to restore the army to its proper state of discipline, the lord lieutenant decreed that no general order should be issued until first submitted to himself. Such a proceeding, with the army in a state of insubordination and licentiousness, and the country itself in a grave state of discontent, was a sure step towards a rebellion in Ireland.

On the 23rd of May, 1798, a general rising throughout the disaffected parts of Ireland was intended by the rebels. Owing to its discovery in many places, however, the movement was not as widespread as it might have been. A partial rising took place in Wexford, Waterford, Wicklow, Kildare and other counties.

> On the outbreak of the rebellion, the 5th Dragoons, standing high in the confidence and estimation of the government, was ordered to march, with all speed, to be contiguous to the capital, and took up its quarters at Lehaunstown Huts, a position within seven miles of Dublin. Although several of the cavalry regiments were quartered in the immediate distance, this regiment was brought upwards of one hundred miles to act upon a duty, the most important perhaps, that has occurred during the history of Ireland.

Though the first effort of the rebels to rise in Dublin had been defeated by the vigilance of the authorities, it was known that another attempt was to be made, which resulted in the publication of the following notice to the inhabitants of the metropolis on the 24th of May:—

> Lieutenant-General Lake, commanding His Majesty's forces in this kingdom, having received from His Excellency the Lord Lieutenant full powers to put down the rebellion, and to punish rebels in the most summary manner, according to martial law, does hereby give notice to all His Majesty's subjects, that he is determined to exert the powers entrusted to him in the most vigorous manner, for the immediate suppression of the same; and that all persons acting in the present rebellion, or in any wise aiding or assisting therein, will be treated by him as rebels, and punished accordingly. And Lieut.-General Lake hereby requires all the inhabitants of the city of Dublin (the great officers of State, Members of the Houses of Parliament, Privy Councillors, Magistrates, and Military persons in uniform excepted) to remain within their respective dwellings from nine o'clock at night till five in the morning, under pain of punishment.

The viceroy, Lord Camden, received news that a body of rebels had risen at Rathfarnham, a village about three miles from Dublin, with the intention of attacking a small force of yeomanry there. Lieutenant O'Reily with a troop of the 5th Dragoons was on May the 23rd ordered off in pursuit, and with him went the Earl of Roden and Lieut. Col. Puleston as volunteers. On arriving at Rathfarnham, the 5th were informed that the rebels had gone towards Rathcool. They rode towards that place, and on the way met the yeomanry, who were retreating, after having attacked and been repulsed by the rebels.

The troop of dragoons halted, and it was agreed that Lord Roden should take half the troop up the road to the right, and Lieutenant O'Reily with the other half troop should go to the left, in order to surround the rebels.

Roden's party came up with the rebels at the first turnpike gate on the Rathcool road, and engaging them, drove them back on to O'Reily's half troop; the latter killed two and wounded a good many more, but the majority managed to escape, the much-enclosed country preventing a pursuit. The bodies of James Byrne and James Keely, two of the leaders who were killed, were afterwards exhibited to public view in the Castle Yard, Dublin.

At Kildare, on the night of the 23rd of May, an old pensioner of the 5th Dragoons named George Crawford, and his grandchild, a girl of fourteen years, were savagely murdered. He and his wife and the girl were stopped by a party of the rebels, one of whom struck the wife with a musket while another stabbed her in the back with a pike. Her husband endeavouring to save her, was knocked down and disabled by repeated blows from a firelock. While the rebels disputed whether they should kill him, his wife stole behind a hedge and hid herself. They then massacred Crawford with pikes, and the grand-daughter, having thrown herself on his body to protect him, received so many wounds that she also expired.

> The fidelity of a large dog, belonging to this poor man, deserves to be recorded, as he attacked these sanguinary monsters, and fought bravely in the defence of his master till he fell by his side, perforated with pikes.

On the 29th of May, two dragoons were sent from Dublin with an express to Lord Rossmore, the Colonel of the 5th Dragoons, at Newtown-Mount-Kennedy. When within about two miles of that place they were fired on by some rebels lining the hedges on the roadside. The dragoon carrying the express was killed, yet his comrade dismounted, and under fire, took the message out of the dead man's pocket, and remounting, galloped off and safely delivered it to Lord Rossmore.

On the 2nd of June a large party of rebels were at Ratoath, some eighteen miles from Dublin, and against these went a party of eleven highlanders and four yeomen. On the way this small party met Mr. Frederick Falkiner and eighteen of the 5th Dragoons, who joined them, and at Ratoath charged and dispersed the rebels, killing thirty-five of them in the pursuit.

On the 4th of June an action was fought under General Loftus near Gorey in Wexford, against a large body of rebels. Fifty men of the 5th Dragoons were on the left of the loyalists. The centre of the force was under the command of Colonel Walpole, whose lack of prudence and military skill resulted in his total defeat; and his neglect to communicate with General Loftus' force on his left, prevented any reinforcements reaching him in time. The defeat of Walpole left Loftus with but the fifty men of the 5th Dragoons, commanded by Capt. Corry, and two hundred of the Dunbarton Fencibles. The situation was an alarming one, for the rebel army from Vinegar Hill had formed a junction with that at Ballymore only a couple of miles or so to the front, and amounted to some twenty thousand men.

The small force then moved back on Gorey, which was found to be in possession of the rebels. Loftus was now between two rebel forces, and he quickly made up his mind that the only way to save his small detachment was to endeavour to fight his way through Gorey. He pushed rapidly on to that town under a heavy fire from the surrounding hills, to which he did not reply. On nearing the place, he. Captain Corry, and Colonel Scott reconnoitred it, and discovered it to be so strongly held that an attempt to force a way through appeared hopeless. The only possible way of escape seemed to be to march round the right flank of the rebel position at Gorey, and to endeavour to join Lord Ancram's force at Carnew, some twelve miles away to the north west, which could only be done by moving south west and crossing the Slievebuoy mountain, and then moving north.

Lieut.-Colonel Scott was at once sent off with the Dunbarton Fencibles, while the general remained behind with Corry and the 5th Dragoons to watch the enemy. Corry managed to engage the attention of the rebels by pretending to move on Gorey, and so enabled Scott to cross the mountain unmolested. Corry then quickly followed, and Carnew was occupied early the next morning. This action was a spirited performance, and to quote from the historian:

Thus this small body fairly marched round twenty thousand rebels; and by the good countenance which they kept, and by preserving their fire, though constantly fired at, they escaped without any injury.

To turn to the doings of the 5th dragoons in another part of Wexford, we find two troops of the regiment, under the command of Captain Irwine and Captain Ridge, who had been on the march from Tallow in Waterford to join headquarters at Lehaunstown, diverted at Kilkenny to reinforce the garrison at Ross in Wexford, in consequence of the preparations of a large force of rebels to attack that town. On the 2nd of June Irwine and his dragoons arrived at Ross, where they found the Clare, Donegal and Meath regiments of Militia, detachments of English artillery and Mid Lothian Fencibles; and the rebels collecting a force some eighteen thousand strong at Carrickbyrne, about five miles south east of Ross.

In consequence of the long and rapid march, many sick and weak horses were left at Waterford, and each troop in the fight which now took place could therefore only mount thirty odd files.

On the 4th of June the County of Dublin regiment marched in to Ross, and on the same day the rebel army moved to Corbet Hill, an eminence about a mile and a half from the town, having driven in the loyalist outpost.

A person who was forced by the rebels to attend the march, stated afterwards that their army was organised into parishes and baronies, each having a particular standard; and on their way they stopped at a chapel, where mass was said by the priests at the head of each column.

The garrison of Ross consisted of some fourteen hundred men under the command of General Johnson, and remained under arms all night. The infantry and artillery were mostly in a line outside the walls of the town. On the east and south sides the 5th Dragoons were on the quay by the river side, and the yeomen infantry on the bridge over the Barrow.

About four o'clock on the morning of the 5th of June, a sentinel on an outpost shot dead a man who was galloping towards him waving a white handkerchief. On his body was found a letter signed by Bagenal Harvey, commanding "the Army of Ireland," and addressed to the officer commanding "the King of England's Forces at Ross," to the following effect:—

As a friend to humanity, I request you will surrender the town of Ross to the Wexford forces, now assembled against that town; your resistance will but provoke rapine and plunder, to the ruin of the most innocent. Flushed with victory, the Wexford forces, now innumerable and irresistible will not be controlled, if they meet with resistance. To prevent, therefore, the total ruin of all property in the town, I urge you to a speedy surrender, which you will be forced to in a few hours, with loss and bloodshed, as you are surrounded on all sides. Your answer is required in four hours. Mr Furlong carries this letter, and will bring the answer.

At about five o'clock, the historian relates, "no less than thirty thousand rebels approached the town, with terrific yells, having four pieces of cannon, besides swivels," their priests with vestments on and crucifixes in their hands marching in the ranks.

They moved with slow but irresistible progress, like an immense body of lava, which issuing from the bowels of Vesuvius, spreads over the plains of Calabria, and from which man alone can escape, and that by flight only.

One column set fire to the suburbs and forced a number of horned cattle before them through the smoke in order to create confusion in the garrison. The first onslaught was met by the Dublin Militia under Lord Mountjoy, supported by the Clare regiment at Three-bullet-gate. A sanguinary struggle now ensued, but the great numbers of the rebels began to tell; the gallant Mountjoy was killed at the head of his regiment, a gun was captured, and the troops forced into the town, A column of rebel pikemen penetrated at another point, and the garrison was thrown into confusion, and retreat became necessary.

Meanwhile Captain Irwine had collected about sixty men of his two troops of 5th Dragoons, and forming them up as best he could, was ordered by General Johnson to charge the rebels at the Three-bullet gate, to gain time for the infantry to retire.

To quote the historian's own words:

This was a service replete with danger, as from the situation of the place, and the continual increase of a desperate enemy, a handful of men seemed precluded from every hope of escaping destruction. Notwithstanding, the order was instantly obeyed, and the detachment, not forgetting that they were a portion of the Royal Irish Dragoons, rode to meet bodies of insurgents advancing against them, armed with pikes from ten to twelve feet long. Nor were the rebels inexperienced in the practice of this formidable weapon. Their instructions were to pierce the horse in the flank, and thus obtain an easy conquest over the rider.

A shot from a twelve pounder at the Three-bullet gate killed Captain Irwine's horse, which fell on his leg, and prevented him from moving for some time. Luckily for him, a loose artillery horse passed, and, laying hold of one of the traces, he was dragged clear of the dead horse and after the retreating infantry into the town. Three times did the dragoons charge with an enormous loss to themselves.

Such was the lot of these brave devoted men who in the action at Ross have written a testimonial with their blood, that might at least have softened the rigorous order which was impending over their regiment, and which in reality was excited more by an unlucky occurrence of unfavourable appearances, and indiscreet reports, than by any actual transgression of its own. We are far from calling the propriety of the order in question, because we are convinced that in calmer times, the grounds upon which that order was given would have been leisurely weighed and maturely executed.

The quartermaster of the 5th at last found himself in command, and with only nine men, he with difficulty managed to retreat to the opposite side of the river, where the infantry were rapidly forming up.

During the retreat of the infantry the rebels poured into the town in great numbers. General Johnson planted guns at several cross roads, but the rebels, in spite of great slaughter, continued to press on.

One rebel, emboldened by fanaticism and drunkenness, advanced before his comrades, seized a gun, crammed his hat and wig into it, and cried out, 'Come on, boys! her mouth is stopped' At that instant the gunner laid the match to the gun, and blew the unfortunate savage to atoms. This fact has been verified by the affidavit of a person who saw it from a window.

The gallant Johnson now rallied the troops on the Kilkenny side of the river and persuaded them to recross into Ross.

He exhorted his troops to recover their ground and concluded by desiring such as were willing to conquer or die, to follow their general. An awful silence prevailed for a few minutes; after which the quartermaster and the few men remaining of the 5th Dragoons who were able to sit on their horses, pressed eagerly forward and exclaimed, 'They were willing to shed the last drop of their blood in support of their general, and to revenge their fallen comrades.' A shout of applause followed from every part of the column and terminated with three cheers and a general cry of 'God Save the King and success to General Johnson.'

The troops, and with them the small remnant of the 5th Dragoons, returned to the charge; Ross was retaken, and an immense carnage of the rebels ensued.

The enemy's losses in killed counted on the field was two thousand six hundred, besides numbers they carried off on cars. The losses of the king's troops were, killed, one colonel, one cornet, one ensign, four sergeants, three drummers, eighty one rank and file and fifty four horses; the wounded were one captain, one drummer, fifty-four rank and file and five horses; while missing were one captain, three lieutenants, one ensign, two sergeants, two corporals, seventy-two rank and file and four horses. Of these losses the 5th Dragoons had in killed alone. Cornet Dodwell and twenty-eight men.

On the 5th of June General Needham led a force, amongst them being a detachment of the 5th Dragoons, to recapture the town of Arklow. The dragoons were sent on ahead to reconnoitre, and were able to take possession of the town without meeting any opposition, and next day the main body marched in.

General Needham had under his command in Arklow a force of some seventeen hundred men, amongst them being one officer and eighteen men of the 5th Dragoons, and four officers and twenty-four men of the 4th Dragoon Guards.

On the morning of the 9th of June at about 11 o'clock news arrived of the advance of the enemy. The garrison turned out, and cavalry patrols were sent off to reconnoitre, and gradually fell back before two strong columns of rebels, amounting to some twenty-five thousand men. A desperate action ensued, in which the rebels made no headway, and finally the cavalry, led by Sir W. W. Wynne, were ordered to charge, which they did with great gallantry. By 8 p.m. the rebel army was in full retreat, with a loss of a thousand killed and a large number of wounded. During the action, a priest named Murphy, to encourage the rebels, took out of his pocket some musket balls, which he said had been fired at him by the enemy, some of which had hit him without wounding; and others he had caught in his hands. He assured them that the balls of the heretics would not hurt them, as they were under the protection of the Almighty, in whose cause they were fighting.

Unfortunately for his promises. Murphy was himself killed by a cannon shot later in the battle, "and the fall of this church militant hero had an immediate effect in damping the ardour of the enemy." The men of the detachment of the 5th Dragoons covered themselves with glory during this desperate action, and worthily upholding the honour of the regiment they belonged to, were publicly thanked for their services by General Needham.

On the 18th of June General Johnson moved from Ross towards Vinegar Hill, where the rebels had their headquarters. Reinforcements had brought his army up to four thousand men, and he was able to leave a small garrison in Ross. A detachment, consisting of the few survivors of the 5th Dragoons from the battle at Ross, a part of Hompesch's mounted riflemen, and two companies of sharp-shooters, were sent on in advance, with orders to reconnoitre the rebel position and drive in their outposts. This was done so successfully, that the rebels were pursued with considerable slaughter to within musket shot of their own entrenchments.

On the 21st of June was fought the battle of Vinegar Hill. General Johnson's column moved against the position on the West side, while General Lake advanced from the North East.

On the evening of the 20th, Johnson was opposed by some rebels who moved out of Enniscorthy, a village on the Slaney on the western foot of Vinegar Hill. The rebels posted themselves on an eminence, against which Johnson fired a few shots from his twelve pounders; "and when the balls lodged on the hill, the rebels vied with each other to lay hold of them." Johnson then fired some shells, which numbers of rebels "having surrounded for the same purpose, exploded, and blew them to atoms."

Early next morning, having driven the rebels from the high ground into Enniscorthy, Johnson commenced his attack on the town. The place, however, was very strongly held and fortified, and Johnson's storming party of infantry was driven back with the loss of the guns which had accompanied them. The general sent up reinforcements, amongst them being the detachment of the 5th Dragoons, and another attack against Enniscorthy began. "The 5th Dragoons being the eldest regiment present," took the post of honour and "led the charge into the town." The rebels were driven out with "considerable carnage," Enniscorthy was captured, and the lost guns retaken. The infantry were then ordered across the bridge over the Slaney, and pressed up the steep sides of Vinegar Hill, driving the rebels before them.

General Lake had meanwhile commenced his attack on the north east side, and now joined hands with Johnson, and the rebels abandoned the hill and fled in "wild consternation."

Captain Ledwell, with another detachment of the 5th Dragoons from Lake's force, now joined their comrades with Johnson, and these representatives of the Irish Dragoons vigorously pursued the rebels.

"Their intrepidity and zeal was not a little quickened by the sense with which they went into action, of the loss the corps had sustained in the deaths of so many of their brave comrades at Ross."

The following paper was found in the pocket of a rebel who had been shot by Captain Hugh Moore, of the 5th Dragoons, A.D.C. to General Needham:—

Jesus I.H.S. Maria
I trust thee

This is measured of the wounds of the side of our Lord Jesus Christ which was brought from Constantinople unto the Emperor Charles, within a gold chest, as a relief most precious to that effect, that no evil or anything might take him which reads it, hears it, wears it, cannot be hurted by any tempest, fire, water, knife, sword lance or bullet. Neither the devil shall hurt him; he shall be victorious, and never die an unnatural death, and shall be a sure safety to women with child"

At Ballymore Ustace and in other places "the same zeal and *esprit-de-corps* for which the Royal Irish Dragoons had been so remarkable for more than a century, were singularly conspicuous."

In the midst of barbarous murders and treason, the 5th Dragoons continued to do their duty, while many of the King's regiments were more or less tainted with sedition, and the entire army in Ireland was in an extremely bad state of discipline. On the 27th of August, General Lake, with some seventeen hundred men and eleven guns, in a strong position on the heights of Castlebar, was confidently awaiting the attack of Humbert and his thousand Frenchmen, who had landed a few days before at Killala Bay. The attack was delivered, and the whole of Lake's force fled in a panic. The Longford and Kilkenny Militia, Eraser's Fencibles, Galway Volunteers, and, we regret to read, a regiment of Dragoon Guards who shall be nameless, fled ignominiously before the disciplined troops of the French general. The artillery, a hundred men of the 6th Foot, and a few of Roden's Fencibles, alone stuck to their ground. The depredations of this force on the march too had "exceeded all description."

To such an ebb had discipline dwindled, that an officer of the guards writing of his men, stated that if kept in the country another six months he would not answer for their subordination.

Again, in July, 1799, four regiments of dragoon guards, amongst them the offenders mentioned above, "were removed to England to relearn the discipline which, through small fault of their own, they had forgotten."

But another fate was reserved for the 5th Dragoons. The regiment had behaved with great gallantry and much self-sacrifice during the rebellion, but trouble was now to come, and a brave and gallant corps was to be charged with the greatest of crimes a soldier is capable of, that of disloyalty to his king.

A number of recruits had enlisted into the 5th with the intention of acting in concert with a party of rebels in attacking a force of troops engaged in stamping out the last dying embers of the rebellion. The plot was discovered in time, but there had apparently been much desertion in the regiment, and it was said that there were men in the ranks who had taken the oath of the United Irishmen. In addition to this, the Lord Lieutenant, Lord Cornwallis, had reported the want of discipline in the corps, and recommended that it should be removed from Ireland. The king, however, took a far stronger view, and ordered its disbandment. The officers of the regiment petitioned for a Court of Enquiry, but this was refused. How the sentence was carried out will be read in the last pages of this chapter.

The following story of the closing scenes in the life of the 5th Dragoons is taken from an account published in the *British Military Library* of April, 1800:—

In reading this brief and unaffected narrative of unquestionable facts, it will not be possible for the man of candour to forbear looking back upon a series of brilliant actions, and after he has passed them in review, to cast an eye of regret upon the fallen state of such an ancient corps.

If being unfortunate constitutes transgression, then the 5th or Royal Irish Dragoons, may truly be said to have been highly culpable; for never did a more unlucky combination of accidental circumstances, happen to overwhelm a body of men; nor was that combination rendered less murderous in its effects by the cordial co-operation of *every* person connected with the corps to avert its consequences. We lament to say, not upon vague grounds, but upon strict, honourable and forthcoming evidence, that the resentment of government was, in all probability, not a little increased by personal misrepresentations and private views. We have been credibly informed that it was the wish, because it was the interest, of some individuals, to get the 5th Dragoons removed from the Irish establishment, for the purpose of enhancing the value of their commissions, in the event of its being sent to England.

It is possible that under such impressions, certain persons might not have been without hopes that should government be deceived into a belief of the corps being disaffected, His Majesty might be induced to order it to the Cape of Good Hope or to the East Indies. In either of which cases considerable advantages were looked for by those persons who consulted their own private emolument at the expense of the corps.

Although we think it right to furnish the public with every authentic particular, which may lead hereafter to a thorough knowledge of one of the most singular instances of censure and disgrace, that has occurred in the military history of Great Britain, nevertheless we are equally aware that nothing should go forth, which may affect the honour and reputation of responsible individuals. Far be it, therefore, from us to insinuate, that anything herein mentioned could possibly allude to the colonel or commanding officer of the regiment. We will not hesitate to say that they exerted themselves to the utmost, in vindicating the character of their corps. Nor should it be forgotten, that at this melancholy period, almost every regiment belonging to the Irish establishment, was more or less tainted by the admission of disaffected persons, who, under the fictitious characters of persecuted Royalists, that had been driven from their homes by the rebels sought refuge in the army. How the regiment in question was visited by this insidious evil, will appear by the following statement.

Some time after the 5th Dragoons had arrived at Lehaunstown Huts an order was received that the strength of the regiment should forthwith march for Dublin. It was, however, directed that a few men from each troop should be left behind to take charge of the heavy baggage, sick men and horses, &c. subsequent to which several small detachments were sent out to different stations. The officers who commanded them were instructed to receive eligible recruits. Many very fine fellows were accordingly enlisted, particularly at a place called Castle Corner, and were sent to headquarters. It is much to be lamented (although in justice to the officers we acknowledge the moral impossibility of diving into the minds of men) that some precautions had not been taken to ascertain the real character of every individual who offered to be enrolled.

Almost all of them, as the event afterwards evinced were rebel partisans, and had insinuated themselves into the 5th Dragoons, agreeable to a preconcerted plan for surprising Lehaunstown; to which place all the recruits and men unfit for immediate service had been transmitted. A conspiracy was accordingly entered into by these newcomers, in concert with the rebels in the adjoining mountains. The design was, that on a certain night an attack should be made on the garrison, whose whole effective strength consisted of about seventy dragoons, many of them invalids, and somewhat more than an equal number of the King's County Militia.

The recruits to a man were concerned in this black plot; and the massacre of every officer and loyal soldier was prevented, only an hour before the scheme was proposed to take place. The conspirators were seized and suffered according to their deserts. The regiment, however, had the mortification to find it announced in the public papers, that several privates belonging to the 5th or Royal Irish Dragoons, had been found guilty by a general court martial of joining the rebels. Some little time alter two brothers of the name of Feney, who had deserted from Drogheda (where the regiment was stationed after the rebellion had been suppressed) and who, under pretence of procuring arms for the rebels, had pillaged several houses in that neighbourhood, were taken by the yeomanry in the act of thieving, and would have been executed on the spot, had they not promised to discover the names of several dragoons, who, they said, were concerned in the same nefarious practices, and were sworn to support the rebel cause.

The influence of scandal is well know to acquire multiplied virulence in its progress. A malignant report, having once obtained circulation, is shortly so much metamorphosed, that the original fabricator can with difficulty recognise his own bantling. The truth of this remark was strongly illustrated in the present instance. It was industriously propagated that a most fortunate discovery had been made relative to the 5th Dragoons. This regiment was stated by some people, to have been corrupted by the rebels, and to have formed a plot to massacre the yeomanry; by others it was said, with equal ingenuity, and no less malice, that the 5th Dragoons had organised a conspiracy to murder their own officers, and afterwards to join the rebels with their horses, accoutrements &c. Such were the gossip stories of the day.

Unfortunately for the cause of truth the commanding officer was at this time absent from the regiment, on leave. It is to be feared that reports, scarcely less exaggerated, were from self interested motives communicated to government by persons of seeming respectability. The Feneys, under a strong escort, were ordered up to Dublin to be tried by a general court martial, and every measure was adopted to bring this serious charge to light. A man of the name of M'Nassar was transmitted along with the two brothers. The Feneys were accordingly brought into Drogheda, escorted by the yeomanry under the charge or having confessed a combination between themselves and several others belonging to the 5th Dragoons.

The commanding officer of the garrison, and some gentlemen belonging to the 5th Dragoons, attended on this occasion for the purpose of receiving their information. The result of this enquiry terminated in the *important* discovery that *one* man, by name James M'Nassar, constituted the whole of this dreadful plot, as far as it regarded the Royal Irish Dragoons. He was accordingly apprehended. It is here necessary to state that James M'Nassar had, for a considerable time, been looked upon as a very bad character; he had been repeatedly punished, and was drafted into the wagon corps, who sent him back to the Regiment as unfit to serve in that capacity.

A general courtmartial was ordered to sit in Dublin Barracks. James M'Nassar having turned King's Evidence, the veracity of the Feneys, and the character of the 5th Royal Irish Dragoons were at issue. The result of this interesting and important trial was, 'That the two Feneys should suffer death, having been convicted of robbery and other evil practices; and that James M'Nassar should be transported beyond the seas.' But not an iota of charge appeared throughout the proceedings that could impeach any other individual belonging to the regiment, which at the time consisted of more than six hundred men. It is incumbent, however, upon us to declare, that a man named Ryan, a degraded sergeant, and a Corporal Gallagher were suspected by the commanding officer, and were confined, but no specific charge of disaffection could be proved against them.

Such were the ostensible marks of criminality under which the 5th Dragoons so unfortunately fell. We have collected the particulars with as strict a regard to truth, as the delicacy of the subject merits, and we make no doubt but we shall stand justified for having so done, in the eyes of every candid and impartial soldier.

On the 10th of April following (1799) the 5th or Royal Irish Dragoons was disbanded at Chatham in conformity to His Majesty's order.

Order for disbanding the 5th Regiment of Dragoons.
Horse Guards, April 8th, 1799.

His Majesty has taken into his most serious consideration, the representation which has been made by His Excellency the Lord Lieutenant of Ireland, of the conduct of the Fifth, or Royal Irish Regiment of Dragoons; and is of opinion that the insubordination, and the departure from discipline, and principles which have ever distinguished the British Army, therein exhibited, require, especially in these times of warfare and exertion, that they should be marked by a punishment which may be severely felt, and be long remembered by those misguided persons, who have been guilty of the atrocious acts of disobedience, which have brought this indelible stigma on the corps; and may serve as an example to all others, of the consequences of such seditious and outrageous proceedings, and of His Majesty's firm determination to maintain subordination and discipline in his army, and to support the authority of his officers in the execution of their duty.

It is on these grounds His Majesty's determination, that the 5th or Royal Irish Regiment of Dragoons, shall be forthwith disbanded.

At the same time that the king judges it requisite for the good of the service, to make this severe example. His Majesty has graciously condescended to direct that General Lord Rossmore shall be assured, that His Majesty is persuaded of the concern which, as a soldier, his Lordship would feel at such a circumstance occurring in any part of the army, and is sensible of the particular mortification he must experience in the present instance, from the event of which, however, his Lordship cannot, in the smallest degree, suffer in His Majesty's estimation.

His Majesty is graciously pleased further to express his persuasion, that there are many valuable officers in the regiment, who have used their best endeavours to restore the order, and to preserve the credit of the corps; and, though in this measure of indispensible severity, it was impossible to make any exceptions, the majority being clearly implicated in the misconduct for

187

which the whole are suffering; yet His Majesty will hereafter make the most pointed discrimination, and those of any rank who are deserving the Royal favour, may rely on His Majesty's disposition to attend to their merits, and to avail himself of their future services. In consideration of the expense to which the officers of the 5th or Royal Irish Regiment of Dragoons have been unavoidably exposed. His Majesty has been graciously pleased to direct, that their full pay shall be continued to them, till the 24th December next, at which period they will be placed on half-pay.

(Signed)   Harry Calvert.
                                      Adjutant General.

The attention which Lord Rossmore uniformly paid to the good order and discipline of the 5th Dragoons, can only be equalled by the heart-felt regret, with which he has been obliged to abandon his trust. His Lordship was, in fact wrapt up in the regiment he commanded; and every officer still concurs in expressing the fullest testimony of his unremitting zeal and personal sacrifices for its welfare.

Previous to this event, the officers had sent in a memorial to government, praying for an investigation of their conduct, and of the character and behaviour of the regiment, before a Board of General Officers. They failed in their petition, and every attempt at producing an enquiry into the business, was rendered fruitless. We are, however, happy to add from very unquestionable authority, that the regiment marched above two hundred miles on foot, through this country (England), in perfect good order. It remained some weeks in Chatham before its final dissolution and was publicly thanked by General Fox for its exemplary good behaviour during the march, and its unremitting regularity whilst it was under his command. The conduct of the regiment was the more praiseworthy on these trying occasions, as it was repeatedly provoked by allusions to the cause or its dishonour, and was frequently reproached by the inhabitants as it marched through the towns, and not a little mortified by the significant whispers of other soldiers.

The privates were drafted into other regiments of the line, in which they have since obtained the best testimonies of good behaviour, cleanliness and discipline. Several among them have since been appointed Non-commissioned officers and continue to prove that the disgrace they suffered, has not diminished their zeal and attachment to the Service.

We cannot conclude without expressing our regret that a regiment which has so frequently deserved well of its country, should have incurred His Majesty's displeasure. Let us hope, that like the Phoenix, it may some time or other rise out of is own ashes, be restored to the army, and add fresh laurels to those of Ramillies and Hochstet.

Time we trust, and a calm reconsideration of presumed delinquency, will restore this Veteran Regiment to the rank it formerly held with so much satisfaction to the different sovereigns under whose banners it fought, and with so much credit to itself.

Such was the end of the Royal Irish Dragoons, Its most distinguished career was not to save the regiment from dishonour The stories of the captured kettledrums at Blenheim, and of the surrendered battalions of Picardie on the field of Ramillies were to pass from the keeping of its sons to the dull pages of the historian, while for years the blank page in the Army List was to remain a standing reproach to the British Army.

Appendices

1

BIOGRAPHIES OF OFFICERS

BRIGADIER-GENERAL JAMES WYNNE.

James Wynne was the eldest son of Owen Wynne by Catherine, widow of James Hamilton, and daughter of Claud, 2nd Baron Strabane. Owen Wynne, who lived in Wales, migrated to Ireland about 1688.

The brigadier's early military service was passed in the infantry. He was a captain in Colonel Stewart's Regiment of Foot, the present 9th Norfolk Regiment, and with that corps he took a prominent part in the relief of Londonderry under Major-General Kirke.

In 1689 James Wynne was one of the officers selected by Kirke to organize the levies which had been doing such strenuous service at Enniskillen. He was appointed a Colonel of Dragoons and raised the famous Enniskillen Regiment known at the time as Wynne's Dragoons, and in later years, as the 5th Royal Irish Dragoons.

Colonel Wynne led his regiment throughout the war in Ireland, which ended with the peace of Limerick in 1691.

In 1694 Wynne took his regiment to Flanders, where he commanded a brigade of dragoons under Marlborough, being appointed a Brigadier-General on the 4th of October.

In an action near Rouselaer he was badly wounded, although at the time it was not thought fatally. He died of his wounds, however, a few days later, on the 15th of July, 1695, at Ghent.

GENERAL CHARLES ROSS.

Charles Ross of Balnagowan was a son of the 11th Baron Ross. He joined Wynne's Regiment of Enniskillen Dragoons as a captain in 1689 on the formation of the regiment, and with it served throughout the war in Ireland.

In 1694, as Lieutenant-Colonel he accompanied the regiment to Flanders. On the death of James Wynne on the 15th of July, 1695, Marlborough appointed Ross Colonel of the Regiment.

In 1704, through the instrumentality of its colonel, the title of the Royal Dragoons of Ireland was accorded to Ross's Dragoons.

On March the 9th, 1702, Colonel Ross was appointed a Brigadier-General of Dragoons, and on January the 1st he was promoted to Major-General. He served throughout Marlborough's campaigns in Flanders and commanded a brigade of dragoons at Blenheim, Ramillies, Oudenarde and Malplaquet.

Promotion to Lieutenant-General followed on the 1st of January, 1707. On the 1st of May, 1711, Ross was appointed Colonel-General of all the Dragoon Forces, and on January the 1st, 1712, he was promoted a General.

In September, 1713, General Ross was appointed Envoy Extraordinary to the Court of France.

He was removed from the head of the Royal Irish Dragoons by George I. on the 8th of October, 1715. He was, however, re-appointed to the Colonelcy of his old regiment on the 1st of February, 1729, which appointment he continued to hold until his death at Bath on the 5th of August, 1732. He was buried at Fearn in Ross-shire.

Lieutenant-General Owen Wynne.

Lt.-General Owen Wynne was the third son of Owen Wynne who settled in Ireland about the year 1688, having previously lived in Wales,' and was a younger brother of Brigadier-General James Wynne who raised the Regiment.

Owen Wynne in 1688 was serving in the army of James II, but being a Protestant, he transferred his allegiance to the Prince of Orange on the breaking out of the Revolution. He was with Major-Gen. Kirke's force sent from England to the relief of Londonderry, and he also took some part in the defence of Enniskillen, and served through the War in Ireland.

Owen Wynne was appointed a major in his brother James Wynne's Dragoons on the 1st of November, 1694, and served with his regiment through the Flanders campaign of 1694 to 1697, being promoted Lieut.-Colonel in July, 1695, taking the place of Charles Ross, promoted Colonel of the Regiment on the death of James Wynne.

He served under Marlborough and was promoted Colonel in 1703, and in 1705 he raised and commanded a regiment of foot. The year 1706 saw him a Brigadier-General, and in 1709 he was promoted to Major-General.

In 1715 Major-General Wynne raised and commanded the regiment now known as the 9th Lancers. From the head of Owen Wynne's Dragoons he was transferred to the Colonelcy of the 5th Horse, now the 4th Dragoon Guards.

Promotion to Lieutenant-General followed in 1726, and in 1728 Owen Wynne was Commander-in-Chief of His Majesty's Forces in Ireland. In August, 1732, he was transferred from the 5th Horse to the Colonelcy of his old regiment the Royal Irish Dragoons, which appointment he retained until his death in 1737.

Owen Wynne represented Ballyshannon in Parliament from 17 15 to 1727, and from 1727 to 1737 was member for Sligo. He was also a Privy Councillor, and in 1736 was Governor of Londonderry. It is stated that he several times refused a peerage.

Field Marshal Viscount Molesworth.

Richard Molesworth was the third son of Robert Molesworth, ambassador at one time to the Court of Denmark and raised to the peerage in 1716.

He was educated for the Law and sent to the Temple, but preferring a more active life, he volunteered for the War of the Spanish Succession, and obtaining an ensigncy in Orkney's Regiment of Foot, now the Royal Scots, went to Flanders on the 14th of April, 1702. He served with his regiment at Blenheim, and at Ramillies he was an *aide-de-camp* to Marlborough.

It was during the Battle of Ramillies that he saved the life of his great chief, an incident which for some reason appears to have been kept somewhat secret at the time, but which nevertheless has been handed down in history. The duke while leading a cavalry charge, was cannoned against when jumping a ditch, and unhorsed, his charger getting away. Molesworth, who was close at hand, came to his assistance, and dismounting, helped Marlborough to his own horse, and remained to face the enemy alone on his feet. The French, however, were so intent upon pursuing the duke that Molesworth escaped with a few sabre cuts. He then recovered the duke's horse, and rejoined him, when Marlborough remounted his own animal. While doing so, the equerry who was holding the duke's stirrup, had his head taken off by a cannon ball.

There is a picture in the August 1901 number of the *Royal United Service Magazine* of a very rare medal struck in honour of the occasion, but the present owner of the medal cannot be traced. The *obverse* bears the profile of Captain Richard Molesworth equipped as a Roman warrior, with the inscription "Richard Molesworth Brit. Trib. Mil." round the margin. On the *reverse* is a figure representing Victory leading by the hand a warrior, trampling on broken artillery with the motto "*Per Ardua*"

In 1708 Molesworth was present at the Relief of Brussels as Captain and Lieutenant-Colonel in the Coldstream Guards, and at Mons in the following year he was blown up by a mine, but not seriously injured.

He next commanded a regiment of foot which was disbanded after the Peace of Utrecht. In 1715 he raised a regiment of dragoons with which he fought at Preston, where he was severely wounded. His dragoons were disbanded in 1718, and in 1725 he was appointed Colonel of the 27th Foot, from which he was transferred in 1732 to the Colonelcy of the present 9th Lancers.

He succeeded to the title in 1726 as 3rd Viscount.

In 1735 Viscount Molesworth was promoted Major-General, and in 1737 appointed to the Colonelcy of the Royal Irish Dragoons, which appointment he held until his death.

Promotion to Lieutenant-General followed in 1739, and in 1741 he was Master-General of the Ordnance in Ireland, and a Field Marshal in 1757.

Viscount Molesworth was a member of the Privy Council in 1733. He was twice married. After a brilliant career he died in October, 1758.

GENERAL THE HON. JOSEPH YORKE K.B.

The Hon. Joseph Yorke was a son of Lord Hardwicke, the Lord Chancellor.

General Yorke commenced his career in the Foot Guards, with whom he served in Flanders in 1743, and was present at Fontenoy and the other actions of that campaign.

He also fought with his regiment during the Jacobite rebellion in 1745.

He was appointed Colonel of the 5th Dragoons, from Colonel of the 8th Dragoons, on November the 27th, 1760, and on April the 4th,

1787 he was again transferred to the head of the nth Light Dragoons. He was a Major-General on the 18th of January, 1758, a Lieutenant-General on the 11th of December, 1760, and General on August the 29th 1777.

SUCCESSIONS,

Successions of Colonels

James Wynne	25th December 1688
Charles Ross	16th July 1695
Thomas Sydney	8th October 1715
Charles Ross	1st February 1729
Owen Wynne	6th August 1732
Richard, Visc. Molesworth	17th June 1737
John Mostyn	18th October 1756
The Hon. Joseph Yorke, K.B.	27th November 1760
Robert Cuninghame,	
Lord Rossmore	4th April 1787

Succession of Commanding Officers.

Lieut.-Colonel Charles Ross		Before 1695
„	Owen Wynne	20th July 1695
„	Robert Hunter	1705
Brevet-Colonel Hugh Caldwell		1707
Brevet-Colonel Jno. Hill		September 1709
Lieut.-Colonel Ric. Gore		1st November 1711
„	Thomas Sidney	Before 5th October 1715
„	Wrioth' Betton	23rd September 1719
„	Alex Rose	12th September 1729
„	William Cope	10th May 1740
„	Christopher Clarges	20th February 1749
„	William Hill	25th August 1760
„	Hugh Cane	31st March 1768
„	James Stewart	7th January 1778
„	Hon. Ch. Wm Stewart	1st January 1797
„	Alex J. Goldie	17th February 1798

Succession of adjutants.

Griffith Lloyd		1st August 1694
Mat. Watts		20th June 1696
David Ross		August 1703
Cornet William Ross		23rd August 1707
„	James Ross	9th April 1756
„	Rich. Wolfe	7th May 1757

Cornet Thomas Bowater		18th October 1764
„	Rich. Wolfe	16th May 1766
„	Richard Vyse	18th March 1767
„	William Broom	28th November 1771
„	Thos. Tickell	17th January 1774
„	Wynne Fawcett	5th March 1783
„	George Broome	31st October 1792
„	John Taylor	12th November 1794

Note.—The above list is incomplete as in many of the earlier Army Lists the adjutants are not given.

DRILL

The exercises and drill of dragoons at the time the regiment was raised are interesting.

When mounted dragoons were exercised as Horse, each squadron was drawn up in three ranks with the officers immediately in front of their men.

The distances and intervals in the cavalry exercises were only three; the Open Order, which was six feet between ranks or files; the Close Order, which was three feet between ranks or files; and the Close Order from Close Order (*i. e.* doubly close) which was head to crupper or knee to knee.

When dismounted, they were formed and exercised as Foot, so far as the evolutions were concerned; for the rest the following were the words of command, the men being mounted, to act dismounted:—

Dragoons have a care (take heed.)
Sling your muskets.
Make ready your links.
Clear your right foot of your stirrup.
Dismount and stand at your horses' heads.
(The six outside men remained mounted to take charge of the horses.)
Link your horses to the left.
March clear of your horses and shoulder as you march.
Halt.
(The dragoons were then formed up in the same way as a foot regiment.)
Have a care of the exercise.
Officers to the right-about.
Take your posts in rear.

March.

Dragoons have a care, (the men pull off their right hand gloves and stow them under their waist belts.)

Lay your right hand on your musket.

Poise your musket.

Rest your musket.

Cock and guard.

Present; fire.

Recover your arms with the cock half bent (*i.e.* half-cock).

Rest upon your musket.

Handle your daggers (*i.e.* bayonets).

Fix them in the muzzle of your muskets.

Poise your muskets.

Charge to the front.

To the right (left, right-about, left-about) Charge.

Recover your arms.

Rest upon your muskets.

Handle your bayonets.

Withdraw your bayonets.

Place (*i.e.* return) your bayonets.

Poise your muskets.

Rest your muskets.

Clean the pan (with the ball of the thumb).

Open your cartridge-box.

Handle your primer.

Sink and prime.

Return your primer.

Shut your pan (with your fore-fingers).

Blow off your loose corns (recovering arms at the same time).

Cast about to charge.

Handle your cartridge.

Take out your cartridge (and shut the box).

Open it with your teeth.

Charge with powder and ball.

Draw forth your scourers (*i.e.* ram-rods).

Shorten them to an inch (against your right breasts).

Put them into the muzzle of your muskets.

Ram down powder and ball.

Withdraw your scourers.

Shorten them to an inch (as before).

Place (*i.e.* return) your scourers.
Poise your muskets.
Shoulder your muskets.
Poise your muskets.
Rest your muskets.
Lay down your arms.
Quit your arms.
To the right about.
March clear of your arms and break.
(The men being thus dispersed, the drum beat and the men
    drawing their swords run to their arms "with a Huzza.")
Return your swords.
Handle your arms.
Rest your arms.
Poise your muskets.
Sling your muskets.
To the right-about.
March to your horses.
Unlink your horses.
Shorten your bridles.
Put your left foot in the stirrup.
Mount.
Fasten your links.
Unstring and advance your muskets (on the right thigh).
Join your left hands to your muskets.
Cock and guard.
Rest your muskets on your bridle-hands.
Present; Fire.
Recover your arms with the cock half bent.

Of individual or setting up drill there was, apparently, very little; the instruction of the recruit being limited to making him hold his head up, to "look lively," and not to swing his arms. In marching the men were to step off with the left foot, and to set their "feet down altogether, so that they may be heard," and were "to march very slowly."

LIST OF OFFICERS WHO HAVE SERVED IN THE REGIMENT

NAME	DATE OF JOINING AND RANK	OUT OF REGIMENT AND RANK	WAR SERVICES AND REMARKS
ABERCROMBIE, Alex	1694. Quarter Master.	No trace after 1709. Lieut.	Flanders 1694-97. Blenheim, Ramillies, Oudenarde, Malplaquet.
ABERCROMBIE, John	13th April 1782.	1787. Cornet.	
ALLEN, James	5th Oct. 1776. Captain.	1791. Major.	
ANDERSON, John	16th Dec. 1775. Cornet.	1778. Cornet.	
ARCHER, Nicholas	3rd May 1786. Surgeon.	1787. Surgeon.	
AYLMER, Gerald	28th May 1794. Cornet.	1799. Cornet.	Disbandment of 5th Dragoons.
BALDWIN, Thos.	17th Nov. 1721. Cornet.	1740. Cornet.	
BALFOUR, Jeremiah	1708. Quarter Master.	Still a Cornet. 1730.	Malplaquet.
BALL, William	8th Jan. 1740. Lieutenant.	No further trace.	
BAMFORD, John	1st July 1798. Cornet.	1799. Cornet.	Disbandment of 5th Dragoons.
BARKER, Robert	24th Feb. 1708. Cornet.	No trace after 1709.	Malplaquet.
BEATTY, Charles	20th July 1695. Lieutenant.	1710. Captain-Lieutenant.	Flanders 1695-7. Blenheim, Malplaquet.
BELLINGHAM, Henry	14th Feb. 1765. Cornet.	1773. Lieut.	
BERNARD, North Ludlow	1st May 1724. Lieutenant.	1754. Major.	Died.
BETTON, Wriothy	23rd Sept. 1719. Lieut. Col.	1730. Lieut. Col.	
BLAKE, Dennis	14th Jan. 1775. Cornet.	1777. Cornet.	

BLAKE, Walter	14th Nov. 1775. Cornet.	1781. Lieut.	
BLAKENEY, William	10th July 1722. Cornet.	No trace after 1736. Cornet.	
BLIGH, Robert	28th Feb. 1787. Cornet.	1791. Lieut.	
BOISRAGON, Danl. Chevalau de	1695. Lieut.	Before 1709. Lieut.	Flanders 1695-7. Blenheim.
BOGGES (or BOGGEST, Fraser.	27th Jan. 1707. Cornet.	(?) 1711 Capt. serving in Evans' Dragoons 1728.	Of Halwey, Suffolk. Malplaquet.
BOLTON, Jno.	14th March 1772. Cornet.	1789. Captain.	
BOWATER, Thos.	31st Dec. 1759. Cornet.	1776. Lieut.	
BROOM, Wm.	13th Feb. 1762. Cornet.	1776. Lieut.	
BROOME, George	31st May 1792. Cornet.	1799. Cornet.	Disbandment of 5th Dragoons.
BROWN, the Hon : Henry	20th Jan. 1764. Captain.	1772. Capt.	
BROWE —	March 1705. Qr. Master.	No further trace.	Blenheim.
BROWNE, Dennis	27th Oct. 1774. Cornet.	1784. Cornet.	
BROWNE, Redmond	31st March 1793. Major.	1799. Major.	Disbandment of 5th Dragoons.
BROWNLOW, Wm.	28th March 1775. Cornet.	1777. Cornet.	
BULLOCK, Jno.	15th Oct. 1757. Cornet.	1761. Cornet.	
BURLTON, Ferdinand	16th Dec. 1775. Cornet.	1779. Cornet.	
BURLTON, Jno. Phillip	5th June 1771. Cornet.	1771. Cornet.	
BURROWS, Robert	1st Augt. 1720. Cornet.	No trace after 1730. Cornet.	
BUTLER, The Hon: Henry	30th Nov. 1791. Cornet.	1793. Cornet.	
BUTLER, The Hon: Sam. Rich.	31st Augt. 1793. Cornet.	1747. Lieut.	

BUTTER, John	23rd Jan. 1746. Captain.	Later a Major in 3rd Horse Carabineers.	
CALDWELL, Hugh	9th May 1690. Captain.	1710. Lieut. Col. Commanding.	Defended Donegal Castle against 2000 Dragoons under Duke of Berwick in May 1689. Flanders 1694-7. Blenheim, (wounded) Malplaquet. Killed at siege of Douay 1710. Son of Sir Jas. Caldwell of Castle Caldwell, County Fermanagh.
CANE, Hugh	12th March 1754. Captain.	1777. Lieut. Col. Commanding.	
CARDEN, John	9th May 1794. Cornet.	1799. Lieut.	Disbandment of 5th Dragoons.
CARTER, Henry Boyle	2nd May 1742. Cornet.	No trace after 1745. Cornet.	
CARTER, John	22nd Aug. 1794. Cornet.	1799. Captain.	Disbandment of 5th Dragoons.
CARTER, Thomas	27th June 1739. Cornet.	No further trace.	
CAULFIELD, Rich.	24th Feb. 1711. Lieut.	No trace after 1730. Lieut.	
CAULFIELD, Wm.	17th Dec. 1757. Cornet.	1772. Lieut.	
CHAIGNEAU, Jno. Clement	12th March 1774. Chaplain.	1777. Chaplain.	
CLARGES, Christopher	15th April 1749. ? Major.	1760. Lieut-Colonel. Commanding.	
CLARGES, George	22nd June 1757. Captain.	Before 1765. Captain.	
CLARGES, Gould	8th Sept. 1725. Cornet.	No trace after 1730. Cornet.	
CLERKE, S. Wm.	25th Oct. 1715. Cornet.	No trace after 1730. Cornet.	
COCKBURNE, George	30th Nov. 1789. Captain.	1791. Captain.	

COCKING, Ralph	21st Oct. 1729. Chaplain.	1776. Chaplain.	
COCKSEDGE, Wm.	1694. Surgeon.	No trace after 1709. Cornet.	Resigned appointment of Surgeon and appointed Cornet. Blenheim, Ramillies, Oudenaerde, Malplaquet.
CONGREVE, Wm.	5th April 1724. Lieut.	No trace after 1730. Lieut.	
CONINGHAM, Henry	1st Dec. 1725. Captain.	No trace after 1736. Captain.	
CONINGHAM, Sim. L.	1786. Lieut.	1792. Capt.-Lieut.	
CONWAY, Henry	27th July 1737. Lieut.	No further trace. Lieut.	
COOKE, Richard	17th Jan. 1774. Cornet.	1796 Captain.	
COPE, Anthony	1st Feb. 1714. Cornet.	1741. Captain.	
COPE, William	1st Feb. 1714. Captain.	1742. Lieut. Colonel. Commanding.	
COPPINGER, Robert.	9th July 1745. Cornet.	1752. Lieut.	Cashiered.
CORNWALLIS—	1696. Captain.	No other trace.	Flanders 1696.
CORR, Francis	29th May 1796. Cornet.	1799. Cornet.	Disbandment of 5th Dragoons.
COURTENAY, Joseph	1799. Cornet.	1799. Cornet.	Disbandment of 5th Dragoons.
COX —	29th Feb. 1796. Cornet.	1797. Cornet.	
CRAMER, Marmaduke	1799. Lieut.	1799. Lieut.	
CREIGHTON, The Hon. Abraᵐ.	31st Dec. 1782. Cornet.	1784. Cornet.	Disbandment of 5th Dragoons.
CREIGHTON, John	9th Feb. 1750. Cornet.	Before 1767. Captain.	
CREIGHTON, The Hon. John	17th April 1784. Cornet.	1791. Cornet.	
CROMMELIN, Alec.	28th Aug. 1753. Surgeon.	1761. Surgeon.	

CURTIS, Robt. Foulkes	25th June 1784. Cornet.	1786. Cornet.	
CURTIS, William	1st Oct. 1784. Lieut.	1787. Lieut.	
D'ARCEY, William	29th Feb. 1796. Cornet.	1799. Captain.	Disbandment of 5th Dragoons.
DAVIS, Simon Farthing	28th Nov. 1767. Cornet.	1777. Lieut.	
DAWSON, Henry	29th Feb. 1793. Cornet.	1794. Cornet.	
DAWSON, Thos.	6th May 1760. Surgeon.	1770. Surgeon.	
DEANE, John	8th March 1780. Cornet.	1789. Lieut.	
DESPARD Rich.	20th Sept. 1789. Chaplain.	1792. Chaplain.	
DILKES, —	1760. Cornet.	1760. Cornet.	Irish War 1689-91 Flanders 1694-7. Blenheim, Ramillies, Oudenarde, Malplaquet.
DODWELL, Michael	1st Oct. 1797. Cornet.	1798. Cornet.	
DRURY (Drewry), Robert	20th July 1689. Lieut.	No trace after 1711. Brevet Maj.	
DRURY, Robert	28th May 1794. Cornet.	1796. Cornet.	
DUNBAR, John	1704. Cornet.	17— Capt.-Lieut.	Blenheim. A Major. in Owen Wynne's Dragoon (9th Lers) in 1715
DUNBAR, Ric.	1704. Qr. Master.	No trace after 1709.	Blenheim, Ramillies, Oudenarde, Malplaquet.
ELLIS, Robert	1799. Lieut.	1799. Lieut.	Disbandment of 5th Dragoons.
ERROLL, George Earl of	26th Aug. 1786. Captain.	1791. Captain.	
ERSKINE, William	14th Nov. 1787. Lieut.	1787. Lieut.	
EVANS, John	1709. Quarter Master.	No futher trace.	Malplaquet.

FARRER, Jno.	1st Jan. 1723. Lieut.	No trace after 1730. Lieut.	
FAWCETT, Benjamin	31st Dec. 1795. Cornet.	1799. Lieut.	
FAWCETT, (?FANFITT) Wynne	5th March 1783. Adjutant.	1793. Cornet.	
FIRMAN, Rich. Flood	6th Nov. 1772. Cornet.	1785. Lieut.	
FITZGERALD, Maurice	31st Oct. 1792. Captain.	1794. Captain.	
FLEMING (Jas.)	29th Sept. 1696. Chaplain.	1704. Chaplain.	Flanders 1696-7.
FLEMING, Thom.	15th Dec. 1771. Cornet.	1788. Capt-Lieut.	
FLETCHER, Richard	1st Oct. 1784. Surgeon.	1786. Surgeon.	
FOLLIOTT, M. Jno.	6th June 1694. Captain.	1694. Captain.	Flanders 1694-7.
FORTESCUE, Mathew.	28th Oct. 1737. Cornet.	No trace after 1745. Cornet.	
FRANKLIN, Terence	27th Aug. 1737. Cornet.	No trace after 1745. Cornet.	
FRASER, Francis	30th Sept. 1787. Surgeon.	1792. Surgeon.	
FRENCH, Arthur	24th Feb. 1775. Cornet.	1778. Cornet.	
FRENCH, Henry	21st Nov. 1747. Cornet.	1753. Cornet.	
FRENCH, John	15th March 1768. Cornet.	1778. Capt-Lieut.	
GALBRAITH, Arthur	1695. Lieutenant.	No trace after 1702.	Flanders 1695-7.
GALBRAITH, Hugh	1689. Captain.	1698. Major.	Irish War 1689-9 Flanders 1694-7. Of the Tyrone Family of Galbraitl

GETHIN, Percy	1689. Captain.	Before 1702. Captain.	Irish War 1689-91. Flanders 1694-7. Married Anna, widow of Sir Fras. Gore of Artaman, co. Sligo, & daughter of Robt. Parke of Newtown, co. Leitrim.
GLEADSTEANE, George	1st Jan. 1760. Cornet.	Before 1765.	
GOLDIE, Alexander	6th Feb. 1788. Cornet.	1791. Cornet.	
GOLDIE, Alex. J.	11th May 1791. Lieut.	1799. Lieutenant-Colonel.	Disbandment of 5th Dragoons.
GOLDIE, Thomas	17th Feb. 1798. Major.	1799. Major.	Disbandment of 5th Dragoons.
GORE, Ric.	1st April 1695. Captain.	No trace after 1711. Brevet Lieut.-Cononel.	Flanders, 1695-7. Blenheim, Ramillies, Oudenarde, Malplaquet. 9th Son of Sir Fras. Gore of Artaman, co. Sligo.
GORING, John	15th March 1798. Surgeon.	1799. Surgeon.	Disbandment of 5th Dragoons.
GORGES, Richard	27th April 1756. Captain.	1761. Captain.	
GOUGH, John	24th Feb. 1708. Cornet.	No trace after 1709. Cornet.	Malplaquet.
GREAVES, George	30th April 1788. Cornet.	1791. Cornet.	
GREEN, Joseph Geo.	31st Aug. 1795. Cornet.	1799. Lieut.	Disbandment of 5th Dragoons.
GREEN, Nuttall	31st Aug. 1791. Lieut.	1799. Captain.	Disbandment of 5th Dragoons.
GRIFFITH, Lewis	8th Sept. 1725. Lieut.	No trace after 1745. Lieut.	
GROGAN, John	5th March 1777.	1786. Lieut.	
GWYNN, Jno.	10th July 1695. Cornet.	1709. Cornet.	Flanders 1695-7.

Name	Commission	Later	Campaigns
HAM (?), Edward	1704. Quarter Master.	No further trace.	
HAMILTON, Edward	1694. Quarter Master.	No trace after 1730. Lieut.	Flanders 1694-7. Blenheim, (Wounded),Ramillies, Oudenarde, Malplaquet.
HAMILTON, Hans.	31st Aug. 1783. Captain.	1790. Captain.	
HAMILTON, Gustav.	17th Aug. 1715. Captain.	No trace after 1730. Captain.	
HAMILTON, James	10th April 1704. Cornet.	No trace after 1709. Lieut.	Blenheim, Ramillies, Oudenarde, Malplaquet.
HARCOURT, Henry	31st May 1790. Captain.	1792. Captain.	
HARRISON, Holton	1st May 1797. Asst. Surgeon.	1798. Asst. Surgeon.	
HATTON, William	13th Jan. 1777. Cornet.	1786. Lieut.	
HAY, Henry	10th March 1730. Cornet.	1737. Cornet.	
HEATH, John	24th Jan. 1733. Captain.	No trace after 1737 Captain.	
HEATLY, Henry	12th July 1777. Cornet.	1784. Lieut.	
HENDERSON, Andrew	9th May 1794. Cornet.	1796. Cornet.	
HENNIKER, B. Trecothic	30th April 1791. Major.	1793. Major.	
HIGGINS, William	11th July 1722. Capt.-Lieut.	1739. Captain.	
HIGGINS, William	1745. Captain Lieutenant.	1754. Captain Lieut.	
HILL, Edward	9th June 1704. Cornet.	No trace after 1709.	Malplaquet.
HILL, John	6th Nov. 1694. Captain.	1709. Lieutenant Colonel. (B-Col).	Flanders 1694-7. Blenheim, (Wounded) Ramillies, Oudenarde, Malplaquet.

Name	Commission	Last Trace	Notes
HILL, William	1st Aug. 1741. Captain.	1759. Lt. Colonel. Commanding.	
HOBART, Robert	17th Nov. 1780. Captain.	1783. Captain.	
HUNT, John	1st Oct. 1781. Captain.	1787. Captain.	
HUNTER, John	1694. Quarter Master.	No trace after 1709. Lieut.	Flanders 1694-7. Blenheim(Wounded) Ramillies. Oudenarde, Malplaquet.
HUNTER, Robert	13th April 1698. Major.	About 1707. Brevet Lieut. Colonel.	Son of James Hunter of the Hunterston family. Is said to have had a command at the siege of Londonderry 1689. Blenheim. Governor of Virginia 1708. Taken prisoner by the French on his way to America, but soon afterwards exchanged for the Bishop of Quebec, then a prisoner in the hands of the English. Governor of New York 1709. Brig. General 1711, Governor of Jamaica 1729. Major General 1729. Died in Jamaica 31st March 1734.
HUTCHINSON, Norton	25th June 1789. Cornet.	1795. Lieut.	
IRELAND, Courcy	1694. Quarter Master.	No trace after 1695. Qr. Mr.	Flanders 1694-5.
IRVINE, William	13th Jan. 1777. Cornet.	1799. Captain.	Disbandment of 5th Dragoons.
JENNEY, Brabazon	7th Oct. 1758. Cornet.	No trace after 1763. Lieut.	
JENNEY, Henry	12th March 1754. Cornet.	Before 1765. Lieut.	

JESSOP, Thomas	3rd Feb. 1776. Chaplain.	1789. Chaplain.	
JOCELYN, The Hon: George	17th April 1776. Cornet.	1786. Lieut.	
JOHNSTON, Allen	1st May 1734. Captain.	No trace after 1745. Capt.	
JOHNSTON, Jno.	8th Dec. 1692. Lieut.	No trace after 1709. Capt.	Flanders 1694-7. Blenheim, Ramillies, Oudenarde, Malplaquet.
JOHNSTON, Ric.	1704. Quarter Master.	No trace after 1709. Q. M.	Blenheim, Ramillies, Oudenarde, Malplaquet.
JONES, Charles	29th Feb. 1796. Cornet.	1799. Lieut.	Disbandment of 5th Dragoons.
JONES, Thomas	19th June 1798. Cornet.	1799. Cornet.	Disbandment of 5th Dragoons.
JONES, William	28th Feb. 1788. Cornet.	1796. Lieut.	
KEILY, Richard	4th March 1769. Cornet.	1776. Captain.	
KENRICK, Thomas	8th Jan. 1740. Cornet.	No trace after 1745. Cornet.	
KING, Gilbert	16th May 1766. Captain.	1783. Major.	
KIRWAN, Andrew	25th Aug. 1760. Cornet.	1781. Captain.	
KNIGHT, Hy. Raleigh	31st Dec. 1790. Captain.	1792. Captain.	
KNOX, James	1709. Quarter Master.	1753. Cornet.	Malplaquet. Died 1753.
KNOX, John	8th Nov. 1737. Cornet.	1756. Captain.	
KYNAIRD, Thomas	14th May 1735. Cornet.	No trace after 1739. Lieut.	
LADAVEZE, John	20th Jan. 1764. Captain.	Before 1767. Captain.	
LALOR, Thomas	30th May 1794. Cornet.	1795. Cornet.	

LEDWILL, William	31st Dec. 1791. Lieut.	1799. Captain.	Disbandment of 5th Dragoons.
LEESON, The Hon: William	25th June 1789. Cornet.	1791. Cornet.	
LENNOX, Wills.	8th June 1749 Cornet.	1755. Cornet.	
LESLIE, Cecil	30th June 1796. Cornet.	1798. Cornet.	
LLOYD, Griffith	1st Aug. 1694. Adjutant.	1702. Cornet.	Flanders 1694-7.
LLOYD, Jno.	8th May 1694. Chaplain.	1696. Chaplain.	Flanders 1694-6.
LOCKHART, Alex.	1702. Quarter Master.	No other trace.	
LORD, Thomas	20th Jan. 1764. Cornet.	1766. Cornet.	
LUCAS, Benj.	8th March 1757. Cornet.	1770. Lieut.	
LUSHINGTON, William	6th June 1741.	No other trace.	
M'CAUSLAND, John	29th June 1793. Cornet.	1799. Lieut.	
McDONNELL, Edward	9th May 1794. Captain.	1795. Captain.	
McKEANE, George	1702. Quarter Master.	No trace after 1709. Cornet.	Blenheim, Ramillies, Oudenarde, Malplaquet.
M'TAGGART, Isaac	31th May 1792. Surgeon	1798. Lieut.	Transferred to combatant rank.
MADAN, Rich.	2nd April 1724. Captain.	No trace after 1730. Captain.	
MAGILL, George (?)	28th Dec. 1784. Cornet.	1792. Lieut.	
MAHER, John	25th July 1795. Cornet.	1798. Lieut.	
MAHON, Stephen	30th Nov. 1791. Captain.	1794. Captain.	

MANGIN, Sam. Hen.	18th April 1766. Captain.	1782. Major.	
MANN, Jno.	16th Dec. 1695. Cornet.	No trace after 1709. Lieut.	Flanders 1695-7. Ramillies, Oude-narde, Malplaquet.
MANNING, Thomas	30th June 1795. Capt-Lieut.	1799. Capt-Lieut.	Disbandment of 5th Dragoons.
MARELLA, John	4th Oct. 1777. Lieut.	No further trace.	
MARSILLY, Peter	10th Dec. 1710. Cornet.	1739. Cornet.	
MASON, Henry Mark	Oct. 1745 Cornet.	Before 1765. Captain.	
MASSEY, Fra. Hugh.	17th Jan. 1774. Lieut.	1791. Captain.	
MERCER, Rich.	17th March 1761. Captain.	Before 1767. Captain.	
METGE, Jno.	30th April 1771. Cornet.	1780. Lieut.	
MILLEFONT, David	29th June 1780. Cornet.	1786. Cornet.	
MILLER, Humphrey	25th March 1705. Captain.	No other trace.	
MITCHELL, Nathaniel	10th March 1753. Cornet.	1761. Lieutenant.	
MOLESWORTH, Richard, Viscount	27th June 1727. Colonel (Major General).	1758. Colonel (Field Marshal).	Blenheim, Ramil-lies, Oudenarde, Malplaquet.
MOLESWORTH, Robert	28th Oct. 1745. Cornet.	1770. Lieut.	
MOLYNEUX, Thomas	1794. Capt-Lieut.	1795. Capt-Lieut.	
MONK, Harry Percy	22th Jan. 1755. Cornet.	1767. Lieutenant.	
MOORE, Lorenzo	9th May 1794. Lieut.	1795. Lieut.	
MOORE, Lorenzo Henry	15th Dec. 1794. Cornet.	1796. Cornet.	
MOORE, Ponsonby	4th March 1745. Cornet.	1752. Lieut.	

MOORE, Thomas	16th May 1766. Lieut.	1776. Captain.	
MOORE, William	16th March 1775. Cornet.	1778. Cornet.	
MORRIS, Charles	28th Nov. 1771. Cornet.	1773. Cornet.	
MOSTYN, Jno.	18th Oct. 1758. Colonel (Major General.)	1760. Colonel. (Lieut-General).	
NESBIT, Francis	15th April 1749. Cornet.	1757. Lieut.	
NESBITT, Thos.	17th Sept. 1761. Cornet.	1765. Cornet.	
NETTLES, William	15th Aug. 1766. Cornet.	No other trace	
NEWCOMEN, Beverley	16th Dec. 1695. Cornet.	1709. Lieut.	Flanders 1696-7. Malplaquet. 5th Son of Sir Thomas Newcomen, of Kenagh who was killed at the Siege of Enniskillen in 1689. Beverley Newcomen was "probably a child" (Dalton) when gazetted to the 5th Dragoons. No trace of him in the 5th Dragoons after 1709. In 1720 he was Lieut. Colonel of Clement Neville's Dragoons. Died 1731. A Beverley Newcomen had held a commission as Ensign of Foot in King James' Army in 1687. (Dalton's King James' Army List).
NEWCOMEN, Charles	1689. Captain.	No trace after 1702. Captain.	Irish War 1689-91. Flanders 1694-7. Son of Sir Thos. Newcomen of Kenagh Co. Longford.

NICHOLLS, John	4th Jan. 1749. Cornet.	1772. Lieut.	
NORCOTT, Arthur	13th March 1767. Cornet.	1772. Cornet.	
OLIVER, Robert	13th Oct. 1798. Cornet.	1799. Cornet.	Disbandment of 5th Dragoons.
ONGE, Samuel	8th July 1794. Cornet.	1799. Captain.	Disbandment of 5th Dragoons.
O'REILLY, James	31st Augt. 1796. Cornet.	1799. Cornet.	Disbandment of 5th Dragoons.
ORMSBY, Phillip	1745. Cornet.	1776. Captain	
PALISER, Richard	11th March 1769. Cornet.	1786. Captain.	
PARKER, Michael	1st April 1695. Cornet.	No trace after 1709.	Flanders, 1695-7. Oudenarde, Malplaquet.
PERRIN, John	8th June 1769. Surgeon.	1776. Surgeon.	
PHILLIPS, John	25th Feb. 1741. Surgeon.	1753. Surgeon.	
POE, Francis	3rd Sept. 1763. Cornet.	1766. Cornet.	
POÉ, James	1694. Qr. Master.	1728. Lieut.	Flanders 1694-7. Blenheim, Ramillies, Oudenarde, Malplaquet. 3rd son of Emanuel Poé of Co. Tipperary. Died 1728.
POE, James	17th March 1761. Cornet.	Before 1765. Cornet.	
POMEROY, James	10th Oct. 1770. Cornet.	1776. Cornet.	
PRESTON, John	30th July 1796. Surgeon.	1798. Surgeon.	
PRICE, James	28th May 1794. Cornet.	1796. Cornet.	
PURDON, Bartholomew	28th May 1756. Cornet.	Before 1765. Lieut.	
PYLE, Sir Seymour	26th Aug. 1737. Captain.	About 1746. Captain.	

REYNELL, John	13th Feb. 1765. Cornet.	1776. Cornet.	
RICE, James	20th June 1753. Cornet.	No other trace.	
RIDGE, J.S.	6th Sept. 1794. Cornet.	1799. Captain.	Disbandment of 5th Dragoons.
ROBINSON, Jocelyn	23rd Feb. 1742. Captain.	About 1752. Captain.	
ROBINSON, Jos.	26th March 1737. Cornet.	1742. Cornet.	
ROSE, Alex.	12th Sept. 1729. Lieut-Colonel.	Given command of a regiment in 1740.	
ROSS, Charles	1689. Captain.		Ireland 1689-91. Flanders 1694-7.
	16th July 1695. Colonel.	1715. Colonel (General).	Blenheim, Ramillies, Oudenarde, Malplaquet. Died
	1st Feb. 1729. Col. (General).	1732. Colonel (General).	Aug. 1732. Son of the 11th Baron Ross of Balnagowan.
ROSS, David	1702. Quarter Master.	1707. Adjutant.	Blenheim (wounded).
ROSS, James	16th Dec. 1695. Lieut.	1702. Lieut.	Flanders 1696-7.
ROSS, James	9th April 1756. Adjutant.	1757. Adjutant.	
ROSS, William	20th July 1695. Captain.	Before 1704. Captain.	Flanders 1696-7.
ROSS, William	20th July 1695. Captain-Lieut.	1705. Capt-Lieut.	Flanders 1696-7.
ROSS, William	1702. Quarter Master.	About 1737. Lieut.	Malplaquet.
ROSS, William	30th Aug. 1739. Cornet.	1761. Captain.	
ROSSMORE, Robert, Lord.	4th April 1787. Colonel (Lieut. General).	1799. Colonel. (General).	Disbandment of 5th Dragoons. Formerly Robert Cuninghame, succeeded to title of Rossmore in 1797.

ROWLEY, Clotworthy	13th Feb. 1762. Captain.	1776. Major.	
ST. LEGER, Richard	9th Oct. 1775. Cornet.	1777. Cornet.	
SANDFORD, Joseph	26th Sept. 1772. Cornet.	1779. Lieut.	
SANDFORD, Robert	1744. Cornet.	1756. Lieut.	
SAVARY, William	14th Feb. 1776. Cornet.	1779. Cornet.	
SAWER, Thomas	26th April 1677. Lieut-Colonel.	1678. Lieut. Col.	
SCOTT, James	25th March 1705. Surgeon.	About 1710. Surgeon.	Malplaquet.
SCOTT, James	27th May 1717. Cornet.	About 1745. Lieut.	
SCROW, James	4th March 1735. Cornet.	1739. Cornet.	
SIDNEY, Thomas	5th Oct. 1715. Colonel.	1729. Colonel.	Died 1729.
SINCLAIR, John	13th Aug. 1879. 2nd Lieut.	1887. Captain.	Suakim 1855
SKAEN, William	24th July 1746. Cornet.	About 1753. Lieut.	
SKEFFINGTON, The Hon. Henry	2nd Sept. 1763. Cornet.	1791(?). Cornet.	
SKEF(F)INGTON, The Hon. W. John	22nd Sept. 1769. Cornet.	1772. Cornet.	
SKEL(S)TON, John	1704. Quarter Master.	No trace after 1709. Cornet.	Blenheim, Ramillies, Oudenarde, Malplaquet.
SKENE, And. Philip	31st July 1788. Captain.	1791. Captain.	
SMITH, Cuthbert	20th June 1739. Cornet.	1772. Captain.	
SMITH, John	27th Aug. 1760. Cornet.	Before 1765. Cornet.	

SMITH-	7th Feb. 1759. Cornet.	1761. Cornet.	
SMITHWICK, Robert	1st Jan. 1774. Surgeon.	1784. Surgeon.	
SMYTH, James	17th April 1784. Cornet.	1789. Cornet.	
SOMERVILLE, Warburton	17th Dec. 1762. Cornet.	Apparently 1763. Cornet.	
SPICER, Thomas	31st Jan. 1791. Cornet.	1794. Cornet.	
STANHOPE, Edward	3rd Aug. 1723. Cornet.	1737. Cornet.	
STANLEY, John	16th Nov. 1785. Captain.	1791. Captain.	
STEPHENS, Daniel	30th June 1787 Cornet.	1799. Lieut.	Disbandment of 5th Dragoons.
STEPHENSON, St. George	1st Aug. 1741. Cornet.	Before 1765. Captain.	
STEUART, Charles	1st Feb. 1728. Cornet.	About 1746. Lieut.	
STEVENSON, George	1695. Lieutenant.	No trace after 1702. Lieut.	Flanders 1695-7.
STEVENSON, William	8th May 1694. Cornet.	1704. Cornet.	Flanders 1694-7.
STEWART, The Hon. Charles W.	1st Jan. 1797. Lieut-Colonel.	1799. Lieutenant-Col. Command.	Disbandment of 5th Dragoons.
STEWART, Francis	18th June 1766. Captain.	1766. Captain.	
STEWART, James	7th Jan. 1778. Lieut-Colonel.	1796. Lieutenant-Colonel.	
STRANGWAYS, The Hon. S. Digby	5th Aug. 1767. Cornet.	1770.	
STRATTON, John	3rd April 1779. Cornet.	1786. Lieut.	
STYLE(S), Charles	21st Dec. 1733. Cornet.	1757. Captain.	
TAYLOR, John	7th Sept. 1771. Cornet.	1785. Lieut.	

Name	First Commission	Later Rank	Service
TAYLOR, John	2nd Nov. 1794. Adjutant.	1799. Adjutant.	Disbandment of 5th Dragoons.
TICKELL, Thomas	14th March 1771. Cornet.	1787. Capt-Lieut.	
TIDY, John	1694. Quarter Master.	1702. Qr. Mr.	Flanders 1694-7.
TOLER, George	16th Feb. 1756. Cornet.	1767. Lieut.	
TOWNSEND, Phillip	30th April 1742. Lieut.	Apparently in 1743.	
TUITE, James	15th April 1749. Cornet.	1756. Cornet.	
USHER, John	1704. Captain.	No trace after 1709. Capt.	Blenheim, Malplaquet.
VEREKER, Amos	20th Jan. 1764.	1778. Lieut.	
VERNON, Edward	27th Nov. 1752. Cornet.	1753. Lieut.	
VESEY, Thomas	16th Feb. 1756. Cornet.	1760. Cornet.	
VINCENT-	26th Aug. 1760. Cornet.	Before 1765. Cornet.	
VYSE, Rich.	13th Feb. 1762. Cornet.	1778. Captain.	
WALSH, James	1709. Quarter Master.	About 1745. Lieut.	Malplaquet.
WARBURTON, Charles	30th Jan. 1718. Captain.	About 1745. Captain.	
WARDLAW, Charles	30th Jan. 1717. Captain.	About 1745. Captain.	
WARRE, John	10th April 1704. Captain.	Before 1714. Bt. Major.	Ramillies, Oudenarde, Malplaquet. Only son of Sir Fraser Warre, Bart. Died at Ghent before 1714.
WATTS, Mat.	20th July 1689. Cornet.	No trace after 1709. Lieut.	Irish War 1689-91. Flanders 1694-7. Blenheim.
WEBB,	1695. Lieut.	No other trace.	Flanders 1695.
WELCH, James	1709. Quarter Master.	No trace after 1728. Lieut.	Malplaquet.

WEST, John	1st May 1797. Asst. Surgeon.	1799. Asst. Surgeon.	Disbandment of 5th Dragoons.
WESTENRA-	1795. Cornet.	same year.	
WESTENRA(Z), Warren	5th Feb. 1787. Cornet.	1791. Lieut.	
WHITBY, William	28th Nov. 1771. Captain.	1776. Captain.	
WHITCHURCH, Percy	1694. Quarter Master.	1702. Quarter Master.	Flanders 1694-7.
WHITE, Mor.	1709. Quarter Master.	No other trace.	Malplaquet.
WILBRAHAM, J. Watkin	15th Aug. 1783. Captain.	1786. Captain.	
WILKINSON, William	6th May 1760. Cornet.	Before 1765. Cornet.	
WILLEY, Edward	31st March 1768. Cornet.	1772. Cornet.	
WILLIAMS, William	6 Oct. 1798. Lieut.	1799. Lieut.	Disbandment of 5th Dragoons.
WILSON, Thomas	10th July 1716. Cornet.	1756. Captain-Lieut.	
WITHERING-TON, Edward	3rd April 1786. Cornet.	1791. Lieut.	
WOLFE, Rich.	16th Dec. 1752. Cornet.	1776. Lieut.	
WYNNE, Fawcett (Faufitt)	5th March 1783. Adjt.	1792. Adjt.	
WYNNE, James	20th June 1689. Colonel.	1695. Colonel. (Brigadier Gen.)	Irish War 1689-91. Flanders 1694-5. Died of wounds received in action near Rouselaer, 15th July 1695-7. He raised the Regiment.
WYNNE, James	20th July 1695. Cornet.	About 1705. Lieut.	Flanders 1695-7. Apparently a son of Brigadier James Wynne.
WYNNE, John	10th May 1740. Major.	No other trace.	

WYNNE, Owen	1st Nov. 1694. Major. August 1732. Colonel (Lieut.-Gen.)	1705. Lieut.-Col. 1737. Colonel. Lieutenant-Gen.	Irish War 1689–91. Flanders 1694 - 7. Blenheim. Died 1737.
WYNNE, Owen	2nd May 1742. Cornet.	No other trace.	
WYNNE, Robert	7th Jan. 1778. Cornet.	No other trace.	
YELVERTON, W. Charles	24th Dec. 1779. Cornet.	1787. Cornet.	
YORKE, The Hon. Joseph	27th Nov. 1760. Colonel (Major General.) From Colonel of 8th Dragoons.	1787. Colonel (General). Transferred to 11th Light Dragoons.	Flanders 1743. K.B. Son of Lord Hardwicke, Lord Chancellor of England.
YOUNG (YONGE) Edward	7th Feb. 1745. Cornet.	1761. Lieut.	

Note:—There is no list of officers who served in the Irish War 1689-91 or in Flanders 1694-7, but it is presumed that the officers on the Roll of the Regiment during those periods served in the campaigns.

The Blenheim Drums

This passage by "Pendragon" was presented for inclusion in this work to Leonaur courtesy of C.R. 16th/5th the Queen's Royal Lancers

During a tour of the Tower of London, the Crown jewels in the Wakefield Tower and those poor pathetic signatures on the walls of the Beauchamp Tower are usually the principal attractions for the ordinary visitor.

In the White Tower, however, there are to be seen some old kettle-drums which sometimes claim attention from casual passers-by, and it is these which have the greatest interest for anyone connected with the regiment who may chance that way.

These drums have painted round the parchment the inscription, "Blenheim, 1704." The official guide book just blandly states that they were "taken at Blenheim and used by Handel for his *Oratorios*," but on inquiry nobody can ever be found who can in any way substantiate a claim that they were ever in the Tower during Handel's time.

A much more likely story is that these are indeed the missing drums of the old 5th Royal Irish Dragoons which were captured at Blenheim and were ordered by Marlborough to be carried at the head of the regiment. For nearly a century this was done, and it is sad to think that it was only a short time before the disbandment in 1799 that confirmation of the privilege was received from Horse Guards in a message which stated that "His Majesty particularly specified this honour for the regiment and hoped that they would long deserve the reputation they had so gallantly required."

And then, on top of all this and only a year after the regiment had again been confirmed in all its ancient privileges, including the Blenheim honours, there suddenly came the disbandment.

The real causes were a somewhat sordid tale of intrigue not unconnected with many of the evils of the purchase system, but the

SIR WINSTON CHURCHILL, FATHER OF
THE FIRST DUKE OF MARLBOROUGH

ostensible reason—the indiscipline of the unit—does not bear a moment's serious consideration; for in the end only one man—James McNissar—could be tried for anything approaching mutiny, the other "ringleaders"—the Feeneys—being tried and convicted of robbery with violence and housebreaking.

When the order came, it is recorded that they marched across England to Chatham in such good shape that their bearing and discipline were admired and commented upon by all who saw them, and none could believe that such a fine body of men was on its way to extinction. But extinction it was, complete and utter, and from then on their uniforms and facings were seen no more.

What then happened to the Blenheim drums?

At that time all equipment would eventually have to be returned to the Board of Ordnance at the Tower of London, and in this particular case would no doubt have included the regimental kettle-drums. But in those days kettle-drums were not, strictly speaking, part of the equipment of dragoons, and only those three regiments—2nd Dragoons (Scots Greys), 3rd (King's Own) Dragoons and 5th (Royal Irish) Dragoons—who had all captured them in battle many years before were allowed to carry them. It is more than likely, therefore, that these drums were never included in the list of "returns," with the result that they were pushed more and more into the background until finally becoming absorbed into one of those dead-end limbos of forgotten things so beloved of any self-respecting Ordnance or Quartermaster's Stores.

And so the legend commenced.

Legends are funny things and originate in a variety of ways, sometimes by an individual with a little authority and a great deal of pomposity airing his personal views and being repeated with embellishments by others too subservient to question his opinion or too lazy to ascertain the truth.

So it was that Handel *did* borrow some drums from the Ordnance for his Oratorios, but they were certainly not these drums, for the Minutes of the Board of Ordnance, dated 17th March, 1748, it was specifically stated that it was "the train of artillery kettle-drums" which were required. These latter had a carriage of their own and were far larger than cavalry kettle-drums. Again, in 1756, Handel specially asked the Master-general of the Ordnance for "the large kettle-Drums," and in any case it would hardly have been necessary for him to borrow anything smaller from Ordnance as there would have been

Battle of Blenheim tapestry showing Blenheim packed with French troops and, in the centre, burning water mills and a casualty station

plenty of drums of such a type readily available elsewhere in London.

But there are several other facts which make the Handel story appear to be completely inaccurate.

In the first place, Grose says:

> In consequence of the good behaviour of the regiment at the Battle of Hochstet (Blenheim) in August 1704, three additional troops were put upon the establishment, making its strength consist of nine troops. The kettle-drums which were taken from the French at this memorable engagement, were directed by the Duke of Marlborough to be carried at the head of the Royal Dragoons of Ireland.

And again:

> The honours which were thus earned by the Royal Irish, were not only established and confirmed, but continued to be uninterruptedly acknowledged through four reigns, without suffering the least diminution during near a century; and the permanency of the nine troops was secured by an order dated 1798.

The again, as is mentioned by Lawson, the clothing lists for 1731 refer to three yards of blue velvet for these drums, while on 3rd September, 1778, Colonel Charles Fitz Roy, commanding the King's Own Regiment of dragoons (now the 3rd Hussars) petitioned Horse Guards, saying that the sixth trumpeter being the kettle-drummer meant that one troop was without a trumpeter, and therefore he begged that another trumpeter be allowed the regiment, "as in the Royal Irish Regiment of Dragoons and other regiments having kettle-drums. The kettle-drummer being a mark of distinction, allowed by Royal Favour.

Now, if in 1778 the Royal Irish Dragoons had a special kettle-drummer, as is obvious from this letter, it is reasonable to presume that the drums were with the regiment, and, as kettle-drums were not normally part of the equipment of dragoons at that time, these must have been the trophies captured at Blenheim. How then could they have been loaned to Handel by the Board of Ordnance in 1748, 1753 and again in 1756, as is stated at the Tower.

So it is, I think, that when we look at those drums in the White Tower we can confidently say to ourselves that here are the very drums which, having changed hands at Blenheim, were proudly carried at the head of the regiment at Ramillies, Oudenarde and Malplaquet.

John Churchill, First Duke of Marlborough

LEONAUR

ALSO FROM LEONAUR
AVAILABLE IN SOFTCOVER OR HARDCOVER WITH DUST JACKET

ZULU:1879 *by D.C.F. Moodie & the Leonaur Editors*—The Anglo-Zulu War of 1879 from contemporary sources: First Hand Accounts, Interviews, Dispatches, Official Documents & Newspaper Reports.

THE RED DRAGOON *by W.J. Adams*—With the 7th Dragoon Guards in the Cape of Good Hope against the Boers & the Kaffir tribes during the 'war of the axe' 1843-48'.

THE RECOLLECTIONS OF SKINNER OF SKINNER'S HORSE *by James Skinner*—James Skinner and his 'Yellow Boys' Irregular cavalry in the wars of India between the British, Mahratta, Rajput, Mogul, Sikh & Pindarree Forces.

A CAVALRY OFFICER DURING THE SEPOY REVOLT *by A. R. D. Mackenzie*—Experiences with the 3rd Bengal Light Cavalry, the Guides and Sikh Irregular Cavalry from the outbreak to Delhi and Lucknow.

A NORFOLK SOLDIER IN THE FIRST SIKH WAR *by J W Baldwin*—Experiences of a private of H.M. 9th Regiment of Foot in the battles for the Punjab, India 1845-6.

TOMMY ATKINS' WAR STORIES: 14 FIRST HAND ACCOUNTS—Fourteen first hand accounts from the ranks of the British Army during Queen Victoria's Empire.

THE WATERLOO LETTERS *by H. T. Siborne*—Accounts of the Battle by British Officers for its Foremost Historian.

NEY: GENERAL OF CAVALRY VOLUME 1—1769-1799 *by Antoine Bulos*—The Early Career of a Marshal of the First Empire.

NEY: MARSHAL OF FRANCE VOLUME 2—1799-1805 *by Antoine Bulos*—The Early Career of a Marshal of the First Empire.

AIDE-DE-CAMP TO NAPOLEON *by Philippe-Paul de Ségur*—For anyone interested in the Napoleonic Wars this book, written by one who was intimate with the strategies and machinations of the Emperor, will be essential reading.

TWILIGHT OF EMPIRE *by Sir Thomas Ussher & Sir George Cockburn*—Two accounts of Napoleon's Journeys in Exile to Elba and St. Helena: Narrative of Events by Sir Thomas Ussher & Napoleon's Last Voyage: Extract of a diary by Sir George Cockburn.

PRIVATE WHEELER *by William Wheeler*—The letters of a soldier of the 51st Light Infantry during the Peninsular War & at Waterloo.

www.ingramcontent.com/pod-product-compliance
Lightning Source LLC
Chambersburg PA
CBHW032052080426
42733CB00006B/251